DUDLEY PUBLIC LIBRARIES

The loan of this book may be renewed if not required by other readers, by contacting the library from which it was borrowed.

Caroline Lucas

Honourable Friends?

Parliament and the Fight for Change

Portobello
BOOKS

First published by Portobello Books 2015
This paperback edition published by Portobello Books 2015

12 Addison Avenue
London
W11 4QR

A CIP catalogue record is available from the British Library

9 8 7 6 5 4 3 2 1

ISBN 978 1 84627 595 1
eISBN 978 1 84627 594 4

Typeset by Avon DataSet Ltd, Bidford on Avon, Warwickshire

Printed and bound by CPI Group (UK) Ltd, Croydon, CR0 4YY

MIX
Paper from
responsible sources
FSC® C020471

For Richard, Theo and Isaac

Contents

With Richard after the election result, Brighton, 7 May 2010

Preface

> 'We can no longer rely on the established parties, nor can
> we go on working solely through extra-parliamentary
> channels. There is a need for a new force, both in
> Parliament and outside it.'
>
> Petra Kelly

When I first read those words nearly thirty years ago they captured everything I felt about politics. Mainstream political parties lacked the courage to adopt radical solutions to the social and environmental problems we face. More than that, they were very often responsible for those problems in the first place. Parliamentary politics seemed incapable of embracing the change that was – and still is – so urgently needed. But protest, though vital, was not enough. We needed what Petra called an 'anti-party': one that would seek power but never sacrifice morality; that would enter Parliament but never become part of it; that would always remain, at heart, a party of the people.

It was a compelling ideal; and Petra Kelly helped bring it to life as a co-founder of the Greens in Germany. As one of the first Green deputies elected to the Bundestag in March 1983, she entered the chamber bearing armfuls of sunflowers, instantly bringing colour and life into the grey world of traditional politics; though her political career was cut tragically short in 1992, she remains an inspiration for many in the Green movement and beyond.

In Britain, there seemed no chance of a similar breakthrough. The three main parties had it sewn up: a political establishment, based on an undemocratic and unfair electoral system, which made it very nearly impossible for smaller parties to break in and shake up the cosy consensus. When I joined the Green Party, back in 1986, my parents were bemused. 'Why don't you join a *proper* party?' they asked. I could see what they meant, for there seemed little prospect of us ever being elected. But the Green Party has always been the only political home I could imagine. And simply by existing, we showed people that there was a positive and hopeful alternative.

The establishment fought hard to keep us out: everything from denying us airtime during election periods, to requiring a deposit of £500 to stand in each constituency – a total of around £250,000 across England and Wales, and far too much for us to raise. Conservatives, Labour and the Liberal Democrats could agree on one thing at least: they wanted to leave no space for alternative voices. Indeed, if politics were a business – and I sometimes wonder whether that is so far-fetched an idea – it would be a prime case for a referral to the Competition and Markets Authority for monopolistic collusion in excluding new entrants to the market.

But on 7 May 2010, the very nearly impossible did, finally, after so much hard work by so many people over so many years, happen – and the Green Party won its first seat in Parliament when I was elected to represent Brighton Pavilion.

It was a moment of history: the first new political movement to enter Parliament in nearly a century. There was so much we wanted to do, so many important issues to raise, laws to try to change, ways to put social and environmental justice at the top of the agenda – and most urgent of all, policies to introduce to address the growing threat from climate change. I was haunted by the words of the actor Pete Postlethwaite in *The Age of Stupid*, a powerful film about the climate crisis: 'Why didn't we save ourselves when we had the chance?'

But in one of the worst examples of bad timing imaginable, at precisely the moment when we most need urgent action by political leaders to address the accelerating climate threat, our political system is broken, and politicians are widely held in deep contempt. And so the issue of political and parliamentary reform was also to become a major focus of my work.

I have come to see, up close, how unless Parliament changes, progress in every other area of our national life faces delay or obstruction. Reform is not an abstract issue, remote from our everyday concerns about job security, or the state of the National Health Service. It is reform that will allow us to take back control of Parliament, and ensure that our government makes decisions in our interest: not just in terms of climate change, but in promoting decent, well-paid jobs rather than the profits of multinationals; or investing in the NHS as a truly public service, not hollowed out through privatization.

This book is a record of progress so far, the challenges and setbacks as well as some successes. It has been put together during late-night train journeys between London and Brighton, it has been scribbled on bits of paper and saved as email drafts. It is built from conversations with colleagues and constituents, and from snatches of diary entries that I'm usually too tired to complete.

It is – probably all too clearly – *not* a conventional political memoir, written during a time of reflection. Nor is it a manifesto. I would have loved to say more about all that my colleagues in the Green Party have achieved over the years, and what the Greens can offer now and in the future. But this is not that book. Rather, it's an 'of-the-moment', from-the-trenches snapshot of the first five years of coalition government. It does not aim to be comprehensive – many things are left out – and if it has the quality of being rough and ready, that's because, of necessity, it is.

But I hope it might have some value as the view of an outsider, inside; in particular, how Parliament needs to change if it is to have any hope of re-engaging with the mass of people it is meant to represent, and rising to the serious social and environmental challenges we face.

Our faith in politics has taken so many knocks in recent years: the MP expenses scandal; the way MPs have colluded to block giving constituents the power to hold their MP to account through the right of recall; the broken pledges on the NHS and tuition fees; and the lies that surrounded the launch of the Iraq War. And people have shown they want a different kind of politics, from the 45 per cent vote in Scotland for independence and how the membership of the Green Party has more than doubled in less than a year; and even the rise of UKIP. If nothing else, it shows that our generation has a unique opportunity to reshape the way we're governed.

The book has three parts. In the first, I am the outsider in Parliament, seeing this institution for the first time, exploring it, trying to understand it, and learning how to make it work. In the second, I am fighting from within, doing my best to tackle vested interests and representing the ideals and interests of those who had elected me in Brighton. And in the third, I try to articulate a vision of how our politics could be different.

Writing this book has shown me how much more is still to be done, and how much I want to be part of that work. There is a danger that our politics will become more corrupt and our society more divided, and that the voice of the people will count for less and less. When I was first elected, I was enormously proud that the people of Brighton should put their trust in a new political movement, and vote for our positive and principled alternative to the politics of division and fear. I hope I have repaid that trust.

This book has also reminded me how much I owe to others. To my husband Richard and my sons Theo and Isaac, whose love and support have been my rock; to the people of Brighton, whose faith in me and whose act of going out to vote has given me the privilege of representing them in Parliament; to Cath Miller, who has marshalled and coordinated all those campaigners, experts, politicians and volunteers I have worked with since being elected, and also managed my office, and all those who have worked with me in Westminster and in Brighton. And finally to Emily Wilding Davison. Each day in Parliament, on the walk from my office to the chamber, I pass the memorial to the suffragettes. I see the scarf that Davison wore when she was killed while campaigning for the vote in 1913. She is a reminder of all those who have gone before in the struggle for true equality and justice; and a reassurance that there will always be others who will join the cause.

Prologue

Election night. It is one of the few national rituals familiar to us all. First the pundits in the studio, the exit polls and computer graphics, marginal seats and swingometers. Then the results themselves: brief scenes of candidates shuffling onto a platform in a draughty hall, their set faces and rosettes somehow placing them apart from the rest of the human race. Even the more colourful candidates, the Monster Raving Loonies or the Miss Whiplashes, are somehow reduced to an anxious dullness, waiting for the returning officer to step hesitantly up to the microphone, for a few minutes under the eyes of the nation, to read out the results.

'I, John Barradell, being the acting returning officer for the constituency of Brighton Pavilion . . .'

I've sat up watching elections for as long as I can remember. As a child, with my parents, it was little more than an excuse for a late night. As a student, it meant more to me, particularly when a woman became prime minister for the first time. Then came a decade of defeats for Labour, which seemed unable to mount a credible challenge to triumphal Thatcherism. Political issues mattered to me then; but not politics.

'. . . the number of votes cast for each candidate was as follows.'

Even after I took the plunge and joined a political party, the Greens, I was still on the outside. We stood to give people an alternative, one they could vote for with a clear conscience, without the compromises and evasions of traditional politics. The height of our ambitions was to save our deposit or win a seat on a local council.

'*Leo Atreides, Independent, nineteen votes.*

'*Nigel Carter, UK Independence Party, nine hundred and forty-eight votes.*'

Now, twenty years later, I have stepped through the glass screen. I am there among them, looking out over the crowds, conscious of the glare of the lights and the TV cameras, as the returning officer continues to read in his dry, formal voice.

'*Caroline Lucas, Green Party, sixteen thousand, two hundred and thirty-eight.*'

A cheer goes up from a section of the audience: my own supporters, who have worked for months and years to convince those sixteen thousand, two hundred and thirty-eight people to vote for me. Only those who have been through a political campaign can possibly imagine the work they have put in, against the odds. They are delighted, but incredibly anxious: they don't know if those sixteen thousand votes are enough to give us victory, or to leave us painfully, horribly, close, as also-rans.

'*Nancy Platts, Labour Party, fourteen thousand, nine hundred and eighty-six.*'

The Labour supporters begin to applaud – in sympathy for their defeated candidate. All their work, just as well intentioned, certainly just as hard, has come to nothing. To the waiting audience, the result is still in doubt.

But not to me. I am learning that politics is full of stage management, and it turns out that the returning officer tells the candidates the result before they all troop on stage for the formal announcement. So we all stand awkwardly on the stage, not saying anything to each other, keeping a poker face. In my case, this isn't hard. I don't particularly feel like laughing or punching the air. In fact, I feel like being sick.

'*Charlotte Vere, Conservative, twelve thousand—*'

His words are drowned out in an enormous cheer from the Greens. We have won. I wait for a rush of triumphant elation, but it's nearly six in the morning, at the end of a draining election campaign, and most of all I feel exhausted. Then soon, deep down, comes a slow-burning realization that we have done something amazing. But there's no time now to reflect or gather my thoughts.

'. . . I hereby declare that Caroline Lucas is duly elected Member of Parliament for the Brighton Pavilion constituency.'

Another great cheer, and they are beckoning me up to the microphone. A sea of faces, some familiar and friendly, some hostile. Mostly, though, the crowd is curious, perhaps relieved that the long night is soon going to come to an end; but also pleased to be part of a small slice of history. Because this is the first time that there has ever been a Green Party MP. We've had councillors before, and Greens in the Scottish Parliament and the Welsh and Northern Ireland Assemblies. We've had Greens in the European Parliament – I've served two terms there myself – but in British politics, the only one that the professionals take seriously is Westminster. That's the breakthrough the party has waited four decades to make. And here, now, tonight, it is me and the people of Brighton.

It's a bit like a dream: feeling you are in the wrong place, that what is taking place around you, though strangely familiar, is nothing to do with you. For a moment, it's hard to concentrate. Even taking the few steps across the stage requires an effort of will. And then the crowd falls silent, with just a few last calls of encouragement, like the audience at Wimbledon settling down to a tense final set.

Thank you. Tonight the people of Brighton Pavilion have made history by electing Britain's first Green MP to Westminster. Thank you so much for putting your faith in me and in the Green Party. Thank you so much for putting the politics of hope above the politics of fear. I pledge that I will do my very best to do you proud.

I've thought about this speech, of course. You don't spend such a chunk of your life, and ask others to do the same, without it crossing your mind that you might win. It would also be awful, in the glare of the lights, to miss anyone out. So I thank the returning officer and his staff, the other candidates and my campaign team and supporters. It's a ritual, but a heartfelt one: particularly in saluting Pete West, who was the first Green councillor elected in Brighton, back in 1996; and Keith Taylor, the previous Green candidate who got nearly 23 per cent of the vote, the base from which to win this time.

And finally of course, thanks to my amazing family. To my supportive husband Richard, who's been with me every step of the way. My incredibly patient kids, Theo and Isaac. Thank you so very much.

These words make me wonder what I've committed them to for the next five years, as well as everything they've done up to now. I've been an MP for about two minutes, but the reality is sinking in.

And I hope the other candidates will bear with me just while I reflect for a few more moments on what the Green Party has achieved tonight. Because this isn't just a moment when one MP out of 650 is elected. It's where a whole political party takes for the first time its rightful place in our Parliament. This has been the closest election for a generation, in the midst of the worst recession since the war, and after people's faith in politics has been trampled into the mud of the expenses scandal. Not the best time to come to people and ask them to take a risk and put their trust in a new kind of politics.

But we asked the people of Brighton to do that. And tonight we have their answer. One that will give hope to communities up and down this country. And so for once, the word 'historic' genuinely fits the bill.

And so I thank everybody from the Green Party and beyond, and particularly the people of Brighton Pavilion, and I'll do my very best to serve you to the best of my ability.

It's a relief to get off the stage and share the victory with so many of the friends and colleagues whose tireless work has made it possible. I also feel an immediate and profound sense of responsibility. It is now my duty to represent the 100,000 people of Brighton Pavilion – a huge privilege, but daunting too. And walking back home in the dawn through the familiar Brighton streets, the sea shimmering, the sun beginning to rise, and with all those supporters and well-wishers around too, I tell myself it will be all right.

PART ONE

Outside In

Passing through the police lines at the Occupy demonstration
outside St Paul's Cathedral, 5 November 2011

1

The Shock of the Old:
How Parliament Looks from the Inside

'You'll get used to it.'

Margaret Beckett

It's the first day at a new school. Over two hundred first-time MPs are directed to various rooms around Portcullis House, Parliament's main modern office block, to be briefed on employing staff and collecting the post, to be given their computer passwords, and to be told about the facilities, from the Library to the numerous bars, there for their use. Only one thing is missing: somewhere to work.

It's a contrast to my first day at the European Parliament, ten years before. There, everything was in place – office, computers and the rest – and I could get started almost straight away. Here, I and the other new MPs are told that we will be allocated rooms in due course. For now we will have to squat in corridors or at cafe tables. It's peculiar because all the rooms in Westminster have been unused for the last three weeks of the election campaign. Once Parliament is dissolved, existing MPs are no longer Members, only candidates, and therefore cannot use the Palace of Westminster. So the rooms can be cleaned and prepared ready for the new intake.

This is not incompetence on the part of the officials who are employed to run the Houses of Parliament. It turns out that they are not the ones who allocate rooms to MPs. This is done by the main parties because, as with so much else in Westminster, rooms are a currency, or a perk. The better rooms go to the more senior MPs, or as rewards to those who do the bidding of the whips. If you are prepared to serve on the less exciting committees, and vote loyally with your party leader, then come the next election you may be rewarded with a room closer to the tea room or further away from the toilets. Those at the top of the tree end up with a view of the River Thames. If you rebel, or don't do your bit, or belong to one of the smaller parties, you can go to the back of the queue and wait for your chance to squeeze into a broom cupboard with limited ventilation. Consequently, the allocation of rooms has to be drawn out while the whips wring the last advantage from this power. We newbies are told we will be lucky to get our rooms within a fortnight. It's a reflection on the status, culture and hierarchy of Westminster, and also the misguided expectation that as new MPs we won't have any serious work to do anyway.

So at the end of my first day I have been given a pile of House of Commons stationery, but have nowhere to store it; a pigeonhole for my letters but no computer to read my emails; and a pink ribbon in the Members' cloakroom on which to hang my sword before entering the chamber. The Member for Brighton Pavilion is open for business.

Fortunately, I wasn't alone. Cath Miller had run my European Parliament office brilliantly and it had been a lurking fear during the election campaign that she might feel that this was the time to move on. We hadn't found a moment to discuss it. It felt like tempting fate to think about the practicalities of being an MP when the voters had yet to speak. But as soon as the results were announced, I had to know the answer. As I came down the steps from the rostrum I had taken her hand and said, 'You will come with me, won't you?'

'Of course,' she had replied, practical as ever. 'We're just going through that door, and then we'll meet the BBC people—'

'No, I don't mean now, I mean come with me to Parliament!'

The job of running an office is incredibly important for an MP or MEP. So much of your life consists of running from one event to another – meeting constituents, delivering a speech, giving an interview, or voting – and in between trying to keep on top of a hundred other issues. So I might come out of a meeting, have no more than half a minute in which to catch up on all this before heading off to catch a train back to my constituency, and there would be Cath, who would know what mattered and tell me briefly all I needed to know.

It also helped to have James Humphreys there. He is one of the few people in the Green Party who had worked in government – in his case five years as a senior civil servant in Downing Street. He was also a source of information on some of the strange customs of the place. One of these concerned the phrase 'honourable friend'. A strange convention of Parliament is that you do not call other MPs by their names when speaking in the chamber. You don't say, 'Eric Pickles . . .' (or Mr Pickles, or Eric) '. . . is talking rubbish.' Instead, you say, '. . . the Honourable Member for Brentwood and Ongar is talking rubbish.' Some MPs are accorded a higher status: so when Eric Pickles joined the cabinet he also became a member of the Privy Council (don't ask . . .) and so is entitled to be called 'Right Honourable'. And if the MP you are talking about is from your own party, then you say 'My Honourable Friend'.

As he was explaining this, it struck me that this was a phrase I would not be needing any time soon. As the only Green MP, I wouldn't have any 'honourable friends'. But I went on to reflect that this need not be a disadvantage. It meant that I was free to speak my mind. I could work across party boundaries, and raise issues that no one else wanted to pick up. But if this was to succeed, I was going to have to learn the rules of the game.

The next day we set up camp at one of the tables in the atrium of Portcullis House, and tried to forget that after spending nearly half a billion pounds on this new building just a few years ago, Parliament still cannot provide MPs with basic office services. Camping, though, was difficult. Cath and James only had temporary passes and the security rules meant that they could not leave my side. If I went to a meeting, they either had to come with me – thereby losing the precious table – or hope none of the police noticed their dubious status if I left them behind. And though Portcullis House is very glamorous – it's where all the new MPs I spoke to were hoping to have offices – the atrium is noisy and very exposed. More positively, it meant that I also saw one or two familiar and friendly faces who came over to offer their congratulations.

Later on in my first day in Parliament, we ventured through the tunnel that links Portcullis House to the main Palace of Westminster. Compared with the modern, glassy, coffee-lounge world I have left, the old Palace seemed rather drab and down at heel. The wood panelling is gloomy, the carpets have come straight from a 1970s pub, and there's a pervading smell of school dinners. But the chamber itself is still impressive: smaller than I had expected, but in a way that only makes the sense of theatre and of history all the more powerful. Even if the tour guides didn't keep talking about it, and there weren't portraits and statues of the towering parliamentary figures of the past at every corner, from Cromwell to Churchill, via Palmerston, Gladstone and Lloyd George, it would still be intimidating. It seemed inconceivable that I was going to sit on those green benches, let alone stand up and cross debating swords with the Queen's First Lord of the Treasury.

In a corridor on the way to the chamber was another piece of history: a small display about the suffragettes and their campaign for votes for women. It even has the scarf worn by Emily Wilding Davison when she was killed by the king's horse on Derby Day at

Epsom. I was particularly touched by how proud the Commons staff are of the suffragettes, always ready to explain how two suffragettes chained themselves to the grilles in the Ladies Gallery; now part of the display. Or how Emily Davison hid in the broom cupboard next to the Chapel of St Mary Undercroft, beneath Westminster Hall, on census night in 1911 so she could legitimately give her place of residence on the census form as the House of Commons. This testimony to their courage has become a source of inspiration each day I pass to and from the chamber, as it has to many men and women before me. (Tony Benn even put up a commemorative plaque outside the broom cupboard: quite illegally, as he later recounted with pleasure.)

Back at my cafe table, we talked about building some cross-party alliances. The more I could work with others, the greater the difference I could make on the issues and causes that mattered for Brighton and for the country: and this would be easier for me than an MP with deep-rooted party allegiances and rivalries. The first of these was with the Scottish Nationalists and Plaid Cymru, who were part of an informal group that pooled information on upcoming government business. They were very helpful and invited me to join this group without any preconditions. At once, I had some honorary honourable friends, and was plugged into the Westminster system a little more firmly.

Another boost was being allocated a room in the Norman Shaw building, which turned out to be the old home of Scotland Yard. It had previously belonged to the eminent backbencher Michael Mates, and my stock rose when some of the more status-conscious MPs learned of my good fortune. I suspect that one of the senior officials in Parliament had a hand in it. They could not have been more helpful in seeing me settled in, and their staff were clearly delighted that the Greens had finally made it into Parliament: 'You'll be a breath of fresh air,' one said. In the immediate aftermath of the expenses scandal, there was a sense of change around Westminster. More prosaically, having a proper office with space for several desks (and windows you could open!) would mean we could work far more effectively: and even in the first few days, I realized just how many letters and messages from my new constituents there would be, some raising very difficult and sensitive issues, and how important it was that each was dealt with properly.

Meanwhile there were more new rules and procedures to absorb. If I were an MP for one of the main parties, I would receive a 'Whip Sheet' detailing all the business of the House in the week to come, and how badly the whips would take it if I were to vote the wrong way, or not turn up at all. The votes are helpfully underlined once, or twice for more important business, or three times if attendance is mandatory – hence the term 'three line whip'. This helps the whips control their 'troops': and means the troops don't have to think about the issues. In fact, they don't even need to know what it is they are voting on, and in my first few trips through the voting lobbies there were plenty of MPs who had run from their offices when the division bell rang without knowing the name of the bill being debated, but sure how they were supposed to vote. And if they forgot, they could always look at who else was going through the 'Aye' or 'No' lobbies, and be guided by whether they were surrounded by their own side or not. (Sometimes even 'old hands' go into the wrong lobby by mistake and have to explain themselves to the whips. You could call it being caught short: you are not allowed to 'reverse' out of the lobbies once you've gone in, so one way of covering up a mistake, apparently, is to hide in the loos in the lobby until the voting is finished.)

It was on one of these early votes that I first wondered why it is that we have such a system. So much about the way Parliament works is obscure or downright weird. (Do MPs really need a snuffbox at the entrance to the Commons Chamber in case they need a quick snort before going in?) This means that it's not always easy to see what is stupid-but-irrelevant and what is comic-but-harmful. Being old and looking odd isn't in itself a bad thing. The guards outside Buckingham Palace in their red tunics and bearskin hats might look like they are from another century, but the soldiers themselves are highly trained professionals and they carry modern weapons, not blunderbusses. After a few weeks I began to suspect that because Parliament is completely stuffed with strange customs, like a cross between Ruritania and a Gilbert and Sullivan comic opera, it's easy to make fun of the whole thing, and not take it seriously. So Black Rod's silk stockings, the archaic, Anglo-Norman language and the right of a single MP to veto a Private Member's Bill all just seem at first sight part of a venerable yet lovable institution, one that might not have kept up with the times but is rooted in solid virtues: the 'Mother of all Parliaments'. Yet while fancy dress is harmless, having a ban on breastfeeding is a terrible signal to send to women thinking of standing for Parliament and are planning to have children or already have a young family. It shows that they are not welcome; and that they are currently so marginalized they have been unable to challenge a ban that almost every other workplace and public space has long since done away with. Similarly, the right to veto Private Members' Bills in effect puts yet more power in the hands of the elected government, and weakens the right of backbench MPs – those who do not receive additional salaries as government ministers or positions on the Opposition front benches – to pursue issues that matter to them or to their constituents.

I was soon convinced that the current voting system in Parliament is not just a piece of inert tradition, but actively malign; and probably kept that way deliberately. The process itself is absurd. When a vote is called – which can happen at any time, though there are set times of day when most are more likely to be held – a 'division bell' begins to clang throughout the Palace (and in various bars and restaurants in the surrounding streets) to warn MPs that they have eight minutes to reach the voting lobbies.

Whether or not you are in the middle of a select committee session or meeting constituents, you have to drop everything and run for it. The MPs then crowd into the lobbies, and file through one of two doors – the 'Ayes' who support the motion, and the 'Noes' who don't – where they are counted and their names recorded. The whole pantomime takes around fifteen minutes for each vote, which means that MPs only have the chance to vote on a tiny proportion of the amendments put forward for each bill. It's excruciatingly inefficient.

After a few days of this, I asked some of my new MP colleagues whether anyone had looked into electronic voting. The answers were not very compelling. Some – presumably keep-fit fanatics, though you might not know it – think it works fine as it is. Others see it as a chance to catch up with other MPs, in particular ministers and other senior colleagues, if you can fall into step with them. What no one wanted to say – and maybe they didn't realize it – is that most people like Parliament just the way it is.

That feeling goes far beyond the voting system and is why Parliament is so resistant to reform. Before I was elected I'd heard it said that the Palace of Westminster is one of the best gentlemen's clubs in London, and the only one you are paid for attending. It certainly offers plenty of comfort, service, and deference, all paid for by the taxpayer. Many MPs work hard, but the combination of status and power is still heady. If you are ready to accept it all at face value, the place will treat you like minor royalty – bringing with it the risk that you lose your sense of perspective (even of reality) and also forget who you are there to serve.

Again, it only took a few days on the inside to understand how it was that MPs got themselves in such a mess over their expenses. There is a sense of entitlement that pervades this place like a colourless and odourless gas, creeping along the corridors and under every door. Some MPs still don't see that the rules that they create for other people have to apply to themselves. For example, if you are given perks in other jobs, you are supposed to pay tax on them as if they were any other form of income. But though MPs voted through the powers for HM Revenue and Customs to enforce those rules, there were those who didn't think they should apply within the boundaries of Westminster.

Even though the scandal had only recently broken, I was already hearing MPs complaining about having to retain receipts and submitting claims to the much-hated Independent Parliamentary Standards Authority. It was as if they had forgotten that for everyone else in this country, collecting receipts if you want to claim anything back is just one of those chores imposed on you by HMRC – in other words, by Parliament. Despite everything, a frightening number of my new colleagues didn't see that you can't have one rule for yourself and one for the other 60 million people in Britain, and still retain their trust.

Fortunately, there were also MPs who saw that things need to change; not just about expenses, but opening up the whole place, making it more efficient, and giving more power to Parliament to scrutinize the government. It was hugely encouraging that John Bercow had been elected by MPs as a reform-minded Speaker. If we were to make further progress, cross-party support would be crucial; and I soon realized that this was perhaps an area where I could play a role, being free of the pressures and blandishments of the whips.

But first, there was one further tradition in the House of Commons that I could not avoid. Every Member must speak in the chamber for the first time, and give what is called their 'maiden' speech. Like everything else, this is wrapped round with precedents. Some of these gave me no problem. You are supposed to praise your predecessor, and I was lucky that I genuinely felt that David Lepper, who had held the seat from 1997 until deciding to stand down in 2010, had been a diligent constituency MP. You also praise the constituency itself, describing some of its finer features, as if standing in for the local tourist board. That was a pleasure too, as I could talk about some of the places and organizations that I was truly happy to celebrate, such as the women's refuge RISE, alongside the charm of the North Laine or the beauty of the South Downs. One tradition, though, was a problem: that you were not supposed to be political. I could hardly utter my first words as the first Green MP to be elected and not mention politics, if only to say something about why this moment mattered, and why a Green voice in Parliament was so important. I was sure there would be a way of doing this that would not create needless controversy or offence: but then came Trafigura.

2

Coalition and Opposition:
How Tory Ideology Goes Unchallenged in Parliament

'When the forms of an old culture are dying, the new culture is created by a few people who are not afraid to be insecure.'

Rudolf Bahro

In 2006, around 31,000 people in the Ivory Coast city of Abidjan were poisoned by the dumping of toxic waste that caused headaches, nosebleeds and stomach pains. At least twelve of them died. Three years later the victims were offered around $46 million in compensation by the owners of the waste. Typically in such cases, the waste had taken a long and devious route to end up dumped on open ground at several locations around Abidjan. Oil from Mexico with a high level of impurity had been shipped via Galveston in the United States and put on a ship where it was treated with chemicals to strip out the impurities. The cleaned oil was sold and the waste was transferred to the ship's 'slop tanks' for offloading in Amsterdam.

Disposing of hazardous waste properly is an expensive business, usually involving high-temperature incineration in specialist facilities. Once the disposal company in Amsterdam realized how contaminated the 'slops' were, they increased the disposal charge and the ship left to find another home for the waste. After trying in Lagos, Nigeria, they found a 'waste disposal company' in Abidjan called 'Tommy', which was set up shortly after the ship left Amsterdam and had never handled this kind (or perhaps any kind) of waste before. The waste was pumped from the ship into road tankers and driven away to be dumped.

The whole affair involved many different companies and agencies in several countries, from Mexico and the United States to the Ivory Coast via the Netherlands and Nigeria. But if there was one place where it was planned and overseen, that place was the offices of the commodity traders Trafigura at 2 Portman Street, London.

The City of London prides itself on being one of the great trading and financial centres of the world. And with that position comes responsibility. London should not be a base for commercial piracy around the world, any more than it should be a base for drugs, child pornography or slavery. Parliament has the ultimate authority, and responsibility, for setting the laws that govern the international activities of the companies and individuals who live and work in London, and for ensuring that those laws are obeyed. For centuries, the law had established the principle that if you let your waste end up on someone else's land you are responsible; and which country that waste was created in, or where it ended up, should not affect that basic principle. But the law, or the enforcement of the law, had failed. And Greenpeace, who were pursuing Trafigura through the Dutch courts, asked if I could help.

Trafigura's lawyers had already sued various UK journalists for libel over the case, had forced the BBC to withdraw a report from *Newsnight* and pay Trafigura compensation, and had taken out a 'super-injunction' against the *Guardian*, preventing them from reporting on the case, or even reporting on the injunction. Trafigura is one of the largest commodity trading companies in the world, with annual turnover in excess of $100 billion and annual profits of over $1 billion. Those are profits worth protecting, and even the fees of London law firm Carter-Ruck would seem modest by comparison. British newspapers and broadcasters weren't the only ones being pursued: from the Netherlands to Norway, Trafigura was intent on challenging any suggestion that they had known that the 'slops' they had pumped into the freshly painted oil tankers belonging to 'Tommy' were hazardous waste.

This was the heart of the Greenpeace case in the Netherlands; but in a further Kafkaesque twist, Trafigura's injunctions meant that the court hearings couldn't be reported in Britain, even if those at the centre of the allegations worked in London. Only one legal principle could trump this block: parliamentary privilege. This says, among other things, that the proceedings of Parliament may be freely reported, and in effect the normal rules of contempt of court and libel do not apply. Clearly this is a privilege that has to be used very carefully; but if I mentioned the Trafigura case in Parliament – even a few words would be enough – the media could then cover it.

I met the Greenpeace team in Portcullis House and listened with mounting horror as they explained just how appalling the situation was. But I was also concerned that if I were to use my maiden speech to talk about Trafigura, it could cause a row about parliamentary privilege that would overshadow everything else I wanted to say about the environment and climate change, and the challenges facing my constituents in Brighton. There were to be over a hundred maiden speeches by new members that session; but only one would be the first time that a whole political movement was speaking in Parliament.

Then I read some of the internal emails that the traders and managers in Trafigura had sent between themselves to set up the oil deal and get rid of the waste. The impetus for the deal was clear. The contaminated oil was '. . . *as cheap as anyone could imagine and should make serious dollars'*. So too were the problems with cleaning the oil with 'caustic washing', as *'. . . US / Singapore and European terminals no longer allow the use of caustic soda washes since local environmental agencies do not allow disposal of the toxic caustic after treatment.'* But Trafigura's dealers did not give up: *'. . . am checking in the US/Estonia and Tunisia, the Caustic supplier disposes the slurry in Fujairah (not sure if in a legal way!)'*. And it's clear why. *'Me and Leon want it cos each cargo should make 7m !!'* And even before the waste arrived in the Netherlands, some interesting ideas are being kicked around the Trafigura email lists. *'Does it make any sense to take on t/c [time charter] a vessel that is about to be scrapped for something like $5k/day (or am I dreaming) and park somewhere in WAF [West Africa] in order to carry out some of the caustic washings over there? I don't know how we dispose of the slops and I don't imply we would dump them, but for sure there must be some way to pay someone to take them.'*

There was then a long exchange under the email header 'PMI shit' – PMI being the company that produced the oil – about disposal options and the risk of 'choking on this stuff'. And as these were copied to Claude Dauphin, the head of Trafigura, it suggested the underlying attitude or culture of the organization that these emails portray is one he was aware of and of which he presumably approved. That in turn showed why the Trafigura case mattered so much. Even if you put aside criminal knowledge or intent, the picture was of a company whose ways of working were likely to lead to further incidents of pollution, and perhaps further deaths, unless something was done. But the determination to make money at all costs came through clearly too; and that was the company we were proposing to take on. Had it been a straight fight, that would not have concerned me. But here was a rich and powerful business with some of the most able legal advisers at their call; and I was in my first few days in Parliament, not sure of the formal rules, let alone the back channels and informal networks that an influential business like Trafigura might have in this place.

In the event, my first words in the House came sooner than expected. Who gets chosen to speak and when is decided by the Speaker, and with so many new MPs to get through, my own chance was somewhat delayed. I had been tipped off that I would be called to make my maiden speech during the part of the debate on the Queen's Speech – in other words, on the new programme of the government – which related to the environment and climate change; which was probably the Speaker, John Bercow, being considerate. But as I sat listening to the debate, and particularly Ed Miliband's depressing views about the need for new nuclear power stations to tackle climate change, I found myself on my feet, intervening in his response to the government (intervening being the polite, parliamentary term for interrupting):

> My Right Honourable Friend says that the challenge of climate change is so great that we need nuclear power as well as renewables and energy efficiency, but given that we have to reduce our emissions in the next eight to ten years if we listen to the scientists, we need to consider what is the most cost-effective and the fastest way to do that. Is nuclear power not a massive distraction in that debate? Even if we doubled the amount of nuclear power, we would cut our emissions by only 8 per cent. Putting money into renewables and efficiency is far more effective.

When I sat down, I could see why it was known as a maiden speech: as in cricket (I have this on good authority – my husband Richard had been a professional cricketer for Warwickshire) once you had scored your first runs, you could begin to relax a little. After that, the speech itself, an hour or two later, was still daunting, but much more straightforward than I had anticipated.

I started by talking about how I was following in some impressive footsteps in making the first parliamentary speech on behalf of a new party:

> When Keir Hardie made his maiden speech to this House, after winning the seat of West Ham South in 1892, there was an outcry, because instead of frock coat and top hat, he wore a tweed suit and deerstalker. It's hard to decide which of these choices would seem more inappropriate today. But what Keir Hardie stood for now seems much more mainstream. Progressive taxation, votes for women, free schooling, pensions and abolition of the House of Lords. Though the last of these is an urgent task still before us, the rest are now seen as essential to our society. What was once radical, even revolutionary, becomes understood, accepted and even cherished.

The Green Party was on a similar journey, and I hoped our principles and priorities, on equality, the fair use of resources, international peace and justice, and protection of our natural environment – would also over time find wide acceptance. I also talked about Brighton and the unique character of the people and the place:

> Brighton has always had a tradition of independence – of doing things differently. It has an entrepreneurial spirit, making the best of things whatever the circumstances, and enjoying being ahead of the curve.

But that was not the whole story of the constituency I now represented.

> There is also a Brighton that is perhaps less familiar to Honourable Members. The very popularity of the city

puts pressure on transport and housing and on the quality of life. Though there is prosperity, it is not shared equally. People are proud of Brighton, but they believe that it can be a better and fairer place to live and work. I pledge to do everything I can in this place to help achieve that, with a particular focus on creating more affordable, more sustainable housing.

I also spoke about the opportunities available to an individual MP:

A single MP can contribute to debates, to legislation, to scrutiny. Work that is valuable, if not always appreciated on the outside. A single MP can speak up for their constituents. A single MP can challenge the executive. I am pleased that the government is to bring forward legislation to revoke a number of restrictions on people's freedoms and liberties, such as identity cards. But many restrictions remain. For example, control orders are to stay in force. Who is to speak for those affected and for the principle that people should not be held without charge, even if it is in their own homes? House arrest is something we deplore in other countries. I hope through debate we can conclude that it has no place here either. A single MP can raise issues that cannot be aired elsewhere.

From there, it was natural to speak about Trafigura and the scandal in the Ivory Coast. No one interrupted, or appeared waving an injunction; and that part of my job was done, because the media could now follow this lead and cover the trial. And I was free to turn to the final part of my speech: our immense, even overwhelming responsibility as MPs to tackle the urgent threat of climate change.

It was hard to know the right note to hit. No audience likes to be lectured; but MPs less than anyone. In theory at least, MPs were committed to the cause. Parliament had adopted the Climate Change Act in 2008, and more recently had signed up to the 10:10 campaign to reduce carbon emissions by 10 per cent by 2010. But how to turn this into a programme of action that matched the scale of the danger? We were not even doing enough on the basics, like reducing the waste of energy from badly built and maintained housing, and where spending money on lagging and insulation would soon pay for itself in reduced bills and more jobs as well as helping to avoid the worst of climate change. For the next five years, we were the 650 people who were ultimately responsible: and looking around me I felt hope and fear in equal measure.

> I have worked on the causes and consequences of climate change for most of my working life, first with Oxfam – for the effects of climate change are already affecting millions of people in poorer countries around the world – and then for ten years in the European Parliament. But if we are to overcome this threat, then it is we in this chamber who must take the lead. We must act so that the United Kingdom can meet its own responsibilities to cut the emissions of carbon dioxide and other gases that are changing our climate, and encourage and support other countries to do the same.

Then it was over. The *Independent* reported the speech under the headline 'A historic moment for anyone who cares about the environment', which was an exciting thought. It wasn't that I would be the only MP in Parliament to care about the environment. Far from it. But I had a unique mandate. And I'd already had my first taste of why the fact that Brighton had elected a Green MP, rather than another Labour backbencher, would make a difference. It had come from my earlier intervention: Labour's loss of nerve over energy policy and climate change.

Ed Miliband had talked about nuclear power for a reason. His own party was in favour of building more nuclear power stations, in part influenced by the engineering unions who represented the interests of many of those working in the nuclear industry. But it also discomforted the Liberal Democrats, who as a party were opposed to nuclear, but were now in a coalition with the Tories, who were very much in favour. The fudge was that nuclear power could go ahead, to please the Tories, but without any public subsidy, to satisfy the Lib Dems. Ed had fun with this in a typically parliamentary way, teasing the Lib Dems about how the Coalition Agreement meant they were part of a government in favour of nuclear power, but which allowed their spokesperson to speak against it, but required Lib Dem MPs to neither support their own government or their own spokesperson, but instead to abstain. It was of course a ridiculous position; but the joking masked the underlying reality. If all three parties were either in favour or neutered, on nuclear power or other issues, then who was going to speak out?

These first days in Parliament, making sense of the arcane procedures, meeting potential allies, and preparing for my maiden speech, had been played out against the backdrop of an election that had left no single party with enough MPs to form a government on their own. Previous governments had seen their working majorities melt away through defections and lost by-elections – Labour in 1978, and the Conservatives in 1996 – but it was the first time that the voters themselves had delivered a hung Parliament since 1974, the previous instance being in the 1930s, which was also the last time the Liberal Democrats had been in power.

I'd followed Nick Clegg's rise with interest since we'd first met in the European Parliament and worked together on trade and international development. He'd left for Westminster in 2005 and in five short years he'd become leader of the Liberal Democrats, given them some stability after the whispering that

had undermined his two predecessors, Charles Kennedy and
Menzies Campbell, and then been propelled into the role of
Britain's favourite politician through the three leader debates
during the election campaign. Now he was the kingmaker –
or so it seemed. But it didn't take long to see that his position
was not quite so powerful. The Conservatives were the largest
party in Parliament, and had also in one sense 'won' the election,
in that they had secured the most votes – over 2 million more
than Labour. Gordon Brown, though still caretaking in No. 10,
was clearly the loser, with Labour's share of the vote down from
35 per cent to 29 per cent. The election felt like a rejection of
Labour, and though it was anything but a clear endorsement of
the Conservative alternative, it was argued that it would be hard
for the Liberal Democrats to keep the losers in power.

The electoral mathematics did not favour a Liberal–Labour
deal. Even a 'rainbow' coalition, in which I soon saw my own
name being included, would only create a tiny majority – perhaps
just three or four seats. That would hardly be the ideal foundation
for a stable, long-term government, though the alternative was
still much worse. There was talk of Nick Clegg having to try to
negotiate a deal with the Conservatives: but such a deal was so
unlikely, a left-leaning coalition of Labour, Liberals and the Welsh
and Scottish Nationalists might well be the final outcome.

During the weekend that followed the election, though, the
latter option faded away. For the rainbow coalition to work,
Gordon Brown would have to accept that he could not continue
as prime minister; and Labour would have to begin to open
channels with the potential coalition partners about a programme
that they could rally around. I took soundings from some of
the other elected representatives in the Green Party, including
Jean Lambert in the European Parliament and Jenny Jones and
Darren Johnson on the London Assembly, to get a sense of how
we should steer through these uncharted waters. My own view
was that we shouldn't join any formal coalition. While I was far

more likely to vote in support of Labour than the Conservatives, the fact remained that Labour's recent record in government had been, in many ways, a desperately disappointing one: not only the Iraq War, but everything from the privatization of public services to serious attacks on civil liberties: and I had no wish to be locked into supporting whatever they came up with next. Instead, I should vote on the merits of each piece of legislation they put forward. This was quite an undertaking. There would be literally hundreds of votes, each one potentially controversial, and each one needing us to work hard to understand the implications.

In the event, however, Gordon Brown did not step aside; and enough of Labour's 'big beasts' came out that weekend dismissing any possibility of working with the 'Nats' that by Monday it was clear to me the rainbow was only going to lead to fool's gold. It seemed astonishing that Labour was not going to make a fight of it.

Even stranger were the rumours coming out of the Tory–Lib Dem talks. Under Charles Kennedy, the Lib Dems had been firmly to the left of Labour. Since then, the party's economic liberal wing – the so-called Orange Book tendency – had become more prominent, but at the same time Labour had been continuing to drift to the right, particularly on civil liberties and on breaking up public services. The idea of the Lib Dems somehow holding their noses and accepting a Tory-led government seemed strange; and yet might they actually *prefer* to deal with Cameron? It was true that he had been burnishing his image in a way that would appeal to Lib Dems – talking up civil liberties, challenging various prejudices among his membership, and pledging to be the greenest government ever. But they couldn't be taken in, could they?

Then came the announcement: a pact that would last for the full five years of the Parliament. A detailed programme for government, welded from their two very different election manifestos. And Lib Dems given ministerial posts throughout government, with Nick Clegg as deputy prime minister. But even more astonishing than the deal's ambition, the cherished policies the Lib Dems would sacrifice, or the thought of Sarah Teather working alongside Michael Gove at Education, was the sight of 'Dave and Nick' in the rose garden at No. 10 as they revealed the deal. The delight they took in each other's company was both an act and genuine – almost visibly leaning towards each other, and away from their respective parties, like people on separate boats, steering a common course, shaking hands over the rail.

As I watched the coverage of this odd event, I felt torn. We had avoided the risk of a Labour-led coalition perhaps stumbling on for a few months, discrediting itself further and making Cameron seem strong and decisive, and then losing an autumn election, giving the Tories five solid years. But much stronger was a sense of grim foreboding. On paper, it might have seemed that the Liberal Democrats had got a fairly good deal: such as a referendum on electoral reform and a block on subsidies for nuclear power. But in return, they had bought into the whole austerity package: the idea that the only credible response to the financial crisis was to inflict deep cuts in public services and benefits. For all their claims that 'we were all in it together', it was obvious that, with George Osborne as Chancellor, the burden would fall on those least able to bear it: women in low-paid jobs, casual workers, and those with disabilities or long-term illnesses. Yet here was the Liberal Democrat leadership, prancing around waving their tails and acting as if they had won the lottery.

The rank and file told a different story. In Westminster, they were looking shell-shocked at finding themselves on the same benches as the Tories, and locked into it for the next five years. This wasn't the kind of coalition politics they had ever imagined, and had it not been for Simon Hughes – who clearly disliked the whole business but persuaded others to stick with it from party loyalty – there would have been trouble. Perhaps it helped that so many Liberal Democrat MPs were being offered the once-in-a-lifetime opportunity of becoming a Minister of the Crown, with civil servants, red ministerial despatch boxes and the rest. Heady stuff.

But the Coalition Agreement had yet wider implications. On a whole host of issues, from climate change to civil liberties and from tuition fees in higher education to protecting the NHS, the Lib Dems had provided the only substantial alternative voice to the populist, illiberal and neo-conservative positions of the Tories and, increasingly, of Labour. But now the Lib Dems were to be absorbed into this new coalition, which would inevitably be dominated by the Tories. Collective responsibility, party loyalty and party discipline would mean that even backbench Lib Dems would be unlikely to speak out forcefully or mount effective opposition. The importance of alternative voices speaking up would be greater than ever. So with Labour contaminated by its own time in government, and the Lib Dems muzzled by the Coalition Agreement, the scene was set for David Cameron to begin an ideological assault on the welfare state.

3

Austerity:
How Bankers' Blunders
Are Being Used to Punish Us All

'We're all in this together.'

George Osborne

The Palace of Westminster is a strange place from which to launch an attack on the country's most vulnerable people. Once you are past the security barriers, you enter a world of privilege and comfort. There are ushers to take messages for you, and police officers at every turn, ready to direct you through the maze of corridors. There is a hairdresser, a gym, cash machines, coffee bars and post offices, so you never need to leave the orderly precincts of the Palace and jostle with the tourists and civil servants in the surrounding streets. There are subsidized bars and restaurants, so that those who want to can apparently start the day with the Westminster breakfast of House of Commons champagne and orange juice, smoked salmon with scrambled eggs and chives, toast, tea or coffee, etc. and finish it with a fine dinner of, say, asparagus, duck, Eton mess and a selection of British cheeses.

To be fair, most MPs probably use the bars and restaurants because they are convenient, rather than because they particularly want to gorge on fine food and wine at the taxpayers' expense. Some MPs have campaigned to have these subsidies abolished or reformed. (Part of the subsidy helps to keep the cost down in the canteens used by staff, reflecting the antisocial hours we expect them to work, and I don't want to see those cut. But there's no reason why MPs couldn't use those same canteens if the House is sitting late.) Even so, the fact that we haven't yet succeeded suggests that the majority of MPs are relaxed about enjoying prices themselves that they deny to their constituents. It was a surprise to me, arriving in Parliament after the expenses scandal. After all, many MPs complained that the public had 'lost trust' and that 'hard-working' MPs were being unfairly criticized for the actions of a few 'bad apples'. But here was a simple reform that would show MPs have learned they shouldn't have one law for themselves and another for everyone else – and they hadn't taken it.

Some might argue, of course, that MPs are not the only ones with expenses and perks and subsidized catering. Business people, the media, celebrities: they too can enjoy a privileged existence, and they don't always have to put their hands in their own pockets to fund it. But MPs write the rules. That makes a huge difference. And if they feel they aren't paid enough, then have the courage to vote through a pay rise and take the consequences at the next election.

But however distasteful the subsidy, it isn't the real problem with the Westminster culture of privilege. If MPs paid the full price for every vol-au-vent and glass of Chablis themselves, it would still be wrong for them to forget that many millions of their fellow-citizens live in a very different world. The subsidy in the Members' Dining Room is only a symptom of a much deeper disconnect between the rulers and the ruled. Over half the members of the 2010 Cameron cabinet went to private school. Over half went to Oxford or Cambridge universities. Over half of them had substantial wealth – that is, over £1 million without taking their family home into account – and in 2012 the total wealth of the current cabinet was estimated at nearly £70 million.

And perhaps most bizarrely – it actually feels physically odd to be writing these words in the second decade of the twenty-first century – a third of the cabinet were in some way connected to the nobility, through descent or marriage.

None of this is necessarily a problem for politicians as individuals: what school you go to should not mark you down as unfit to represent the country, whether it has the best reputation in the country, or the worst. Rather, the problem is the cumulative effect of drawing our rulers from so narrow a stratum of society. I don't want Parliament dominated by forty-nine-year-old white male Oxbridge graduates, which is the average profile at the moment. Nor do I want them all replaced with people like me, and so filled with fifty-four-year-old white female graduates of Exeter University who used to work for Oxfam. Britain is a far more diverse country than you would guess from meeting those who run it. We need a different kind of richness in Parliament: one that comes from drawing fully on all the regions of Britain, all the many differences in background and education and experience. We need a Parliament of all the talents – and all the perspectives too.

But whatever the faults in the political system that make it so unrepresentative, there is a moral dimension to the wealth and privilege that many MPs enjoy. They – we – are the fortunate few, coming in the main from comfortable backgrounds. Many have benefited from the best education that the country can provide, and rubbed shoulders with others in business, the professions, arts and society. And though some may claim otherwise, MPs are well paid: the basic salary is more than twice the national average, and ministers receive even more. Having been given all this, politicians should be the last people to despise those less fortunate.

And yet, British politics has become reinfected with the idea of the 'undeserving poor'. The cliché of the greedy, uncaring and hard-hearted Victorian politician or industrialist, blaming the poor for their own improvidence, has been reborn in a post-Thatcherite form. The top hats and side-whiskers may have gone, but the attitudes are still the same. The tools of the nineteenth-century social reformers – statistics and reports – have been taken up and twisted by a new generation of think tanks and lobby groups to argue that poverty is a lifestyle choice; that offering financial support breeds dependency; that poverty is passed through the generations, like the modern equivalent of genetic or racial determinism. In this warped ideology, the poor become first a problem, then a threat; they need to be controlled, pressured and punished; they are treated as an underclass, no longer part of the fabric of society.

This has been a growing theme of politics and society since the 1980s. It provided some of the mood music for New Labour's approach to welfare reform, particularly once the honeymoon that followed the 1997 election had begun to turn sour. Talk of balancing rights with responsibilities could seem quite reasonable – but under this cover, the belief that those who were receiving benefits were in some way taking advantage of everyone else could grow and spread. After May 2010, though, we had a government not being pulled in this direction by right-wing think tanks or the media, but deliberately pushing on to see how far they could drive the poor to the margins. For them, the economic crisis that had erupted in 2008 was a golden opportunity to shrink the state. They claimed that it was necessary to cut the welfare budget and to slash public sector jobs in order to reduce public debt, even though the effect of the cuts was to remove money from the economy. This in turn meant less money being spent, and so less tax coming in to the Treasury.

The net result (and an entirely predictable example of J. M. Keynes's 'paradox of thrift') was that cutting public spending actually made public debt not better but worse in the long run. As Professor Victoria Chick and Ann Pettifor more recently concluded, based on an analysis of a century of data, '. . . cutting expenditure increases, rather than cuts, the levels of public debt as a share of GDP. As public expenditure increases, public debt falls; and vice versa.' Sure enough, in 2013, three years in to austerity, the national debt was rising again and Britain lost the AAA credit rating that George Osborne had supposedly made these sacrifices to protect.

Some Tories were honest about what they were doing. They maintained that state support was not only bad for the country, but for the people who were receiving what they called 'handouts' (so ignoring that every single person in the country, including those on benefits, contributes to the welfare system through indirect taxes such as VAT, and many have paid in directly through income tax and National Insurance contributions). For these Tories, making working-age benefits as miserly as possible was a good thing in itself, whatever it did to the economy. Doing so would force people into work by making the alternative so unpleasant that they would take any job under any circumstance, whatever it might do to their health, or those who were dependent upon them, such as their children. For these welfare-to-work zealots, cutting benefits and harassing those receiving them was a moral issue. And although I think they were and are profoundly wrong, they at least weren't trying to hide it.

The difficulty for the coalition was that most people in Britain didn't think this way. Most people weren't vindictive to those receiving benefits: they had to be moulded to think this way and so support what the government planned to do. For some years, think tanks and campaigners on the right – particularly those aligned with the neo-conservative movement in the United States – had been seeking to 'reframe' the debate about welfare. In their hands, even an innocuous phrase such as 'hard-working' could be used to convey a subtle and destructive message. Those in work were described as 'hard-working', and by implication those who were not in work were not 'hard-working': as if there was work to be had, but they chose not to take it because they were not 'hard-working'. This was a distortion of reality. It ignored the fact that many were unable to work, perhaps through illness. It also ignored or belittled the efforts of those who wanted to work but could not find a job. In Brighton, I have many constituents who have been searching for work for months or years, applying for dozens, even hundreds of jobs. They work immensely hard to find employment; but their efforts are belittled and they are dismissed as not 'hard-working'. And so what seems to be a bland sound-bite of the kind that politicians utter every waking moment becomes a way to suggest that those on benefits are 'work-shy' and so undeserving of the support of the rest of the country.

Set out in this way, it seems almost childish: yet these framing techniques can be immensely powerful, in part because they tap in to quite widespread and understandable feelings. As the full extent of the financial crash of 2008, and its impact on the real world of jobs and wages, became apparent, so people became fearful about their own futures, and the prospects of those who depended on them. To find a group you can blame for the economic and social anxieties of a nation is an old technique, but still effective: even more so if that group is already at the margins, lacking in power and unable to strike back. So demonizing those on benefits helped direct attention away from the real causes of the crash – greed and mismanagement in the City, and ill-judged cuts that were making the recession worse by undermining people's confidence – and to direct it instead onto a group who were in no position to make their case effectively.

This rhetoric was supported by a conscious effort to use statistics to bolster the case that the current welfare bill was 'unaffordable'. Partly this was by playing a three-cup trick, by using terms like 'welfare' very loosely. When it suited the government, they would quote frightening figures for the 'welfare bill' as a sign that there were far too many people receiving working-age benefits, without explaining that most of the money in fact went to paying the state pension. There was no acknowledgement that many of those on 'welfare' were in fact working, but being paid so little that the state needed to top up their pay. Nor was it pointed out that many of those out of work had paid into the system for many years, through National Insurance. And although working-age benefits rise during a recession, this hardly makes them unreasonable: the whole point of such benefits is to tide people over through hard times. It is like an insurance company taking your premiums during the good years, when your roof doesn't leak or your car stays in one piece, and then refusing to pay out when you have to make a claim because that would be 'unaffordable'.

Perhaps because the figures rarely supported their case, the government went further and deliberately set out to manipulate them. It was done knowingly, and went far beyond a question of differing interpretation. The main culprit was Iain Duncan Smith, the Secretary of State for Work and Pensions, and if you think that the definition of a liar is someone who sets out deliberately to mislead, then he has a case to answer. The only other explanation is that he simply doesn't understand the very basics of arithmetic, or has no idea how his own benefits work, or doesn't read the many official statements and press notices issued under his name.

To take one example, on 24 April 2013 Iain Duncan Smith said: 'Around one million people have been stuck on a working-age benefit for at least three out of the last four years, despite being judged capable of preparing or looking for work.' Surely you could only utter those words if you wanted people to think that there were a million people who had been out of work for most of the last four years, even though they were capable of working. That is certainly how the *Daily Mail* covered it. But in fact this was far from the truth. The one million figure was created by taking those receiving Jobseeker's Allowance (which isn't far from most people's idea of those 'capable of working') and adding to it those receiving Income Support for Lone Parents and those in an even more Orwellian category called 'Work Related Activity Group'. WRAG means people with long-term sickness or disabilities who have been assessed as potentially having some chance of returning to work in the future. You can be on dialysis, chemotherapy, be diagnosed as having an incurable illness or even be lying in a hospital bed and still be in WRAG.

So the 'one million' includes terminally ill people and single mothers with very young children, as I see all the time in my constituency surgeries in Brighton. But this is still not the really dishonest bit. Iain Duncan Smith also includes 187,000 people in the 'ESA Assessment Phase'. For those who have the good fortune never to have had anything to do with ESA, I should explain that this is the Employment and Support Allowance created to replace Incapacity Benefit and encourage more people of working age who are ill or disabled to return to work. It includes the medical assessment which was handed to a company called Atos to administer and which has generated more misery and suffering for its victims than any other part of Britain's often malign and uncaring welfare system. But the point about being in the 'assessment phase' is that you have yet to be assessed. In other words, Mr Duncan Smith had no idea if these 187,000 people are fit for work or not. As a majority of assessments find that former Incapacity Benefit claimants are not, in fact, fit to work, it would be very odd if every single one of these 187,000 assessments decided that they were. So does Iain Duncan Smith not understand this? Or was it that he was prepared to do whatever it took to get to the magic 'one million' figure that would delight the *Daily Mail*?

This is not accidental, it is a modus operandi: take groups of people from a fiendishly complex welfare system, play fast and loose with dates and processes, and come up with an eye-catching number or sound-bite. Then simply ignore the criticism from the Office of National Statistics, independent analysts, select committees and the rest.

There are countless more such truth-crimes. In November 2010, Iain Duncan Smith told the House of Commons that 'according to the Office of National Statistics', rents in the private sector were down around 5 per cent while rents linked to Housing Benefit had gone up by 3 per cent, and that this gap justified cracking down on Housing Benefit. In fact, the ONS does not produce statistics on private sector rents. It turned out that the 5 per cent figure was taken from that slightly less official source, www.findaproperty.com.

On 12 April 2013, Iain Duncan Smith told the *Daily Mail*: 'Already we've seen 8,000 people who would have been affected by the [benefits] cap move into jobs. This clearly demonstrates that the cap is having the desired impact.' The head of the UK Statistics Authority, Andrew Dilnot, later confirmed that this claim was 'unsupported by the official statistics'.

In fact, challenging distorted and misleading statements coming from government ministers has become an industry in itself. The campaigning group Disabled People Against Cuts (DPAC) produced a report on thirty-four of these, none of them trivial, and all checked against independent commentators such as *Channel 4 News* and www.fullfact.org. These include claiming that Job Centres had 500,000 new jobs coming in each week (but the Department for Work and Pensions later admitted that it was actually around 50,000); that fraudsters from around the world target Tax Credits (but HMRC do not record the nationality of claimants so there is no way of knowing); that inter-generational worklessness is a curse (but Iain Duncan Smith had to admit in a letter to Paul Goggins MP shortly before the latter's untimely death that the existence of families where no one has worked for three generations was based on 'personal observations' and not on any evidence).

Governments and politicians lie and exaggerate: no shock there. But this is different: a conscious programme of deception to establish beliefs that are simply not true. It is only dishonesty over the true cost of the welfare state that creates the climate in which such odious processes can go unchecked. For example, that hotbed of Marxist revolution, the Methodist Church, pointed out in an excellent report on mythmaking in poverty and welfare that the amount spent on propping up the banks during the financial crisis could have covered the cost of benefit fraud for a thousand years; that benefit fraud runs at a fraction of the rate of tax fraud; that there is no evidence that those receiving benefits then rush off and blow it on booze, fags, gambling, Sky or other addictions, despite the claims of Tory MPs and newspapers; and that many of the claims about the poor, made by Cameron and his 'team', are simply untrue and can be demonstrated as such with a few minutes of basic research. The problem is not the facts, it is the lack of willingness to challenge the myths.

Of course, some of those claiming benefits might never have worked, and so may never have paid in to the system through National Insurance; and some might avoid the chances to work that came their way. But in my experience – and as an MP I meet many people who receive state benefits – most people want to work, if there is work to be done, and if they can overcome the many barriers that lie in their way, such as the cost of travel and the lack of affordable childcare.

The deceit and the rhetoric are harmful in other ways. In my advice surgeries and in the rallies about welfare form in Parliament, I regularly meet constituents who have been undermined and demoralized by a system that is based on forcing them to 'prove' their disability. Instead of this relentless focus on what they cannot do, they would rather show to an employer or to society what it is that they can do. And by excluding their talents and endeavour, these 'reforms' impoverish us all.

This is not only about Iain Duncan Smith. The rest of the government – Cameron and Osborne, Clegg and Cable – adopted the same approach but wrapped it up in crocodile tears with their talk of 'all being in it together'.

Nothing could be more symptomatic of the coalition government than that empty phrase. The rich in Britain have enjoyed a series of tax breaks over the last five years, while those with the least have suffered most from the cuts in public services and the incompetence of its administration. Every week I have constituents coming to me who have found themselves, through no fault of their own, in distressing and often frightening circumstances. One had to wait eight months for her medical assessment, and in the meantime had funding for her electric wheelchair removed. Another was assessed as fit for work in 2012, won an appeal, and was then assessed as fit for work again in 2013: it took him almost a year to have that second decision reversed as well. I even had a case of a child of five with cystic fibrosis who needed twenty-four-hour care having her Disability Living Allowance withdrawn before Christmas and her family waiting months to see if they could have it reinstated so that they could care for her properly.

A large part of my time goes in doing what I can to represent my constituents by raising their cases with ministers and chasing up progress with the Department for Work and Pensions. I also work with local voluntary agencies, who are a vital defence for the city's most vulnerable people. But while we have some successes, it is an uphill battle. Parliament sets the rules, and even though every single MP will have cases like this, not all learn the obvious lesson: for every 'chancer' or 'scrounger', there are hundreds of innocent people caught up in a nightmare of the government's making. I remember another case, a man who had worked all his life but was now suffering from cancer. He was astonished at how long his claim was taking: like so many of us, he had paid his dues and believed that the state would look after him when he needed it; but he had been caught up in a malicious war on an illusory enemy.

By trying to evoke some kind of Blitz spirit with talk of being in it together, the government also hoped they could equate the impact on those who had contributed to the financial crisis with those who were being punished for it. But no bankers were required to come each day to the Job Centre to sign on, even though there were no jobs to be had. No property speculators were made to take unpaid work, helping to swell the profits of multinationals, or risk losing their benefits. No specialists in tax avoidance were forced to undergo intrusive medical examinations to see if they were fit to work.

In this last case, the treatment of those who were claiming benefits related to illness or disability has been shaming: no other word will do. Atos was given a contract by the Department for Work and Pensions to administer 'Work Capability Assessments'. Not only did the test discriminate against those taking part, but the way in which it was administered was a shambles. In Brighton, the proportion of appeals upheld was 56 per cent: in other words, Atos was proved to have got it wrong more than half the time.

The government has remained unrepentant, still claiming that welfare cuts were a necessary response to the financial crisis. But this was the big lie of austerity. In fact, despite the debt, we in Britain are still rich enough that we can, as a nation, afford the things that really matter. The NHS is affordable, even when people are living longer and health costs are rising, and even during a recession. After all, the NHS was established in 1947, in the midst of the post-war financial crisis, when there were fuel shortages and even bread was rationed. It is all about choices. So when politicians say that something is 'unaffordable', they really mean that they would rather spend the money elsewhere.

The choices made by the coalition government, and Labour before it, show this. They believed that a replacement for the Trident nuclear missile system was affordable, even though it will cost £100 billion over its lifetime. They could have cancelled this, or postponed it. But instead they decided to write the first cheque for £3 billion. They were happy to commit the country to an open-ended financial liability for the nuclear power plant at Hinkley Point, together with yet more subsidies. They were happy to spend billions of pounds on an unnecessary, top-down restructuring of the NHS. And there was money for Academies and Free Schools, for tax breaks for businesses and for a raft of other policies favoured by the coalition.

These were political decisions: in many cases, they were ideological decisions, based not on evidence or consensus about the needs and priorities facing the country, but on a narrow, almost sectarian view of the world. To take £1.5 billion that could have gone into mainstream education and spend it on an experiment such as Free Schools, and not even link these new schools with areas of need, was an indulgence that gives the lie to the idea that welfare payments were 'unaffordable'.

The coalition government also paid no attention to the cumulative effects of these cuts, and where the burden would be greatest. The most striking imbalance was the way in which so many of the coalition's decisions and policies would affect women disproportionately. Over two-thirds of local authority employees are women: so the cuts to local services have hit them particularly hard. In the same way, three-quarters of those claiming allowances as carers are women, so they suffered most from the cuts to those allowances, and the wider chaos of Atos, welfare reform and the rest. Childcare support, Sure Start centres, refuges from domestic violence: in a hundred ways, the position of women has been worsened by the decisions taken by Cameron, Clegg and Osborne. Locally, groups such as Brighton and Hove Women Against the Cuts have done what they can to highlight the injustices and campaign for them to be reversed; and organizations like the Fawcett Society have done the same nationally. But for women, already paid less than men and taking on many more unpaid responsibilities, the reverses of the last few years have been completely unjustifiable.

For those plunged into difficulty and distress by austerity, the final safety net should have been the local council. But councils have been particularly hard hit by the coalition, who have slashed their funding and capped their ability to raise their own revenue. Now, even if local people elect a council on the basis of their manifesto pledge to raise the Council Tax more than 2 per cent, this still has to be ratified by a separate (and expensive) referendum. It makes a mockery of the idea of local democracy.

In Brighton and Hove the council is required by law to do more and more each year, and yet is given less and less. The city had one of the worst deals from Whitehall of any council in Britain. In 2011, the Greens became by a small margin the largest single party on the council, but a long way off an overall majority. This meant that the Green administration had to rely on the support of one of the opposition parties to make any significant decisions. Faced with these drastic government cuts in funding, the Greens concluded that the only way to protect vital services was to increase the Council Tax by 4.75 per cent. Disappointingly, Labour joined the Conservatives to vote down this proposal. The result is a set of cuts to services that neither the Greens nor local people want.

The coalition's ideological commitment to austerity is wrong. Their methods are immoral. And all of this is being done by politicians who are paid whether they turn up or not, and are free to take second, third and fourth jobs if they wish, or take eight or nine weeks over the summer as holiday. Listening to them say that the problem the country faces is 'layabouts' is almost comical. When ministers and their cheerleaders rail against 'gold-plated' civil service pensions, and yet have the most generous pension arrangements this side of the City of London, you begin to feel you have stumbled into a looking-glass world in which the very words – let alone morals and ethics – have been stripped of any meaning.

There is one fact that captures this combination of privilege and detachment from reality perhaps better than any other. In the first two years of the coalition government, when the cuts were being voted through night after night, sales of champagne in the restaurants and bars of Westminster rose from £31,000 to £35,000 a year. Queen Marie Antoinette would have been proud.

Throughout my first year in Parliament I was constantly taken aback by this kind of moral myopia. Each evening, while debates on welfare reform were taking place literally over their heads, the Strangers' Bar was still packed with Honourable Members, creating a waft of beer and good cheer that would float along the corridors; and when the division bell sounded, those same MPs would stumble out and make for the lobbies, to vote with the government.

And there were and are alternatives. A start would be to collect the tax that is owed or evaded. For every £100 due in tax, around £7 is not paid, and even retrieving a proportion of that missing money – £35 billion in 2012 – would have helped avoid the worst of the cuts. HM Revenue and Customs already have extensive powers, but they often choose not to use them, preferring more cosy deals with their rich and powerful 'clients' – a far cry from the attitude taken to those who are overpaid tax credits and other benefits through no fault of their own and then find it hard to pay it back. But there are additional and simple ways in which the tax system could be tightened up. For example, we worked with Tax Research UK on a draft bill that would require banks to notify HMRC about new commercial accounts, so that HMRC could trace companies more easily that come and go without ever paying tax or even submitting their annual returns to Companies House. There were 500,000 companies who vanished in this way in 2011, and even if only a quarter of these owed the average company tax liability of £30,000 when they were struck off, it would still be £4 billion in lost tax reclaimed. But the chances of us ever seeing that £4 billion are getting less each year. In 2011 the government decided to cut 250 posts from Companies House, so making enforcement even weaker. Now less than half of UK companies file their tax returns on time, or at all, so making the task of collecting tax more and more difficult.

As well as tax owed but never collected, there is new money created electronically by the Bank of England. At the height of the crisis the Bank used this to purchase £375 billion of high-end financial assets like government bonds (government promises to repay money borrowed from the private sector, known as 'gilts'). By purchasing these bonds, removing them from the market and placing them on its own balance sheet, the Bank helps to increase their price. When the central bank purchases assets, the money holdings of the bond sellers (including wealthy institutions and overseas investors) are increased. These money holdings can then be used to purchase other assets, such as stocks and shares – in turn boosting the prices of those assets. The process goes under the uninformative name of 'quantitative easing' (QE). However, the main beneficiaries of QE are wealthy institutions and individuals that deal in bonds, and invest in shares.

The value of shares moved around 20 per cent higher as a result of QE. As it is generally the wealthy who own assets, QE helped the already-rich become richer. According to the Bank of England, about 40 per cent of the gain went to the richest 5 per cent of people in Britain.

That's the bad news. Wealth created by the publicly owned, nationalized Bank of England and intended to stabilize an economy destabilized by bankers, was unjustly channelled to the rich.

The good news is that QE operations helped lower the costs of government borrowing. Unprecedented low interest rates could have presented the coalition government with an historic opportunity to borrow to invest in the transformation of the economy away from fossil fuels. This increased investment could have supported thousands of high-skilled, highly paid jobs – and that in turn would have increased government tax revenues to repay the debt, making the borrowing sustainable.

There is an argument that QE was necessary, and that without it we might have faced an economic collapse in which the poor would certainly have become poorer. But the money created to fund QE could have been much better used to direct public investment that would not only have supported the economy, but also spread the benefits more fairly, and led to positive Green outcomes.

When I wrote to the Governor of the Bank of England, Mark Carney, asking him for confirmation that QE could have been used in this way, his reply was instructive: it could, he said, be aimed more directly at public infrastructure investment – but only if the government authorized the Bank of England to do so. To its shame, since the coalition was hell-bent on downsizing the state, and imposing austerity, it had absolutely no intention of using the Bank of England's money-creation powers in this way.

As long ago as July 2008, before the collapse of Lehman Brothers, a small group of economists and environmentalists published a report called 'The Green New Deal' in which we outlined policies, including what we called 'Green QE', to finance investment which would tackle both economic failure and the growing environmental crisis.

A programme of Green QE could fund a massive investment in energy efficiency, for example, ensuring every home in Britain was properly insulated, and in the process cutting carbon emissions, reducing energy bills, and creating hundreds of thousands of quality, well-paid jobs. It could also have been invested in a much-needed programme of affordable housing, providing homes for the huge numbers of people consigned for years to local council housing waiting lists. And since employment generates income, including revenue for the government, the investment of Green QE would effectively pay for itself.

Whether or not QE was the right answer to the threat of outright depression in 2008, there is no doubt that Britain is less equal as a result. Furthermore the failure to use Bank of England resources to invest in sound public infrastructure, meant that the 'recovery' was drawn out, and agonizingly slow. That is why QE should have been accompanied by other measures – such as a capital levy on the richest, who made around £400 billion from it – to pay back some of those windfall capital gains. It is a glaring irony that those responsible for the financial crisis were those that gained most from the chosen remedy: but not, perhaps, surprising. We were never 'all in it together'.

A further alternative to the government's austerity also lies in the financial world. The crisis of 2008 that kicked off the recession and left each household in Britain with a share of the national debt of over £40,000 was largely caused by reckless lending and by ever-more complex international financial transactions. These transactions – derivatives, forward and future contracts, and the rest – were increasingly created not to support trade or investment in the real world but to create illusory profits and allow the banks to cream off a percentage of the turnover in fees. A modest tax on each transaction would discourage the froth, calm the markets and make a future crash less likely. It would also raise revenue in a cost-effective way, without the distortion and unfairness of other taxes, such as VAT. And best of all, it would not mean targeting individual groups, such as those bearing the brunt of welfare cuts, but would spread the cost more fairly, and in particular ensure that those who had created the problem in the first place would help to put it right.

Usually, a proposal of this kind would leave the public cold. It would feel too technical, and too remote, to build up the kind of momentum needed to overcome the opposition of vested interests. But something about the transaction tax proposal caught the public imagination, helped by the imaginative campaigning of a coalition of NGOs and by its nickname: the Robin Hood tax. You didn't have to understand credit default swaps to agree that a tax that took from the rich and gave to the poor was just what was needed. And the idea of a hero who puts themselves outside the law to protect the vulnerable and fight corruption in high places had a universal appeal. Soon, around the world, protesters were gathering to put pressure on their governments under the banner of Robin Hood.

I received hundreds of letters and emails about the Robin Hood tax from my constituents – one of the biggest postbags so far. And I met a group of Robin Hoods myself on Parliament Green, just before the G8 summit at Camp David, who included some campaigners from my old workplace, Oxfam. Later that morning I was back in Parliament, putting a question to David Cameron in Prime Minister's Questions. 'Will the prime minister listen to both the demonstrators outside Parliament today and the 80,000 people who have emailed him in recent weeks and commit to becoming a leading advocate for the introduction of a Robin Hood tax at the G20 summit in Cannes with the revenue earmarked to address sustainable development and the growing climate crisis?'

Cameron did not answer the question, of course. That's not what PMQs is about. But I was particularly proud to be representing the campaigners I'd met outside and the constituents who had written to ask me to put pressure on the government. For a moment, their commitment and idealism disturbed the cloying atmosphere of Westminster like a fresh breeze from Sherwood.

4

National Ill-Health:
How Privatization is Hollowing Out Our Public Services

> *'Deregulation is a transfer of power from the trodden to the treading.'*
>
> George Monbiot

During the 2010 election campaign in Brighton, I spoke to hundreds of people who were fearful about the future of the National Health Service. For some, it was because they depended on it day to day. For others, particularly those who were living in poor-quality homes, or in low-paid jobs, the NHS was one area of their life where, if the worst came to the worst, they would get the same quality of care as the very rich. For them, that reassurance was priceless. And those who were fit and healthy and weren't relying on the NHS now, saw how important it was to others and to the country.

For all those people, the election meant uncertainty. Whoever won would have the power to sustain and improve the NHS, or to wreck it. They could maintain it as a service free to all those who needed it, and paid for by those who could afford it; or they could strip out the founding principles and let those with more money push their way to the front of the queue. No wonder the parties fell over themselves to offer their pledges on health.

The biggest and boldest of these came from David Cameron. At the very start of 2010 he came out with a charter for the NHS, including pledges to improve maternity services to give mothers more choice, end same-sex wards, and divert more NHS cash to deprived areas that needed it most. He placed his own personal credibility behind the claims that funding for the NHS would increase in real terms under a Conservative government; and that there would be no top-down reorganization. He even authorized spending on 1,000 poster sites to get this message across.

And it worked. In Brighton, many people felt that, whatever else the Tories would do if they got into power, they'd leave the NHS alone. To do otherwise would be electorally disastrous. These were not weasel words, they thought: these were clear commitments. Clearly, the logic went, the Tories have learned that the NHS is untouchable, and self-interest would be enough to protect it. And doctors seemed to feel much the same. A poll in the magazine *Pulse* had over 50 per cent of GPs saying they would vote Conservative in the election, and only 8 per cent would vote Labour (only just ahead of those voting Green, on 5 per cent). One GP was quoted as saying he didn't have any evidence to think the Conservatives would be better than the current Labour government – 'but they couldn't be any worse'.

In the week before that poll was published, David Cameron had given a speech to the Royal College of Pathologists in which he said: 'With the Conservatives there will be no more of the tiresome, meddlesome, top-down restructures that have dominated the last decade of the NHS.'

You might have been forgiven for thinking that this was some kind of response to the widespread sense of disengagement towards politics in the country. For what the Conservatives were saying was just what people on all sides of politics wanted. Yet it still felt unreal. There were and are two reasons why the

Conservatives could never truly be the party of the NHS. First, the NHS has too much of a collectivist ethos. To provide healthcare on the basis of need rather than ability to pay, and to fund it from progressive taxation, is a little too close to the idea popularized by Karl Marx and Friedrich Engels: 'From each according to their ability, to each according to their need.' (Maybe those Americans who rail against the NHS model as 'socialist healthcare' are on to something after all.)

Second, for many Conservatives, the NHS is too big to be allowed to thrive without the 'assistance' of the private sector. It is an affront to those who believe that only the pursuit of profit can motivate employees and managers to provide a decent service. The NHS provides world-class healthcare at a reasonable cost, judged by the support for it from the British public and by independent international comparisons. So what's to stop a similar organization doing the same in other areas, such as water, or railways, or housing?

These ideological prejudices often misunderstand the NHS. It is not a monolith. It is not even a single legal body. In a way, the NHS is more like a flag, under which individuals and organizations come together to deliver health care. GPs, for example, are not employees of the NHS. A doctor's surgery is a little like a small business, being paid by the NHS to treat patients. Hospitals were semi-independent long before the creation of NHS Trusts. Ambulance services were once so independently minded that they found it hard even to agree on what kind of ambulances to buy. But what held this all together was a shared sense of purpose: that everyone standing under the banner of the NHS wanted to provide the people of Britain with the best health service they could. There was a professional commitment to individual patients; and a pride that the NHS was free for everyone who needed it, and provided the best-value – and often the very best – health care in the world. The NHS didn't always live up to these ideals.

There were examples of incompetence, neglect, waste and cover-ups. But that did not mean the ideals themselves were wrong. And the one ideal perhaps mostly strongly uniting those providing the service and those making use of it was that it was not driven by the desire to make money at the expense of people's health.

That is why, whatever you might think about private health care, it was wrong to introduce it into the NHS. Dress it up as a partnership, or making use of extra capacity, it came to the same thing. With the NHS, you knew where you stood. If a doctor gave you a particular medicine or referred you to a particular hospital, it would be the decision that he or she thought was best for you – taking account of the usual problem with funding and capacity. But introduce a new issue – what medicine or treatment centre will make someone the biggest profit – and you have a complete transformation of the relationship at the heart of the NHS.

We saw something similar with the sell-off of the railways. The old British Rail was often inefficient. The trains were not always on time, the carriages were sometimes dirty, and the sandwiches might have been curled up at the edges. But no one was making a profit from these failings. And these faults could be weighed against the dedication and sense of public service of so many of the staff who ran the railways, putting up with low pay and under-investment as they kept the trains running. It might not have had the glamour or slick marketing of the airlines, but British Rail provided a vital public service with only a modest public subsidy.

Fast-forward to our post-privatization world. There are new trains, flashy paint schemes and occasional bargain prices. But this requires a much greater level of public finance than in the days of British Rail, even though we have some of the most expensive fares in Europe. And we also have an immense and costly new structure of regulators, clearing houses and watchdogs to try to make sense of a vast, bureaucratic and often irrational system. And it turns out that the task is beyond them. The fare system, despite attempts at reform, is fiendishly complex. There is still no rational vision for rail services, meeting public need, supporting social objectives, or freeing people from having to use their cars to get about. And the financial structures still give franchise holders a one-way bet: bid low, and you can watch the cash roll in without any requirement to invest your extra winnings in new trains or keep the fares down. Bid high, and if it turns out that you can't make a profit, you just hand the franchise back to the government and walk away.

The companies who have done this, though, have exposed the crucial flaw in the model for privatized railways. The trains keep running, of course: but they are run and managed by a public sector body. And as it happens, it turns out that the public sector is rather good at running trains.

In 2003, the private firm Connex was running the south-eastern franchise so badly that it was handed to a new, state-owned company called South Eastern Trains. In the next three years, South Eastern Trains improved reliability and customer satisfaction and updated the rolling stock. By some measures, it was the best-performing of all the rail franchises in Britain. But ideology struck again (even though this was under a Labour government) and in 2006 the private sector was invited to bid once again to run the trains. South Eastern Trains was not allowed to bid, and the franchise was won by Govia and Keolis (the latter, surreally, is actually a state-owned enterprise, being an offshoot of the French railway provider SNCF) and is now known as Southeastern.

And in 2009, the Department of Transport took back the franchise for the east-coast main line from London to Edinburgh from National Express and once again found no difficulty in running the trains itself. The publicly owned East Coast service performed well and even managed to make more money than its private-sector predecessors. The only difference was this money all went back to the Treasury.

So however you look at it, the public sector has shown that it can be just as good at running a public service as the private sector. (And to be fair, the private sector can do a good job too: but that's usually when firms have developed a culture of truly placing the customer first, treating their staff fairly, planning for the long term rather than a quick profit, and being open and accountable for their actions.) It is the dogmatic claim that the private sector will always outperform the public or not-for-profit sectors that is so damaging. On the railways, the private train operators point to increased numbers of passengers, better reliability and new trains. What they say is true: but it is hardly fair to compare their performance in 2015 to British Rail in 1991. The true comparison is against the kind of railways we would have had if they had stayed in public hands, with the same investment and the same economic context leading to more passengers.

The public understand this: that is why there is such widespread support for taking rail franchises back into public hands when they come up for renewal. This is a straightforward and affordable proposition. In fact, it won't cost the taxpayer a penny, because rather than having to buy out existing franchise-holders, it would simply ensure that once these expire, or if the operator cannot provide an adequate service, the services are taken over by the state. The approach is so simple that when I introduced a bill into Parliament to put it into effect, the lawyers only needed forty-three lines to set out all the necessary powers. Compare that to the hundreds of lines of primary legislation needed to privatize the railways in the first place.

The discussion about the bill showed it was a practical and sensible approach. This makes the Labour leadership's reluctance to adopt this as party policy so odd and so depressing. They fear that if they commit to public ownership, this will be used against them by the right-wing media, portraying them as firebrand socialists ready to nationalize every business in the country, and upset their relationship with the City of London. But a majority of Labour Party members and supporters also want the railways to be publicly owned. So they have adopted a fudge, saying that public sector and not-for-profit bodies will be allowed to bid for franchises alongside private sector firms. The Labour leaders know this will never work. Where will these public sector bidders come from? Where will they find the millions of pounds needed to put a bid together? And even then, you would still have to leave in place all the pointless layers of bureaucracy needed to administer the bidding process and regulate the winning franchises, and which costs us around £1 billion a year. So the official opposition adopt a policy that is only intended to con the public and thwart the democratic wishes of their own party members. And then they wonder why politicians are held in contempt, and party membership is in decline.

Keeping public services in public hands is not just about ownership and profits. It is also a matter of accountability. It is no coincidence that the businesses most often caught ripping off their customers are the same ones who hide behind the screen of 'commercial confidentiality' – even when providing what amounts to a public service. For most of us, life in modern Britain means being reliant on phone companies, energy companies, Internet service providers, banks and insurers. We know, because we've all lived through it, that many of these businesses engage wholesale in dishonest and manipulative practices: deliberately misrepresenting their products, creating impenetrable pricing structures to rip off customers who loyally stick with the same provider, thwarting attempts to gain redress and incentivizing their employees to mis-sell their services, even to vulnerable customers.

But these same companies, though providing a public service, are entirely unaccountable. They deny everything until the evidence becomes overwhelming; then order an internal inquiry and announce that they have discovered a few junior rotten apples and that they are taking steps to ensure it does not happen again. There is no National Audit Office or Parliamentary Ombudsman to take up the case. Nor can you apply to the courts for judicial review. Sometimes firms will answer my questions, but an MP has no rights to demand answers on behalf of their constituents.

At least the NHS remains accountable to Parliament. But one of the dangers of the coalition's plans was that, by bringing in the private sector, we would lose much of that protection. We saw that with education. In my first few months at Westminster, I put down dozens of amendments to the Academies Bill, seeking to preserve the right of citizens to know what policies academies were adopting, in everything from admissions to maintenance contracts, and also how well they were performing. Building on this, I used a speech to the Green Party Conference to call for the Freedom of Information Act to be extended to private firms operating as monopolies or near-monopolies, and also to those providing specified public services such as mobile phones or banking. The Information Commissioner would determine classes of information that companies would have to publish, such as risk registers, payment to subcontractors, or tax payments made overseas. This would be quicker and more flexible than the current situation, where extra disclosure requirements on businesses have to be enacted by Parliament in primary legislation – which can take years.

The public would not make requests directly to companies, as they would to a government department or agency under the current Freedom of Information Act. Instead, members of the public could make requests to the Information Commissioner to add to the classes of information that major companies must release. This would help the public see the impact – for good or ill – which companies have on our economy and society: anything from their employment policies to cases of taking excess profits from their poorest customers. Well-run companies would have a good story to tell; badly performing ones would be shamed into mending their ways.

This proposal caught people's imagination perhaps because if we'd had FOI covering the banks in the run-up to the financial crash – the right to ask for information, for example, about new financial instruments or lending policies – then their irresponsible methods might have been exposed before the crisis hit. Extending FOI would mean giving the public, academics, think tanks, the media and campaigning groups the right to scrutinize powerful corporations and so improve the way they serve their customers and society as a whole. No company – or government – should be afraid of such a necessary move.

There was the usual chorus of 'impossible': but since then, the idea has caught on and a number of campaigning groups and even other MPs have taken up the cause. It also led to my working with Cat Hobbs and her colleagues at We Own It, which is campaigning for public services to be publicly owned and accountable. The way that private providers can avoid the openness and accountability that goes with freedom of information requirements is one example of how the 'playing-field' is slanted against public providers, along with the emphasis on low-cost bids rather than maximizing quality or public benefit. We Own It have done great work on understanding what the public wants from their public services, and this is reflected in their Public Service Users Bill. In brief, this would ensure the public was consulted about public services – what they should be and who should run them – and would introduce a presumption in favour of service provision by public sector and not-for-profit entities. Whoever won, they would have to be open to proper scrutiny and the public would have a 'right of recall' if the service was below the expected standard. It's a simple, elegant and fair alternative to the current obscure deals and biased tendering processes. Research shows this approach is overwhelmingly popular with the public – 79 per cent of people want to be consulted about privatization and contracting-out of services, and 88 per cent want the right of recall. So I was extremely proud to present the bill to Parliament in 2014, backed by a cross-party group of MPs.

Accountability was just one of the battlegrounds when the coalition government began its reform of the NHS. Another concern was the coalition's claim that they wanted to put more power in the hands of GPs, taking it away from the 'bureaucrats' in the Primary Care Trusts (PCTs). On the surface, who could object to this? GPs would know their patients and could ensure they got the best possible care. In polls, the public said they were in favour of this. But to anyone who'd seen up close how the health service actually worked, the proposal was deeply alarming. For a start, commissioning is a very complex business – not just a GP picking up the phone and booking you into one clinic rather than another. Also, most GPs came into medicine because they wanted to make people better, not to manage a health commissioning system. The government's plan was that GPs would come together in a new Clinical Commissioning Group that would in turn buy in administrative services from new bodies called Commissioning Support Units. So what came out of the reforms was not power in the hands of individual doctors, but a new layer of administration replacing the old PCTs (which also had GP representation).

This was an example of one of those issues where those closest to the situation – in this case, the health professionals – could see the problems coming; but by the time the public had grasped that they had been misled, and could see the awful consequences, it would be too late. The Conservatives knew that if they had put a 'for sale' sign on the NHS – offering to sell shares in it, as they had done in years past with the water and electricity boards, or British Gas – the public would have marched on Parliament with pitchforks and blazing torches that same night and turfed them out of office. But by breaking it up from within, giving private firms the chance to slide in and snap up the most profitable morsels, they could maintain the fiction that the NHS was running on just as it always had been, only a little bit better. Because the reforms were so complex, many people were put off from getting involved. And because the trappings of privatization were missing, others felt the health professionals were crying wolf.

This meant that those fighting to save the NHS would have to cooperate together, and work harder than ever to overcome the deceptions at the heart of the NHS reforms. The unions and the Royal Colleges had a crucial role. But it also needed a strong, cross-party movement within Parliament. There were individual MPs across all the parties concerned about the situation, and as the proposals affected Wales, Plaid Cymru was up for the fight. I was ready to chain myself to the Speaker's chair if I thought it would save the NHS for a single day. But, realistically, Labour would need to be on-side too: and therein lay a problem.

When they were in government, Labour had gone far further than the Tories had ever dared in bringing in the private sector, particularly when Alan Milburn was at the Health Department. Throughout, they had been warned that their reforms to allow private firms to bid for NHS work would be a Trojan Horse for much greater privatization; and so it proved. When the coalition took power and began to break up the NHS, Labour were then caught between either opposing private provision on principle – so opening themselves to the charge of hypocrisy – or complaining about the detail of how it was being done, which would have very little impact on the debate. The Labour leadership's response could never be fully effective because of this toxic legacy.

But within the wider Labour movement, there was much more appetite for the fight. After all, Aneurin Bevan had established the NHS in the face of huge opposition. Working alongside concerned MPs such as Labour's John Healey and with campaigning groups like 38 Degrees, meant we could try to delay the reform process, and give more time to explain to the public what was being done to the NHS. One huge advantage was that the coalition had no mandate and no popular support for their reforms, and a bruising passage through Parliament would remind them of this and give a chance for some of their backbenchers to have second thoughts.

Even after the bill had been passed, there was still a mass of secondary legislation to enact to put it into force. For example, section 75 of the bill gave the Secretary of State powers to set the rules on competitive tendering within the NHS. The government promised that these would not be used to force the new Clinical Commissioning Groups to go out to competitive tender, rather than simply use the local NHS hospitals; but when the draft regulations were published in the form of a Statutory Instrument, they did exactly that: a significant push for the privatization of the NHS. Campaigners were rightly up in arms about both the principle and the deceitful way it was being handled. Statutory Instruments of this kind will come into force unless someone 'prays' against them: in other words, demands more scrutiny. So we put down an Early Day Motion to block the Statutory Instrument, and we contacted Opposition MPs and some Lib Dem backbenchers to try to get as much cross-party support as possible.

Throughout the battle, it felt as if we were being pushed back by an opponent who, though unable to win the arguments, simply had more brute force. But by digging in our heels we could slow it down, and every day or week of delay was a victory because it meant the NHS stayed a little closer to its true purpose. Despite the changes under the coalition government, our National Health Service is largely intact. This makes it all the more important that we fight and win the battle against privatization and market forces.

5

A Voice for the Environment:
How Vested Interests Threaten Landscape and Wildlife

'*The badgers have moved the goalposts.*'
Owen Paterson, BBC interview, October 2013

It's a strange experience to hear a politician on national radio bring his career to a close with six ill-chosen words. But Owen Paterson was perhaps not ideally suited to being Her Majesty's Secretary of State for the Environment in the first place. He had no affinity for the environment; nor did his political judgement inspire much confidence, in that he was given the job to try to calm down the British public after his predecessor had tried to sell off Britain's forests; and yet he decided that his flagship policy would be shooting badgers.

In fact, Owen Paterson's one qualification for the job was also his downfall. His business background was leather; and leather comes from cows. He also represents North Shropshire, which is dairy and cattle country. Owen Paterson knew a lot of farmers, and had listened to their concerns. And one of the key concerns, understandably, was bovine tuberculosis. Bovine TB is a horrible disease: the infected cattle have to be killed, and even with a compensation regime for affected farmers, it is heartbreaking to see a herd that you have tended for years, built up, and taken immense pride in, being rounded up and sent to the slaughterhouse.

The question was, what to do about it. For years, many farmers had linked the rise of bovine TB to badgers, who can also be infected with the disease and play a role in passing it back to cows. Many farmers, and particularly the National Farmers Union leadership, wanted a programme to 'cull' badgers to reduce the chance of infection. In response the government had run a Randomized Badger Culling Trial between 1998 and 2006 but this had concluded in 2007 that '. . . badger culling can make no meaningful contribution to cattle TB control in Britain. Indeed, some policies under consideration are likely to make matters worse rather than better.'

If this seems counter-intuitive, it's because of the 'perturbation effect': that is, the way culling is linked to increased bovine TB in cattle directly outside the cull zone, as fleeing badgers spread the disease further afield. Fortunately, there is an alternative programme based on badger vaccination, improved biosecurity, more restrictions on the movement of cattle and changing the increasingly intensive farming practices that make animals more susceptible to disease. Badger vaccination reduces the probability of infection by 70–75 per cent. Even allowing for the fact that not all badgers can be reached, and vaccination needs repeating year on year to include new cubs, it's still more effective (and more cost-effective) than shooting – not least because it allows the badgers' population structure to remain in place, so helping to contain the disease.

The 2010 election brought Caroline Spelman to the Department for the Environment, Food and Rural Affairs (Defra) and she authorized what she called '. . . a science-led cull of badgers in the worst affected areas'. But the most recent review of the science, the Bovine TB Eradication Group for England (which included officials from her department, Defra, as well as vets and farming representatives), had concluded in 2009:

Our findings show that the reductions in cattle TB incidence achieved by repeated badger culling were not sustained in the long term after culling ended and did not offset the financial costs of culling. These results, combined with evaluation of alternative culling methods, suggest that badger culling is unlikely to contribute effectively to the control of cattle TB in Britain.

So a 'science-led' cull would have consisted of everyone just putting their guns away and trying something more sensible. Instead, farmers were authorized to start blasting away, while Defra (or rather, the taxpayer) funded a monitoring scheme to see what would happen. The main result was a series of legal challenges to the government's irrational policy, thousands of people on the streets marching in protest, and the conversion of a rock icon into the champion of Team Badger.

In any list of the greatest guitarists of all time, Brian May will be there. His charisma and public standing, and his passion for animal welfare, made him an impressive champion for the cause. Badgers have huge latent support among the public. (You have to wonder at the wisdom of a government setting out to shoot badgers, given a badger is the emblem of the county wildlife trusts, who have something like 700,000 members.) But it was Brian and Team Badger, supported by conservation and campaign groups with over 2 million members, that helped turn that support into political action.

Soon there were badger-masked protesters outside No. 10; badger-suited campaigners outside Parliament; and badger-savers disrupting the cull itself, at considerable personal risk, given that the government, in a bid to save money, had authorized the 'free' shooting of badgers, and crashing round in a wood to try to stop a marksman from shooting badgers in the twilight was not for the faint-hearted.

A less committed politician might have looked at this and

decided the game wasn't worth the candle. And when Owen
Paterson succeeded Caroline Spelman as Environment Secretary
in 2012, it looked briefly like he might be about to reach the
same conclusion. I led a debate in the House in 2012 on the
motion that the government should drop the cull and explore
a more effective, evidence-based and humane solution. Over
160,000 people had signed the e-petition on the No. 10 website
that forced the government to grant the debate, and 147 MPs
voted for our motion with only twenty-eight voting against. Just
two days before the debate, in an effort to neutralize the issue,
Paterson had announced that the cull would be delayed until
2013, and there was optimism that this was a prelude to quietly
dropping the whole thing.

But Paterson was made of sterner stuff. To widespread
astonishment, the following year he said the cull would go ahead.
And it rapidly turned into a fiasco.

First, the claim that the badger cull was 'science-led' looked
pretty thin once it emerged that only a tiny number of the
1,800 or so badgers killed were tested for bovine TB. Only a
very small proportion were examined to see if they had died
'humanely': that is, had lived for less than five minutes after being
shot. In the event, it seemed that a worryingly high proportion
did suffer a horribly lingering and painful death: exactly as had
been predicted by the campaigners against the cull and the
scientific experts. And the greatest blow to the credibility of
the cull was that they could not find enough badgers to kill;
which in turn showed that Defra's understanding of the badger
population in these areas and the effects of mass shootings were
wide of the mark.

Although Defra initially tried to cover it up, it soon emerged
that, judged against its original aims and targets, the cull was
a failure: the government had not given an overall figure, but
the costs were at least £7 million, spent on two 'trials' which
one of the leading experts on bovine TB admitted would tell us

nothing new. Owen Paterson attempted to 'redefine' the 'success measures' for the cull, as he tried to build support for extending it from two to forty areas. But when asked if this wasn't 'moving the goalposts' for the trial, Paterson replied that it was the badgers who were moving the goalposts. Somehow, the image of these animals outwitting Paterson and his army of officials and marksmen caught the public's imagination. You have to have a strong track record in politics to overcome that kind of gaffe. Paterson's credibility never recovered.

It was an irony that Paterson had been put in the job partly to try to take the political heat out of the environment. In Parliament and in public, he tried to say the right things; or say nothing at all. But in less guarded moments, among friends, he was less careful. This is what he said to a fringe meeting at the Conservative Party Conference in 2013 about the latest report from the UN's Intergovernmental Panel on Climate Change:

> People get very emotional about this subject and I think we should just accept that the climate has been changing for centuries. I think the relief of this latest report is that it shows a really quite modest increase, half of which has already happened. We need to take [the report] seriously, but I am rather relieved that it is not as catastrophic in its forecast as we had been led to believe early on and what it is saying is something we can adapt to over time and we are very good as a race at adapting.

His words are revealing in several ways. Firstly, his interpretation of the report is wrong; of which more later. But the second revelation is his attitude of mind. If you are a wealthy man, and part of the political elite, then climate change could well seem like something you can adapt to over time. Wealth can insulate you from many dangers; and power means you can be first in line for protection or compensation. For the rest of us, though, adapting to climate change may not be so straightforward. He said that: '... we are very good as a race at adapting'. If by 'race' he meant 'species', then that is true. You could say we adapted well to the Black Death: but having up to half the population of England killed off within a couple of years is still something you'd avoid if you could, however well you might 'adapt' to it. With climate change, our adaptability should be employed now, to avoid making climate change worse; not after it is too late, trying to rescue something from the wreckage.

Still, that is what he believes. And you can accuse Owen Paterson of many things, but not inconsistency. He does not think that climate change is a big problem; and so when he became Secretary of State for the Environment, he oversaw reductions in spending on flood defences, the loss of 550 staff from the Environment Agency (responsible for flood protection) and a cut in the number of officials working on how Britain should adapt to climate change from thirty-eight to six. Certainly a politician who puts his beliefs into action.

There have been a great many documented Paterson gaffes on climate change: these are not questions of opinion, but of plain facts. For example, he said on BBC Radio 4's *Any Questions* in June 2013 that the earth's temperature had not got any warmer in the preceding seventeen years. This is a favourite timescale for those who are sceptical about climate change, because a variety of short-term factors obscure the long-term upward trend (and if you cherry-pick your dates, you can 'prove' anything). In fact, even over this carefully chosen period, the most credible estimate is that mean atmospheric temperature rose by 0.11°C a decade; while the warming of the oceans – where around 90 per cent of the earth's warming takes place, and which is less affected by short-term effects such as El Niño – continued too. Presumably Paterson was relying on something he'd read in the *Daily Mail*, and not his own scientific advisers.

It's worth seeing exactly what he said that day, following on from a response by the Labour MP Peter Hain:

> Well I'm sitting like a rose between two thorns here and I have to take practical decisions. The climate's always been changing. Peter mentioned the Arctic and I think in the Holocene the Arctic melted completely and you can see there were beaches there ... when Greenland was occupied, you know, people growing crops. We then had a little ice age, we had a middle age warming – the climate's been going up and down – but the real question which I think everyone's trying to address is: is this influenced by manmade activity in recent years and James [Delingpole] is actually correct. The climate has not changed. The temperature has not changed in the last seventeen years. And what I think we've got to be careful of is that there is almost certainly – bound to be – some influence by manmade activity but I think we've just got to be rational [audience laughter] ... rational people ... and make sure the measures that we take to counter it don't actually cause more damage. And I think we're about to get ...

At this point Peter Hain could take no more and interrupted him; and no doubt many people around the country were shouting at their radios too. For what sounds like the ramblings of a bloke in the pub, a bit confused by what he's read in the *Mail* and repeating a couple of facts he's picked up about the Vikings in Greenland growing crops in the Holocene era, is actually (as Peter Hain said in tones of disbelief) the Secretary of State for the Environment. Doesn't he read his briefs? Doesn't he talk it over with his chief scientist?

It was a standing joke in his department that if you put up a submission to him with the words 'climate change' in it, that submission would come back unread. A series of Freedom of Information requests reported in the *Independent* have revealed that he also turned down an offer to be briefed on the science of climate change by David MacKay, who was then the chief scientific adviser to the Department of Energy and Climate Change as well as the Regius Professor of Engineering at Cambridge University. He did once have a short meeting with Jonathan Tillson, Defra's head of Sustainable Business, to talk about climate change; and one other meeting with an unnamed official; but that was it for meetings on climate change in his first fourteen months in the job. He didn't even have the time or the inclination to consult Defra's chief scientist, Sir Ian Boyd, about the subject.

Had he done so, Sir Ian might have cleared up a couple of points that have caused Paterson some confusion. For example, we are living in the Holocene era now: it began 12,015 years ago. The Vikings did settle on parts of the coast of Greenland in the eleventh century, but they did so on the existing coastline (you can visit some of the former settlements and see for yourself) not on some mythical 'beaches'. Then, as now, the interior of Greenland was covered by the ice cap (and has been for 400,000 years) but there is a narrow fertile strip by the sea. And the Vikings would have found the Arctic Ocean frozen over, just like now. The evidence for this does not come only from climate scientists 'in the pay of the IPCC': but from archaeologists, historians, and from the accounts of the Vikings themselves: and surely they at least cannot be part of the Great Climate Change Conspiracy.

Paterson was said to be interested in only three things at Defra: killing badgers, yoghurt, and fox hunting. The rest of the department's responsibilities, such as biodiversity, animal welfare, conservation, coastal defences, pollution control, and the rest had to fend for themselves. To put it another way, from early on Paterson decided to park the environment and concentrate on the 'fra' part of Defra's name: 'Food and Rural Affairs'. Killing badgers was part of this: a cause dear to the hearts of the leadership of the National Farmers' Union, who had staked their reputation on the idea that only a mass cull of badgers could deal with bovine TB. The wild card of yoghurt arose not because of any hippy leanings on Owen's part, but rather because he thought that farmers should diversify into 'higher margin' foods (not a bad idea) and yoghurt was the example that had lodged in his mind and tripped out whenever he mentioned the subject. And fox hunting? Well, again Owen Paterson was consistent. He'd voted against the ban, campaigned against it, and wanted to see it repealed.

This meant that under Paterson's rule, I spent a lot of time fighting Defra as well as those seeking to damage the environment or cause suffering to wildlife. It makes a contrast to those departments that only seek to represent their special interests within government. Defra, or at least its ministers, seemed just as intent on marginalizing the environment, conservation, animal welfare and biodiversity as any multinational, let alone the Treasury. But this didn't start with Paterson. His predecessor, Caroline Spelman, had a mixed record. Her commitment to resist pressure for another runway at Heathrow was admirable: but she was also prepared to sacrifice the natural environment to pursue the pro-big business agenda of the government she served.

Our first clash came on timber. The Coalition Agreement had pledged to crack down on the illegal trade in timber from endangered species: in other words, trees that should have been standing in the rainforests of Brazil and Indonesia, providing food and shelter for a whole ecosystem, but had somehow turned up in builders' merchants and garden centres in Britain. It was already illegal to import certain species of trees, but once inside the UK they could be freely bought and sold: even though it was obvious they could not have entered the country legally. This was the loophole the government had promised to close and it mattered for two reasons. First, many more companies with reputations to protect would check more carefully up the 'supply chain' that the timber they bought was legal. And second, it would mean campaigners or even individuals could spot illegal timber in the shops and raise the alarm, rather than relying solely on HM Revenue and Customs spotting an illegal shipment among the thousands of tonnes of timber that pass through British ports each year. Customs officers are conscientious and have had some notable successes in detecting environmental crime: but they have a lot of other responsibilities, including illegal drugs and weapons.

But for some reason – at a wild guess, lobbying by major retailers who didn't fancy having to bother seeing if the timber products they sold were legal or not – the government dropped this commitment. It was the first coalition pledge to be broken, and when I and others on the Environmental Audit Select Committee quizzed Caroline Spelman about this, she became very defensive. Her line was that a ban on importation was enough; she could not bring herself to admit that the pledge had been broken. This was a pattern that the government adopted with increasing frequency over the years: simply denying the facts again and again even though the evidence was clear, and no one who knew anything about the situation believed them.

I brought forward my own bill to make buying and selling timber from endangered species illegal within the UK. As expected, it was 'talked out' by a group of Conservative MPs: but it showed how easy it would have been for the government to do what it had promised. It was an issue that brought together a wide range of campaigning groups working in Britain and internationally. Unless we could cut back on the demand for illegal timber in the UK, it was hard to protect the rainforests in Brazil, Indonesia and elsewhere. With the forests cleared, there would be no future for critically endangered species such as the Sumatran tiger, the mountain gorilla, and Lear's macaw. And it would mean more carbon dioxide fuelling climate change.

Threats to the environment were coming thick and fast. Most damaging, the government set out to scrap most of the protection to our countryside provided in the planning system. Those protections were already inadequate: people would often assume, for example, that designating an area as a Site of Special Scientific Interest would mean it could not be built upon – but no. The system already had a presumption in favour of development, and on top of that developers always had more money than local communities or conservation groups to commission reports and studies to 'prove' that what they were doing was acceptable, or to pay for PR firms to pump out propaganda about the jobs that developments would create. This was particularly frustrating, because there were no matching studies of the jobs lost on the local high street when a supermarket claimed to be 'creating' jobs; and even the BBC would lap up and reproduce these biased claims without challenge.

The government argued that planning regulations had to be ditched because they were an obstacle to more house-building. But while there is a serious housing crisis, protection of the countryside is not the cause, and removing planning controls is not the answer. The roots of the crisis include the way that successive governments have deliberately fuelled property booms that made homes unaffordable for many people; an appalling under-investment in social housing; and Britain's low-wage economy, where people were simply not paid enough to afford a decent home; and where those lucky enough to own a property could be manipulated by politicians into thinking that they and their country's real wealth was increasing as house prices rose ever higher.

In Brighton and Hove, these tensions are all too visible. Because the city is a very attractive place to live and work, and is within easy reach of London, an increasing number of people want to come here and that tends to push up prices. But there is still a lot of deprivation, as well as more and more people who have grown up in the city being unable to afford a place of their own, even though they are in work. As a result, there are over 18,000 people on the council's housing waiting list. There are no easy answers, because these are problems created in Westminster and Whitehall and in the City of London. But there are some things that local communities can do, including encouraging employers to pay a 'living wage' so that rent or mortgage payments are a little more affordable. The council took a lead on this after the Greens became a minority administration in 2011, and the city now has one of the most thriving living-wage economies in the country. But the irony is that the same elite in London who created many of these problems also deny local authorities the remedies – for example, the ability to lift the borrowing cap to raise more finance for house-building, or the opportunity to increase Council Tax beyond a minimum threshold to reflect the additional responsibilities thrust upon them.

In spite of this, in their first council tenure, Brighton and Hove's Green administration oversaw the development of over 500 affordable homes within the city's housing developments, with a further 232 for completion over the following year. By July 2014 it had also brought 876 empty properties back into use (nearly half of them council homes), and one of the Greens' earliest acts as a council administration was to build the first new council homes in the city for a generation.

Some people claimed to be surprised that a Green-led council should have made housing one of its main priorities. But Green politics is deeply concerned with the places where we live: whether it is a one-bed flat or the entire planet, it is all part of our environment. It is also about how humanity can live in balance with our home the earth, and that is all humanity, wherever they live, and whatever their circumstances. The claim that concern for the environment is 'middle-class' is bogus and manipulative. Socialism and conservation grew from the same soil. Labour in its heyday led the fight for free access to open spaces and created the National Parks. And it is those who are financially worst-off who suffer most from noise, air pollution and crowded conditions. You don't have to be middle class to treasure the South Downs, whose timeless beauty extends right to the edge of my constituency. They are there for everyone, and enjoyed by people from all backgrounds.

Nor is animal welfare an exclusively 'middle-class' concern. Anyone who makes such a claim has clearly never joined one of the demonstrations against the export of horses to be slaughtered for the meat trade on the Continent, or against the use of animals for cosmetics testing or other needless experiments. A gathering of animal welfare campaigners is more of a social melting pot that any Labour meeting could ever be, because the recognition that by mistreating animals we fundamentally diminish ourselves does not rely on one particular political creed. It is, or should be, a universally acknowledged part of our own humanity.

When I worked with Animal Defence International and other NGOs on the cause of wild animals in circuses, it was as part of a cross-party campaign, working with MPs such as the Conservative Mark Pritchard and Labour's Jim Cunningham, who cared about the issue themselves and also knew how much it mattered to their constituents. Polls showed that three-quarters of people in Britain were in favour of a ban, and only 8 per cent against, and MPs voted in favour of a motion banning wild animals in circuses. And David Cameron even promised such a ban: only to go back on his word later.

This U-turn (poor Mark Pritchard had already announced to his local paper his 'delight' that the Queen's Speech would contain a Circus Animals Bill) was a long way away from David

Cameron visiting the Arctic for a husky-dog photo-opportunity and pledging that his would be the 'Greenest government ever'. This 'Vote Blue Go Green' strategy had only one purpose: to convince voters that the Conservatives had changed and were no longer the 'nasty party' of Margaret Thatcher, Norman Tebbit, Iain Duncan Smith or Michael Howard. Pretending to care about the environment might win some votes in itself; it would also please those Conservatives who genuinely cared; but most importantly for the Tory strategists and spin merchants, it would help 'detoxify' the Conservative brand. It was no coincidence that the torch of freedom logo was replaced by an oak tree.

So it was a further irony that the mask should slip on an issue concerning trees. Once it had been elected, out of the blue, with no consultation, the government announced that it planned to sell off large parts of the Public Forest Estate to raise up to £250 million. The outrage was immediate and entirely spontaneous. People could not believe that the government would even consider doing such a thing. But selling off the Public Forest Estate was a long-term aim of the right-wing free-marketeers, who were affronted at the idea that a 'business' such as forestry should be in public hands. They had tried before, but under Margaret Thatcher and Tony Blair, the thought of a sell-off of the nation's forests had been proposed internally and soon squashed when the politicians considered the probable public backlash. This time, though, the proposals had become public and the government seemed surprised by the hostility: a sign of how out of touch they were with ordinary people.

It also revealed the sheer incompetence of the government. Trying to wrap up this asset sale as part of Cameron's 'Big Society' initiative, they suggested that some of the most treasured forests – the New Forest, Sherwood and so on – could pass into the hands of some of the conservation charities, such as the Woodland Trust. But in its arrogance the government had not consulted these groups, and soon found they would not play ball. With a petition gathering over 500,000 signatures, radical environmental activists marching alongside the Archbishop of Canterbury, and every conservation group united in condemnation, the sell-off was stopped dead. There was the usual face-saving review, and the government decided to try to forget it had ever happened, in the hope the public might do so as well.

To that end, Caroline Spelman herself was dispensed with, to make way for Owen Paterson. This also had the bonus of removing one of the opponents of the expansion of Heathrow airport. This again had been a useful stance for the Tories in the run-up to the 2010 election; but now their friends in the aviation and construction industry – the only business sectors that stood to benefit significantly from Heathrow – were anxious to get on with increasing noise and air pollution for millions of Londoners.

So began Owen Paterson's calamitous reign at Defra. As well as the badgers, he was a huge fan of genetically modified crops, and also very excited about the opportunities for fracking. He promoted 'offsetting', by which the most precious parts of our countryside, ancient woodland or unspoilt meadows, can be trashed so long as the developers promise to plant trees or flowers elsewhere. George Monbiot was provoked by Paterson's hopeless response to the decline of Britain's bees into declaring him the 'worst Environment Secretary this country has ever suffered': and given that other holders of this post have included Nick Ridley, Tom King and Michael Howard, that's some accolade.

But in the end, reality broke in on Paterson in the form of some of the worst flooding in England in living memory. Although any single storm cannot be directly linked to climate change, the increase in the frequency and intensity of storms and flooding is exactly what climate scientists have predicted, and exactly what we are now experiencing. Even more predictable was that, if you cut back investment in flood prevention, floods will be worse. Owen Paterson could not claim this was some 'Act of God' that no one had foreseen.

Most of the country was affected, but for sheer misery, the plight of the communities on the Somerset Levels, inundated for over a month, stood out. The consequences of years of under-investment in the Environment Agency were laid bare in the lack of sandbags, high-capacity pumps, and other equipment. Worse, the genuine expertise of the agency was ignored too. Anyone who knows anything about flood management will tell you that you can't rely on river dredging alone: it is incredibly expensive, and within a year or two, the river will have silted up again. A proper plan would have included changing farming practices on the Levels to reduce soil erosion; giving up some land to act as a natural sponge to absorb more of the floodwater; and better pumping capacity. But dredging looks good on the news; and so dredging was the chosen option.

But the public were not fooled as to the competence, or otherwise, of the government: Cameron had to tell honourable friends Owen Paterson and Eric Pickles to stop bickering, and his 'money no object' pledge was in stark contrast to the penny-pinching that had undermined the effectiveness of the response to the floods, or the wider run-down of public services under the banner of 'austerity'. Owen Paterson was discarded at the next cabinet reshuffle, to be replaced by Liz Truss. With Parliament already beginning to run down in the shadow of the 2015 election, she had little chance to make her mark, for good or ill. Instead, we are left with the legacy of her predecessors: years in which the degradation of our countryside could have been reversed; standards for animal welfare improved; the richness of our biodiversity given proper protection; and a start made to avoid the worst of climate change and protect ourselves from the changes already upon us.

These were chances that may not come again. No wonder people marched for the forests, and for the badgers; and campaigned for circus animals and for the bees. Even when so much else the government was doing was dishonest, immoral or plain daft – on austerity, welfare, education or human rights – the environment remained an issue that inspired passion and commitment. I was proud when, after making my maiden speech, the *Independent* journalist Mike McCarthy called me a voice for the environment in Parliament; but I was never a lone voice. There were many other MPs who cared; and outside were hundreds of thousands of people who gave their support through charities and campaigning groups, who would write letters and talk to their MPs and even come to protest outside Parliament. However much the government wanted to stitch up the environment behind closed doors, their voices could not be drowned out.

6

Taking to the Streets:
How Parliament's Failings Are Driving People to Protest

'I pledge to vote against any increase in fees in the next Parliament and to pressure the Government to introduce a fairer alternative.'
Candidate Pledge, 2010 General Election

A honeymoon should give you memories you want to treasure forever; whatever might follow. And perhaps, when the Cameron–Clegg coalition of 2010–2015 has become a footnote to modern history, 'Dave' and 'Nick' will still be able to look back on the good days, when it was all new and fresh. The days before the shadow of tuition fees, and before 'coalition' became a dirty word.

It's not surprising that the betrayal over tuition fees has discredited the idea of coalition government. On the one hand, people like the idea of politicians working together. They don't like the 'Punch and Judy' character of political debate, and they want politicians to govern in the interests of the whole country, not just those who voted for them (let alone paid for their election campaign or invited them for holidays in exotic locations). But people are also suspicious of politicians, and see the manifesto as a kind of contract that they can use to try to hold them to account, and make them stick to their promises. And if you can use a coalition agreement to set aside those manifesto pledges, not as a necessary compromise but because you never wanted to do them in the first place, then it can look as if this is another trick of the political class to avoid having to keep their word.

In a coalition, you will always have to sacrifice some of the things you want, in order to get the others. And in a way that's a good thing for democracy. After all, the only reason you have to join a coalition is that you have not managed to convince a majority of voters to back your programme for government. So you are looking for the issues or approaches that will gain consensus among political parties, and their supporters: potentially a more unifying process than one party gaining a small majority and using it to impose its will on everyone else.

Conviction politics became fashionable with Margaret Thatcher, and some people are still misty-eyed at the idea of the Iron Lady dominating her male colleagues and scorning the notion of working with others or settling for anything less than 100 per cent. She was happy to continue her neo-liberal and divisive economic and social policies, even after losing every Conservative seat in Scotland, because it did not matter to her that her vision for Britain had such little support north of the border. It placed Scotland and England on diverging paths – one towards a neo-con, Atlantic future, the other towards a Scandinavian social democracy.

Conviction, though, lost its shine under Tony Blair. He was a politician who led from the focus group, projecting a fuzzy vision of a better Britain but adjusting to the nuances of public opinion and the demands of the elites. But power corrupts, and in the end he began not only to have convictions, but to believe he had the right to impose them on his colleagues and even on the public. Iraq was the consequence, and the idea that the true test of leadership is to ignore the views of the people you are leading was finally discredited.

This should have given the 2010 coalition a good start in life.

But the tuition fee pledge shows the difference between having to accept some compromise so that you can reach a workable programme for a coalition government, and positively welcoming the chance to dump a position which you never really believed in. The Liberal Democrat leadership did not like the cap on tuition fees long before the 2010 election. Those around Nick Clegg, on the economic-liberal wing of the party, believed that higher fees for higher education were inevitable. The tuition fees introduced by the Labour government had clearly deterred many able young people from poorer backgrounds from taking a place at university, and changes to the system – such as increasing the availability of bursaries – could have made a dud system a little less dud. But the rank and file of the Liberal Democrats were set against tuition fees, as were students themselves, and the leadership did not want to have that fight. So instead of making the case for their package of supposed reforms, they agreed among themselves that they would go into the election pledging no increase in tuition fees, and then hope to change the policy later on.

There were enough clues that the Liberal Democrats might not stick to their promises to lead the National Union of Students to try to persuade every individual Liberal Democrat candidate to sign up to a personal pledge not to raise tuition fees. The wording could not have been more clear-cut, and was not about the party's position or what would happen in a coalition, but a personal pledge as to how each individual MP would vote:

> I pledge to vote against any increase in fees in the next Parliament and to pressure the Government to introduce a fairer alternative.

The signatories included Vince Cable, Menzies Campbell, Danny Alexander and Nick Clegg – not surprising as the Lib Dem manifesto went further, saying: 'We will scrap unfair university tuition fees so everyone has the chance to get a degree, regardless of their parents' income.' But during the coalition negotiations both pledges were abandoned. The Lib Dem leadership might say that they had no choice. Yet this is not a question of outcomes, but of motives. Given that Nick Clegg had tried in 2009 to ditch the pledge to abolish tuition fees, and Danny Alexander had been recommending doing the same as part of the preparations for coalition before the 2010 election, it is hard not to see this as a sacrifice they were all too ready to make.

The effect was to make tuition fees the flashpoint for the coalition's first few months, reflecting the sense of betrayal and also the anger that a generation might miss out on their one chance of higher education. For most young people, if they don't go to university within a year or so after their A-levels, then they never will. And so this decision to load those potential students with massive debts, right in the middle of what the government itself was calling the worst recession since the 1930s, felt particularly vindictive and short-sighted. And for me, it also symbolized how far the welfare state had already been undermined since the 1980s and my own days at university.

When I go to speak at schools and colleges, there are plenty of things that can make me feel how much time has passed since my own schooldays. But usually it isn't changes in fashion or music or even technology; it is the way our perspectives have shifted so far, and so fast. When I talk to young people about what university can offer them, this feeling of a mix of gain and loss is particularly sharp. More young people have the chance to enter further or higher education; but their choices are in other ways more limited: partly by the quality of what is on offer, and the loss of courses that did not produce an 'economic return'; and also by the fact that they have to fund it. They are incredulous at the idea that I – and almost all MPs – were once paid to study. When, and why, did having educated people stop being good for the country, and therefore something the country as a whole should pay for? And when was the idea lost that courses should be offered not to make money for the university but because academics believed that it was an area of human knowledge that should be cherished and expanded?

So raising tuition fees crystallized many young people's feelings of betrayal by their elders. They were not the ones who ran up massive debts or screwed up the economy, but they were being asked to pay to clear up the mess. To take to the streets felt like the only way to make politicians understand their depth of feeling and their frustration with a political system that meant that a majority in the country could vote against any increase in tuition fees, and yet the fees increased from £3,000 to £9,000 a year for most courses. And the lies and evasions of those trying to justify it only inflamed the situation.

In November 2010, that challenge came to Parliament itself, when the NUS and other student bodies organized a number of major demonstrations. The first, on 10 November, saw between 30,000 to 50,000 protesters marching down Whitehall from Trafalgar Square to Parliament Square. In the afternoon, as they passed the Houses of Parliament in the direction of Tate Britain for a rally, several thousand broke away and surrounded 30 Millbank, the headquarters of the Conservative Party. The police lost control of the protesters and later the Commissioner of the Metropolitan Police, Sir Paul Stephenson, had to apologize for the ensuing chaos.

Two weeks later, the demonstration on the 24th, the police were determined to see no repeat. An extra thousand officers were drafted in, and steel barriers used to close off Parliament Square. This left many of the protesters trapped in Whitehall, penned in as if in a huge, open-air police cell.

I'd been working in my office that day and I'd planned to join the march when it reached Parliament Square. But I was soon getting concerned messages from friends and colleagues on the march about the police tactics. With Westminster Underground station closed, and the streets cordoned off, Cath and I weren't at all certain if we would be able to reach them. However, we'd underestimated the power of our magic passes.

Leaving by the Derby Gate exit, we found the road empty except for the police. Ironically, the police could not have been more helpful: 'Where do you want to go, ma'am?' They let us through their lines, into what might have been the set from a disaster movie: the familiar landmarks of the Houses of Parliament, Whitehall and the entrance to Downing Street turned into a deserted wasteland, with no traffic, no tourists or scurrying civil servants. In fact, there was very little moving at all except for the police snatch squads running past; but, like the distant sea, you could hear the crowds all around.

We crossed through the lines, and were quickly surrounded by people coming up to tell us about their experiences, many in a state of shock, never having believed that they would ever be on the receiving end of police 'crowd control'. They had been harassed, pushed around, and 'kettled', the name the police use for their tactic of forcing a crowd into a confined space for hours at a time, not able to come or go, fetch a drink or go to the toilet: not arrested, but not free either. The name is revealing because, although claimed to reduce the risk of disorder, kettles are known for boiling over, and oppressing hundreds of people into a confined space leads to fear, distress and panic.

One of those caught this time was Jenny Jones, the redoubtable Green member of the London Assembly (and now in the Lords). There was the added irony that as well as being an elected representative for the city, she was also a member of the Metropolitan Police Authority and therefore one of those responsible for overseeing the Met's actions. It sounded as if she was getting a pretty good view of their tactics up close, judging by her tweets, for she was stuck by the Treasury, just across from Derby Gate: but the police were ten deep and there was no way to link up with her. The following day, though, she was to launch a stinging attack on Commissioner Stephenson, who was trying to defend police tactics at a meeting of the Metropolitan Police Authority: 'When you imprison thousands of people, which is essentially what you did yesterday, you do have a duty of care to them,' she reminded him. 'You kept people for nine and a half hours. You punished innocent people for going on a protest.'

What made me so angry that day was how unnecessary these police-state tactics were. There had been many other protests around the country, and few had led to trouble. In Birmingham, when students occupied the council chamber in protest, the authorities had gone out of their way to praise the way the protesters had conducted themselves. You could see from the people at the Whitehall march that they were predominantly students, including many sixth-formers, and were not there to cause trouble but to show their strength of feeling. Yet the police tactics were bound to inflame the situation. Flight or fight is a basic human instinct. If you make people scared, it is natural for them to become more hostile, especially if you also prevent them from getting away. Had the police allowed the marchers to file past Parliament, they could have made their point and rallied elsewhere. But containing them in Whitehall was in effect treating every single protester as a criminal.

I talked to the police, trying to persuade them to let people out of the kettle, but it was clear they intended to keep the marchers there – including children – for several more hours, despite the biting cold and the lack of even the most basic facilities. Meanwhile, at the other end of Whitehall, they had mounted police charging the imprisoned marchers. It was gone six o'clock when I went back into Parliament. The mood there was very strange: both insulated from the chaos outside, but also fascinated by it. There was a kind of electricity in the air, yet everyone also wanted to pretend that the protests were not happening. I made my way to the chamber to see what the government was going to do in response to the protests that you could still sense going on outside, even in the panelled, thick-carpeted corridors of the

Palace. But in the chamber there was a debate on political reform, of all things, and listening to business as usual seemed to reveal everything that was wrong about Parliament.

'However, we have not moved to the suggestion in other committees of ten sitting days, because if the House were adjourned, there would be a specific problem. I hope that the minister will say what he thinks should happen if the House had been adjourned for a recess – for example, the day after a motion of no confidence. Should there be a requirement for the government to bring the House back, and should there be a specific provision for the Speaker to be able to require the House to be recalled within the two weeks? We will come to prorogation later.'

As is often the case, I couldn't bite my tongue. Parliament was besieged by thousands of students who were challenging us to explain how it could be that, despite everything that MPs had pledged during the recent election, a majority of MPs looked ready to vote to raise tuition fees in just a few weeks' time. To protect those same MPs from the supposed threat from their own electors, the police had adopted the most heavy-handed and illiberal response. And here we were, discussing the minutiae of a hypothetical constitutional wrangle. I found myself on my feet, catching the chair's eye.

'On a point of order, Mr Amess. Have you received any indication from the Home Secretary that she might be coming to the House tonight to make a statement on whether she believes that police tactics outside the House are proportionate? Many hundreds of students and schoolchildren have been kettled for more than four hours and, according to the police, will be out there for several more hours in the freezing cold. Whatever one thinks about the student protest, holding people against their will for no reason is neither proportionate nor effective.'

Mr Amess responded, as I suspected he might, that this was not, technically, a point of order; but he also hinted that the government should think about doing just that. But of course the government had no intention of making a statement. Nor was Ed Miliband more forthcoming – perhaps because he had been a special adviser to Gordon Brown when tuition fees were first introduced. Instead, he came out with a line on the BBC that seemed to sum up everything about his good intentions, yet his failure to take a lead: 'I was quite tempted to go out to talk to them.'

This failure to engage with public anger reminded me of the Stop the War march, when over a million people had taken to the streets of London to protest about the invasion of Iraq. Those marchers had represented many millions more across the country and around the world who did not believe that the case for war had been made, or that the last chance for peace had been exhausted. That day, it had seemed as if people power must surely make the government think again. Yet they had carried on regardless, putting support for the US President above the concerns of the British people. Instead of listening, the Blair government had set out to deceive us: first about its own intentions (having decided, it turned out, to back the United States whatever happened, when they were still telling us that nothing was decided); and second, about the intelligence itself (weaving a few scraps of evidence into what was presented as a cast-iron case for war).

Those million people were not the 'usual suspects'. They were people who had looked at the facts and at the characters and motives of the main players, and particularly at George W. Bush and his entourage, and at Tony Blair. They held no brief for Saddam Hussein; but they could see that the United States was not proposing to invade because Saddam was a bloodstained dictator, but for economic and geopolitical reasons of their own. And they knew that Tony Blair was not being honest about why he thought Britain should be involved. I was privileged to have the chance to speak at the rally in Hyde Park that day about how the impending war was illegal and immoral, and would only lead to further suffering and violence. Then, everything I said that day could have been spoken by one of my Liberal Democrat colleagues. But the 2010 coalition deal meant that their voices were now silenced.

Democracy depends on our hearing different points of view, different ways of seeing the world, and then deciding which we trust the most. But when the political parties only offer one viewpoint, then democracy can start to flounder. The Scottish and Welsh Nationalists had a proud record of questioning military adventurism; but would naturally struggle to engage or represent English voters. Individual MPs can and do make a stand against their own party's positions; but they risk being labelled as mavericks and losing some of their impact. And having a rebel in Islington or Ipswich is not much good if you live in Jarrow or Kensington. What people want, on the really big issues of the day, is that there are parties they can vote for who represent, explain and express the differences in view that exist in the country.

During the 2010 election campaign in Brighton, the issue of Iraq had come up again and again on the doorstep. Partly it was a sense of betrayal. Whether or not they had voted for Tony Blair, there had been a feeling that his victory in 1997 was a rejection of a certain kind of politics: of corruption, deceit and self-interest. And for this to end in an act of deception every bit as shabby and expedient as anything John Major had presided over – and far more harmful for the country – was a shock. But there was also a feeling that we had been let down by Parliament itself. Yes, Blair had lied. But what about the rest of the cabinet? What about all those MPs who had voted for war? What questions had they asked? Had they really done all they could to put the arguments for war to the test?

The parliamentary recess in the summer of 2011 gave me a welcome chance to reflect on this. For a year, I had seen Parliament from the inside. And I had also seen the protests staged on the streets around Parliament: on tuition fees, academies, welfare reforms, the break-up of the NHS and many more. There should have been no need for those people to take to the streets, if Parliament had truly reflected the wishes of the public. And that meant that Parliament itself remained the ultimate barrier to change. It had been captured by the elite, and was being run for their benefit, not for the good of the country.

That summer, when several English cities were struck by a series of riots of exceptional savagery that left the nation in shock, we saw the consequences of some of that same disengagement and frustration. Instead of being turned to something positive, a statement of belief or principle as the students and anti-war protesters had done, it had become entirely negative: wanton destruction and, often, an outflowing of greed and violence. But it was still a symptom of the underlying disconnect between the rulers and the ruled. Looting and arson are crimes; but crime has its roots in society. The more that people have a proper stake in that society, the more they feel it is run by and for us all, the less likely they are to turn to crime.

But there was also the far more positive response of the Occupy movement. More and more, we face challenges that are themselves very complicated, and also face opponents with limitless resources to pay for skewed research and bad science, and to twist evidence in their favour. Increasingly, protest is about deepening our understanding of the issues as well as communicating them to others. I spent some time at the Occupy camp outside St Paul's Cathedral in London and the quality of debate and appreciation of the challenges facing our country was so much deeper there than back in Parliament. Most MPs would never have faced up to the need to provide, in Tim Jackson's phrase, prosperity without growth, or acknowledged the impossibility of providing infinite economic growth on a finite planet; but this dilemma was taken for granted at Occupy, and the discussion was about our response to it. At times it seemed like a People's University, with visiting experts in conservation, science and the new economics finding a ready audience.

The reform of Parliament and politics is often portrayed as a distraction from the 'real issues', or the concern only of policy-wonk 'pointy-heads' and cranks. But this line was often pushed by traditional politicians, commentators and by other stalwarts of the establishment: the very people who benefited most from business as usual in politics. I was beginning to see how Parliament really worked, and how it defended itself from criticism and reform. Everything that I cared about, from peace and the environment to social justice and human rights, passed through a single decision-making process that, if hostile or biased, would always go the wrong way. So part of the fight was to change Parliament itself by setting out why we needed reform; and the one advantage I had was that I was an outsider on the inside.

PART TWO

The Fight from Within

Speaking in Parliament about sexism in the media, 12 June 2013

7

Power for Sale:
How Big Business Drives Government Policy

*Remember the Golden Rule: those who have the gold
make the rules.*

Anonymous

The invitation came on crisp, expensive card, printed in a rich
and tasteful purple, welcoming me and a guest to an event at
the ExCeL centre in London's Docklands. The only clue that
there was anything to set this apart from the hundreds of other
invitations that come the way of an MP was the logo: DSEi, with
the 'I' set in the kind of target you would have on a sniper's rifle.
Look closer, and under the acronym is the name of the event:
defence and security equipment international. Even this might
not mean much; except that I had come across DSEi before,
because I had joined protesters outside the event in previous
years, trying to draw attention to what goes on inside. For DSEi
is the world's largest arms fair: the place that the armed forces and
security services of the world come to shop for tanks and guns,
missiles and handcuffs, drones and stun grenades and a thousand
other weapons of war.

Clearly the event organizers had simply sent out invitations to
every single MP, along with any other members of the supposed
great and the good they could think of, without realizing that
some of us might turn out to be unwelcome guests. Why not

89

go along and see for myself? I knew some of the campaigners against the arms trade well. Some were high-profile ones like the comedian Mark Thomas, who I'd first met at a 'die-in' in Whitehall in 2002 to protest against the planned invasion of Iraq, and who had a routine in one of his shows about chaining himself to a tank outside one of the previous DSEi events. There were also groups such as Omega and CAAT – the Campaign Against the Arms Trade – who had done a fantastic job in raising awareness of the appalling waste and suffering associated with arms exports and even making some companies scale back their involvement.

As an MEP I'd worked to highlight the awful consequences and the double standards of governments that claimed to have rules to ensure weapons did not fall into the wrong hands, yet refused to take responsibility when things went wrong, saying the trade was beyond their control. But to go further, we needed to convince people in Britain that the trade had to stop, so they in turn would put sufficient pressure on governments to overcome their inertia and the influence of the major arms companies such as BAE Systems (the former British Aerospace).

Now, because I was an MP, I was being offered unprecedented access. I decided to accept the kind invitation from Clarion Events and go along with Cath.

A few days beforehand Cath came in with the delegate's pack sent over by the organizers. In it were our 'Access All Areas' passes, our guide to getting there without being caught up in the protests, some further invitations to special events on the day that various merchants of death were keen that we attend, and a mass of background information. From this we learned that DSEi would be hosting thirty-five national pavilions, including for the first time Brazil and India, and with over 1,300 companies displaying their wares. There would be a special focus on unmanned aerial vehicles – drones to you and me – and a vehicle park showcasing, among many other delights, the 'PIRANHA 3 with HITFIST

Overhead Weapon Station, mounting a 30 mm automatic cannon, co-axial 7.62 mm machine gun and the SPIKE anti-tank missile launcher'. All in all, a kind of Ideal Homes Exhibition for killing people. But none of this was preparation enough for the day itself.

We arrived in good time for registration, and there were the protesters, corralled at some distance behind steel fences. The police do this to try to make the protesters feel they are wasting their time. With something like an arms fair, you protest to draw attention to the issue, but also to reach out to those on the other side of the barrier. When I had joined the peace campaigners at the Greenham Common air base in the 1980s, the hope was that just by being there it would cause the men and women guarding the cruise missiles inside the wire to think again about the moral implications of weapons that could only ever be used to kill civilians indiscriminately. If the police can push you far enough away from the actual event, it is a kind of victory for those who don't want protest. Increasingly the police like to create an area where protest is 'allowed': if you won't use it, they then feel justified in arresting you. But the right to protest is not the right to protest where the police decide you can. If it were, then we would soon be told we can all 'protest' at home, in our baths or beds, but that anywhere else is a 'problem' and on grounds of 'public order' it must be stopped.

This thought made our ninja-style infiltration of this arms fair all the more satisfying. There were scores of security guards in every direction, all there to stop my friends and colleagues from making their point, and we were being waved through, greeted with smiles and deference.

Inside, it felt more and more surreal. If you haven't been to ExCeL, or a similar exhibition hall such as the NEC, you have to imagine a vast building, bigger than the largest hypermarket, but laid out with wide aisles along which are set up exhibition stands or, even larger, structures like stage sets they call pavilions. No money has been spared on making these as glitzy as possible, with bright spotlights and gleaming chrome. On each stand are the sales people, all smiles and handshakes, ready to sell you a guided missile or a box of grenades. And the goods they are pushing are not discreetly hidden away. They are everywhere. Guns, pistols, missiles, mock-ups of the latest fighters or patrol ships, all in pride of place. They are usually on white plinths or inside glass display cases, so it's a bit like walking around a gallery displaying 'found art'. Everything is very clean, with no hint of the reality of war, though sometimes their efforts to 'normalize' what they trade are deeply disturbing: particularly when these vendors of destruction have paid women in bikinis to drape themselves over the guns and tanks.

On the surface, everyone we talk to is very pleasant. They are mainly men, and you could imagine them taking their kids to rugby or helping to raise money for good causes at a local fete. The younger ones are keen that you should like them and their products: there's no sense of doubt or embarrassment about what they have to sell. In fact, it's the banality of it all that makes me queasy. We could be looking at displays of photocopiers or office furniture. The reality of the trade is hidden: and this means that these decent people can feel comfortable about taking part in a business that kills and maims tens of thousands of people around the world every year, that devastates whole swathes of countryside or leaves it scattered with dangerous munitions, so that even walking to school or ploughing a field might mean losing a limb. It is a business that feeds on itself, because the more that one country spends on arms, the less safe those around feel until they too have spent far more than they can afford. And it is a business that depends on governments, both to ensure it is protected from proper scrutiny and to subsidize these sales, and that dependency is reflected in the way in which the arms trade ensures it can exert the maximum influence on politics.

The arms trade has a long history of bribery and corruption. In fact, it is so routine that only the most grotesque examples make the news – such as the conviction of the Japanese prime minister, Kakuei Tanaka, over payments from US arms manufacturer Lockheed, or the millions paid to the Saudi elite as part of the massive Al-Yamamah arms deal. The latter revealed how deep the tendrils of corruption can go: when the Serious Fraud Office brought charges against BAE Systems, the Saudi government threatened to cancel further arms purchases and even to stop cooperation with the UK on counter-terrorism. The Labour government then forced the SFO to drop the investigation on 'national security' grounds, citing Saudi Arabia as a key British ally and how withdrawal of cooperation might mean 'British deaths on British streets'. You might ask what kind of 'ally' would threaten to suppress knowledge about potential terrorist attacks in this way. But there was little doubt that BAE had made 'irregular payments': soon after, the US Department of Justice hit the firm with a $400-million fine.

The upshot was that the government had strong suspicions that a major crime had been committed; but rather than let justice take its course, it halted the investigation. In part, this was BAE's famous lobbying power in operation. Some of the many MPs who have BAE factories in their constituencies were naturally asking questions in the House about the risks to British jobs if the investigation went ahead. BAE and its public relations advisers were also well placed to stir up the firms who supply them with materials and sub-assemblies, and these included other major employers such as Rolls-Royce. The sheer scale of arms sales – the Saudi sales alone are now over £40 billion – puts huge power in the hands of BAE.

The whole sorry saga shows the impact of lobbying in modern politics. The techniques now in current use by multinational firms cover everything from arranging meetings between business leaders and the MPs in whose constituencies those factories are based, to loaning your staff to work in a government department, so extending your influence right into the heart of where the decisions are taken. They have been proven to work time and again. The only question is, do you have the money to pay for them?

One vulnerable point for politicians is through the funding of political parties. The more you spend on campaigning – on leaflets, poster sites, on local and regional organizers, on clever software to identify your potential supporters – the more likely you are to be elected. In our first-past-the-post, winner-take-all political system the temptation to spend every last penny that you can in an attempt to secure victory is overwhelming. But raising that money is hard. Membership of the big three political parties has been falling for years. In an attempt to keep members, the cost of membership has been kept down, so the actual funds coming in have fallen even faster. The danger is that these parties are more and more reliant on a few major donors. Even if the donations are declared, there is still a question of what they think they are getting for their money. Some donors do not expect anything in return; but there are plenty of examples of money changing hands in return for political favours. Lloyd George used to sell peerages: the going rate was £40,000 for a baronetcy. Nowadays it is more subtle; but there remains a remarkable correlation between those who make large donations to political parties and those who are awarded peerages, knighthoods and other 'honours' by those same parties. In a way, it is unfair on those who give with honest motives, because it taints the whole system with a hint of corruption. But honours are a powerful form of patronage: one that party leaders are loath to give up by placing all such awards in the hands of an independent panel, who could choose recipients on merit.

It doesn't have to be like this. Even political appointments to the House of Lords could be fair and transparent. When the Greens were offered a seat in the Lords, we did not think 'Has X given us some money?' or 'Does Y need to be bought off with a seat in the Lords to stop them making trouble?' The whole membership of the party voted on who should be our nominee. And, proving that if you trust the membership, they will usually do the right thing, they chose Jenny Jones, who had shown her ability and commitment in the London Assembly and on the Metropolitan Police Authority. Until we have an upper house directly elected by the people, this is the best we can do.

With party funding, it seems as if some politicians lose their moral judgement because the money isn't going directly into their own pockets. A contribution to party funds may seem less seedy than accepting an attaché case of used fivers to blow on foreign holidays or a new swimming pool. But there are also examples of politicians taking money for themselves. The recent cases that have come to light tend to be backbench MPs or members of the House of Lords who agree to represent a business interest or a campaign (or sometimes another country) in Parliament, through behind-the-scenes lobbying or even asking parliamentary questions, in return for payments. But this is rather crude. Buying influence is more subtle. Usually there is no need to break the law.

The route of choice these days is to take advantage of the way the civil service has been run down to loan or 'second' your employees to work in the heart of Whitehall. For companies who do this, the advantages can be enormous. First, their staff can see all the papers and attend all the meetings. Second, they can use their status and experience to influence the views of their colleagues and the advice that goes to ministers. And when their secondment is over, they return with unrivalled knowledge of the inner workings of government, and a host of contacts. As with the honours system, there are people who come into government on secondment and do a good job and do not abuse their position. But the heart of the problem is that a secondee's loyalty is not to the civil service, but to their employer.

This concern also arises when career civil servants leave to join the private sector. For them, when allegiances change, it can be very difficult not to use their knowledge and contacts to the advantage of their new masters. The same, of course, applies to ministers. And the risk is that the knowledge that you can do very nicely working for a bank or hedge fund or arms company in the future will influence you when you are still in government. Will you be quite as tough, negotiating with Serco or PricewaterhouseCoopers or Barclays, or holding them to the terms of their contract, if you are thinking you wouldn't mind getting a job with them a few months or years down the line?

This is how the political system is subverted, British-style: something between outright corruption and a twenty-first-century version of the old boy network. Unlike the more dramatic examples of 'cash for questions' with their brown envelopes stuffed with tenners, this is a world where there is nothing so sordid as money changing hands. Instead it is done through influence, and establishing a common way of seeing the world in which people's personal interest, the interests of their party or employer and the interests of the country shade into each other. When a company director authorizes 'informal commissions' to win an export order, they might be thinking about the bonus he or she will earn, or the benefit to the company, or the employment boost it will bring to Britain, or a mix of all of these. In the same way, when a major British company seconds one of its high-fliers into the Department for Business, Innovation and Skills, no one will be sitting stroking a white cat and laughing in a sinister way because they have infiltrated a bastion of British power. But for all that, they will still hope to exploit the situation in ways that help them make money and shape the law to benefit themselves. And the greater the prize, the more they will invest in gaining this kind of access.

Even when lobbying leads to a scandal, further lobbying can avoid the consequences. It wasn't chance that horsemeat found its way into British supermarkets labelled as 'beef'. The coalition had cut funding to the Food Standards Agency and to the National Equine Database, making it much easier for unscrupulous firms to introduce horsemeat into products like burgers and lasagne and get them onto supermarket shelves. There are some obvious contributory factors, such as the ever-more complex supply chains and the rising price of beef on international markets: but exactly how the supermarkets were caught out we don't know. I and many others have been calling for a public inquiry, so we can learn the lessons and ensure this does not happen again. But thanks to further lobbying by an industry that wants us all to forget about the horsemeat scandal, the government is adamant this will not happen.

One of the greatest of all prizes in lobbying is the National Health Service. Its very size makes it attractive to the private sector, and the way that politicians have lined up to kick it – Thatcher, Major, Blair and even Brown – have left it vulnerable. The lobbying effort by potential private providers of health services has been immense. Lobbying in this context is not merely industry representatives meeting ministers or civil servants. It is a battery of techniques from commissioning research to shape public opinion to seconding staff to work on developing policy or even to sit on advisory and regulatory committees. Charities and other third sector providers, and public service providers, by contrast, cannot spend vast sums on influencing ministers and civil servants – and probably wouldn't want to either.

The combination of lobbying, the erosion of the independence of the civil service and the capture of the political elite by big business has made for a toxic combination. Ministers are already predisposed to favour business (the 'wealth creators' and providers of the job-creation announcements and photo-opportunities that politicians thrive on). Lobbying turns that into subsidies, tax-breaks, deregulation and a hundred other benefits. And the civil servants who might have given ministers an alternative viewpoint, one that would look at the costs and benefits to the country as a whole, have less influence and are themselves having to toe an increasingly corporate, pro-business line.

Take the Department of Energy and Climate Change. In 2011, I tabled a number of freedom of information requests and was alarmed to discover that there were no less than twenty-three policy advisers in the department who were employees from outside organizations, including Centrica (owners of British Gas) and the German energy company RWE. This is a pattern across government, and reflected in the number of civil servants who are seconded to businesses. And while the government claim that it is important that civil servants understand the perspective of business, there is no similar push to ensure civil servants understand the charity or third sector.

This is not to be anti-business. It is to defend the principle that our civil and political masters should act in the interests of the country as a whole, not one section of it. What is good for 'UK PLC', as business leaders like to call our country, is not necessarily good for the rest of us. When businesses pay for lobbyists, it is like one side in a trial having the cash to pay for the best team of lawyers, and the others being left to try to explain their case and understand the rules of the court unaided. And when businesses start funding political parties, then it's as if one side were handing money to the judge to get the judgment they want. It's particularly acute in planning cases, where ministers do in fact act like judges when they decide to uphold or overturn planning decisions. They are supposed to look at the issues dispassionately, considering the effects on local communities as well as the profits that may be made by developers. But most politicians are happy to go on record as having economic growth as their overriding priority: so local communities face the equivalent of 'hanging judges' who have already made up their mind on the outcome.

HM Revenue and Customs is another department where those who advise large firms and rich individuals on minimizing their tax – the 'big four' auditing and accountancy firms – are keen to second staff and to employ ex-HMRC officials. This revolving door is supplemented by the firms providing many more senior people to sit on endless working parties and advisory groups. The net effect is a corrosive cosiness: the more that HMRC staff work alongside colleagues from KPMG, PwC and the others, the more sympathetic they will be towards them. They will instinctively side with them rather than the edgy protesters of the Tax Justice Network or Occupy.

And so it is that too many politicians and civil servants – one group elected and the other appointed to serve the country – can end up captured by the rich and the powerful. How else could we explain companies such as Amazon and Starbucks paying almost no corporation tax in the UK? Yes, international taxation is complex and requires global cooperation. But where is the evidence that politicians or officials were doing anything to lead this international effort before War on Want, Oxfam and other campaigning groups forced their hand? Indeed, the Chancellor, George Osborne, continues to fight the Robin Hood tax tooth and nail, including an unsuccessful challenge in the European Court of Justice (paid for by the taxpayer, of course). The fact that a Eurosceptic such as Osborne, who has made a fetish of the idea that the EU should have no jurisdiction over British taxes, should go to the ECJ to try to stop the eleven members of the Eurozone from introducing the Robin Hood tax themselves, shows how strongly he objects to it.

Of course, the majority of civil servants and politicians resist the obvious lures of lobbyists and their paymasters. They still believe in 'public service', in the sense of serving the public as a whole, not favouring one section of it. But we have had so many decades of pro-business rhetoric that it shapes and distorts all our thinking. Too often businesses want to detach themselves from the very communities that sustain them, as if the people who own and run them are immune from the moral code that governs how humans should treat each other, or somehow superior to the common herd. Even an everyday phrase such as 'wealth creators' contains powerful assumptions. The chief executive of a supermarket would probably see themselves as a 'wealth creator': but what of the staff who work for them? At what point do employees stop creating wealth? A store manager? Someone on the checkout? And what of the engineers who maintain the electricity network that lights the stores? The health workers who keep the workers healthy? The farmers who grow the food they sell? The thousands of other roles that are essential to our complex modern lives? The notion of 'wealth creators' is simply a way for the rich and powerful to claim a higher status that truly has no basis. And when those who chose to make guns and tanks and bombs, and sell them to anyone with the cash to pay for them, also aspire to be wealth creators, then the invidious nature of this kind of linguistic brainwashing becomes clear.

For years, politicians have ducked the responsibility of bringing lobbying out into the open and under some kind of control. Not all lobbying is necessarily bad: organizations, whether charities, businesses or campaigners, will have legitimate reasons to meet decision-makers and set out their views. But when it is done behind closed doors, and the advantages all lie with those who have the most money, then reform is needed. But perhaps because of the very power of lobbying, nothing effective has been done: instead, in one of the coalition's most breathtaking acts of hypocrisy, it went after the charities and campaigners who struggle to get a hearing in the current system. The Transparency and Lobbying Act has placed a quite astonishing range of requirements on campaigning organizations in the run-up to elections. It puts huge barriers in the way of those seeking to raise awareness on issues of public interest, whether they are on NHS reform, housing policy, or wildlife conservation. Campaign spending limits for 'third sector' organizations – such as charities and pressure groups – have been cut drastically and the definition of what constitutes campaigning broadened. The Act's reach even extends down to community groups involved locally in what Parliament considers 'political' issues.

There was huge opposition to the new law and you might wonder why the government would go to such trouble to legislate about a 'problem' that hardly exists in the UK (though 'third-party' campaigns that try to avoid campaign funding limits are a serious issue in the United States). The government never succeeded in making a coherent case for the bill. Lord Tyler was particularly unconvincing when he gave evidence to the Commission on Civil Society on 14 October 2013: 'If you went to Brighton and spent a lot of money trying to make sure that Caroline Lucas lost her seat because you thought that she was too antagonistic to the oil companies, I think you should be registered.'

A touching concern: but was this the best they could come up with? It was hard not to conclude that the Act was designed to protect the government from the inconvenient questions that a vast array of campaigning groups, from Oxfam to the TaxPayers' Alliance, might put to them. The power brokers have already corrupted politics and bought most of the mass media. They could not take over every charity or pressure group in the country, but an Act of Parliament to discourage them from being too forceful or face legal sanctions would be almost as good. In the run-up to the 2015 election, many were concerned about the 'chilling effect' on the ability of charities to make their voice heard. Freedom of speech applies to groups of people just as much as to individuals. It is crucial that, in the new Parliament, charities and campaigning groups must be able to speak out without the fear of legal sanctions.

Our day trip to ExCeL had a bizarre conclusion. We had been tipped off that one of the companies was advertising cluster munitions for sale. These are particularly unpleasant weapons, because once dropped or fired they scatter dozens or hundreds of little 'bomblets' over a wide area. It's common for a high percentage of these to fail to explode, leaving them scattered over the countryside, putting civilians at risk (and particularly children, who are drawn to these fascinating, often brightly coloured objects). This is one reason why it is illegal to use, manufacture, buy, sell or even display them for sale: including at DSEi.

Sure enough, we found the stand and the glossy, illegal brochures. It was infuriating, because any of the dozens of police officers standing around outside the ExCeL centre could have wandered in and found the same illegal marketing material. I made a fuss, and as I was a bona fide guest they produced a rear admiral to hear my complaint and shortly afterwards the company advertising these weapons was escorted out of the exhibition. My friends and colleagues protesting outside could only suspect the law was being flouted: as an MP, I was in the fortunate position of being able to go inside and get the evidence.

8

Climate Change and the Politics of Hope:
How We Could Still Avoid the Worst if We Act Now

'Why didn't we save ourselves, when we had the chance?'
The Age of Stupid

More than any other single issue, it was climate change that brought me into politics, and it is climate change that keeps me awake at night. And these words, spoken in the film *The Age of Stupid* by Pete Postlethwaite as the Archivist, the last person left alive, looking back from the 2050s through the mass of films and documents and other evidence of the accelerating risks of climate change, still make the hairs rise on the back of my neck. Climate change is frightening. It is in some ways the mirror-image of the threat of nuclear annihilation: but instead of a single catastrophic moment, disaster is creeping closer day by day; and instead of ordinary people living helpless under a nuclear threat built and owned by military and political elites, it is something that we are all helping to bring about, in the way we live our everyday lives.

Fear also shapes how we respond to climate change. For those of us convinced by the threat and desperate to do what we can to avert it, the risk is that we talk in such apocalyptic terms that we simply generate a sense of helplessness in those we need to inspire and motivate. For many others, the easiest reaction to a

103

danger for which the remedy appears to be out of their hands is simply to ignore it, just as in the Cold War we pushed the nuclear threat into the background and got on with our lives. And many of those who deny that the climate is changing, or now more often deny that the changes we see around us are caused by human activity, are also gripped by fear: it seems more reassuring to deny the threat than to accept it.

In one sense, we are right to be fearful. The effects of climate change on our lives will be dramatic. The weather will become more extreme, with heatwaves, droughts and storms causing death and destruction. The underlying climate will change too, so in the UK our winters will probably be wetter and summers hotter and drier, and this will mean some species will die out and others spread, bringing diseases with them. And although international climate goals are based on a commitment to keep warming at no more than 2 degrees above pre-industrial levels, many experts believe we are already on course for a 4°C world – an outcome that would be, in the words of many scientists, 'catastrophic'.

Alarmingly, we have not yet seen the full rise in temperature that will occur as a result of the greenhouse gases we have *already* emitted. The earth's average surface temperature has risen by 0.8°C since 1900. The concentration of CO_2 in the atmosphere is increasing at the rate of around 2 ppm per year. Scientists tell us that even if CO_2 was stabilized at its current level of 390 ppm, there is at the very least another 0.6 degrees 'in the pipeline', since the planet takes several decades to respond to increased CO_2 due to the thermal inertia of the oceans.

It is also quite possible that climate change will spin out of our hands and take on a life of its own: for example, as the Arctic permafrost melts, it will release methane gas, which is itself a significant cause of further warming. While the basic science of climate change is beyond question – more robust, it's said, than the science behind evolution – the precise impacts of a change in our climate are less predictable. For example, we don't know exactly what will happen to ocean phenomena such as El Niño or the Gulf Stream; and so we can't be sure if the climate of the British Isles will become more Mediterranean or more like that of northern Canada or Norway. This unpredictability is why this subject has a unique horror attached to it: by releasing vast quantities of carbon dioxide, methane, nitrogen dioxide and other gases into the atmosphere, we are in effect conducting one vast experiment upon our planet and upon ourselves, with no way to reverse it and nowhere else to go.

But all of this is not yet inevitable – there is still time, both to avert the worst of climate change, and to enjoy the many real benefits that a transition to a zero-carbon economy would bring. One of my favourite cartoons shows a professor in a lecture theatre, standing in front of a white board, on which he's written a list of all the advantages of a shift to sustainable living: renewable energy, green jobs, liveable cities, rainforests preserved, clean water and air, healthy children, more local, organic and nutritious food. And one student has his hand up with a speech bubble which reads: 'But what if climate change is a hoax, and we create a better world for nothing?'

Focusing on the prospect of that better world which we can create is likely to be a far more effective motivator for action than fear. There are good reasons to be hopeful. On this issue, the public are ahead of the politicians. People want leadership on climate change. Two-thirds of us have cut down on our electricity use, and around half buy locally produced food. Almost everyone recycles, and often people complain that the recycling facilities provided are not good enough to maximize the environmental benefits. Every contribution, however small, is worthwhile; and many individuals, organizations and (particularly through the Transition Towns movement) even whole communities have gone further, aiming to become 'carbon-neutral'. They are making a difference themselves and also showing others that a zero-carbon world can be a reality and bring with it an enhancement, not a reduction, in our quality of life. The will is there: but we cannot do this alone. We urgently need more ambitious collective action as well.

In Britain we have a legally binding Climate Act – a triumph of cross-party working under the last Labour government, where only four MPs (three of them Conservative) opposed the legislation when it was passed. Since those heady days of 2008, however, the cross-party consensus has been unravelling, and the targets in the Act, which aim to cut carbon emissions by 80 per cent on 1990 levels by 2050, are hopelessly inadequate. According to Kevin Anderson of the Tyndall Centre, evidence-based policymaking would require an 80 per cent target not for 2050, but for twenty years sooner, 2030.

It is that calculation that has led him to declare the EU's climate pact, agreed towards the end of 2014, which demands a mere 40 per cent cut by 2030, as being 'in direct breach of the EU's repeated commitment to reduce its emissions "consistent with science and on the basis of equity"'. In a letter of stark warning to the prime minister, he writes:

> The reasons for today's climate dilemma reside in our prolonged abject failure to set in train an effective programme of mitigation. A quarter of a century on from the IPCC's first report, the carbon intensity of a typical EU citizen's lifestyle remains unchanged. I urge you to resist the vested interests calling for continued inaction and instead drive for an ambitious policy framework . . . Ultimately, this will be the legacy we bequeath future generations.

If we are to meet these more ambitious targets, we need a clear and comprehensive framework for action, based on a massive investment in renewable energy and energy efficiency; and carbon taxes (replacing the current policy of subsidizing coal, oil and gas) to help take account of the benefits of preventing climate change and the costs of pollution, so that low and zero-carbon energy sources can be developed on a large enough scale to become commercially viable. We also need the right infrastructure to create a circular economy, based on reusing, repairing and recycling. There will be a role for regulation, with some curbs on our behaviour, whether it is reducing the national speed limit to promote fuel efficiency or limiting the expansion of aviation; and for a re-localized food system which is far less dependent on oil-based pesticides, plastics and global transportation.

Collective action here in the UK depends on Parliament: and this is where, for me, the greatest fear now lies. Unless Parliament plays its part, there is every risk that we will fail to overcome the danger of climate change. Yet our political system seems singularly ill-equipped to rise to the challenge. Relentlessly focused on the short-term, it fails to consider the potential impacts of policies not just five years hence, but 50 years or 150. It has no interest in, and no mechanism for, factoring inter-generational equity into decision-making. Its structures reinforce a silo mentality which is then passed on to politicians themselves: the fact that the prime minister can say in one breath that he will do everything possible to protect the country from flooding, and in the next, that he welcomes the expansion of the fracking industry, without any sense of irony, indicates a devastating failure to connect.

Indeed Parliament is so unrepresentative of the people, and so much under the influence of lobbyists who want to resist the changes we need to make, that it has become a brake on our collective response, rather than a way of enabling it. Part of the problem is that in many cases MPs are selected by a very narrow group of people. Conservative MPs in particular are detached from public opinion on climate change. Despite all the mud stirred up by the energy companies and some contrarian 'deniers' over climate change, three-quarters of people in Britain believe the climate is changing because of human activity; but among MPs, this falls to half, while in 2014 a staggering 71 per cent of Conservative MPs thought that human-induced climate change is either unproven or 'environmentalist propaganda'. So those who should be leading the country on this issue are actually dragging us backwards.

I saw this first-hand when I attended the parliamentary debate on climate change ahead of the UN climate conference at Cancún in 2010. Although it's hard to think of a more important issue for the future of Britain, that debate was not held in the main chamber, but in Westminster Hall: a venue reserved for less important debates. And although climate change will affect every citizen in Britain, only twelve MPs could apparently make the time to attend. Those who were there spoke with passion and eloquence, and put some very specific proposals to the government: all of which were ignored. The cabinet minister responsible for climate change couldn't find the time to be there either, and it was left to a junior minister, Charles Hendry, to reply for the government.

The practical proposals raised by those MPs who were there included a phasing out of fossil fuel subsidies which, globally, receive around $700 billion, or 1 per cent of world GDP, which would lead to a 10 per cent reduction in carbon emissions. Another was the redeployment of the substantial funds which the government has set aside for an international agreement on protecting rainforests: since no international agreement was in sight, that money could be released straight away to fund bilateral agreements, as Norway has recently done. And since aviation is one of the fastest-growing sources of greenhouse gas emissions, Britain should have pushed for it to be included at Cancún, demonstrating that we were serious about making significant changes ourselves, as well as asking developing countries to take more responsibility.

The minister, in reply, ignored the first two and brushed the third aside, claiming this would put Britain at a disadvantage compared with other countries. With no right of reply for backbenchers, and no vote to hold the government to account, that was the end of the matter; and a few weeks later, Cancún came and went without making any progress towards a meaningful international agreement.

Just a month before the Cancún debate, I had tried to put down an Urgent Question on deep-water drilling off Shetland. To do this you need to persuade the Speaker to summon the minister responsible because it is an issue of immediate concern: in this case, the announcement that the government was issuing new drilling licences. This was shortly after the *Deepwater Horizon* disaster in the Gulf of Mexico, when an oil rig working for British Petroleum had exploded, killing eleven people and causing the worst offshore pollution in US history. Like the nuclear industry, oil firms are very good at reassuring people after such incidents that all the lessons have been learned and that there is no chance of a repeat. But experience shows that some external scrutiny is needed of such claims. Until the full story was known about what had gone wrong with this 'ultra-deep' oil well, it hardly made sense to encourage the exploration off Shetland, where the wells would also be 'ultra-deep' and conditions even less suited to safe drilling. The sea off Shetland is rougher and wilder than in the Gulf. It is potentially more dangerous, not less. And oil disperses less quickly in colder waters, so making the effects of any spill that much worse.

I'd worked closely with Greenpeace on this, and the case for a moratorium on Shetland drilling was compelling; but in the event, the Speaker refused to make time to call ministers to account. Because I've learned that tenacity sometimes pays, I had another go at raising the issue by holding an adjournment debate. Again with help from Greenpeace and other campaigners, I set out in detail why allowing new drilling to go ahead was mistaken, when we still didn't know why the BP platform exploded. But the minister responsible fell back on a bland restatement of policy: the claim that Britain has the best safety regime in the world for offshore drilling and so nothing that happens in the United States need bother us here.

Still determined to find some way to get the issue onto the political agenda, I proposed to colleagues on the Environmental Audit Select Committee that we hold an inquiry into the issue, and was delighted when the committee unanimously agreed a workable proposal for a moratorium: but as is so often the case with the current forms of parliamentary scrutiny, if the government is bent on ignoring cross-party advice, it is free to do so.

The Shetland oil exploration saga is an object lesson in the government's complacency over the growing climate threat. They say they have plans to reduce carbon emissions and so help stabilize our climate – but then encourage companies to go and find more oil wherever they can, whatever the cost in tax breaks or pollution, or the lives of oil workers.

Of all the troubling analysis about our dependency on oil and gas, one in particular stands out. The Carbon Tracker Report has estimated that, if we are to avoid the risk of runaway climate change, we need to leave around four-fifths of the known reserves of coal, oil and gas in the ground. The report revealed that existing fossil fuel reserves already far exceed the carbon budget to avoid global warming of 2°C, but in spite of this $674 billion was spent in 2012 to find and develop new ones – which could then turn into potentially stranded assets. Investing in companies that rely heavily on constantly replenishing reserves of fossil fuels is therefore very risky. So the sooner we can break the carbon habit, the better: as the economist Nicholas Stern pointed out so cogently in his groundbreaking 2006 report, taking action now to avoid the worst of climate change is good economics as well as good for the environment. But we have to do it, sooner or later:

because if we don't, then our modern society, with all the advances and benefits we take for granted, is in effect committing suicide.

Given this, the last thing we need is a fresh source of addiction. Yet we face the frankly insane plans of using 'fracking' to squeeze more gas and oil out of the ground. This is a technique pioneered in the United States in which a mix of chemicals and water is forced into the rocks beneath at high pressure. It literally fractures the ground, allowing pockets of gas to escape and, hopefully, find their way to the surface via the well. It is one of those techniques which is always prefaced by a chilling phrase such as 'completely safe if properly managed': like nuclear power, chemical plants and unsinkable ocean liners. Of course, no one builds a nuclear plant or chemical works expecting it to blow up. When it does, and it is discovered that it was not 'properly managed', those responsible are contrite and the industry sprinkles the usual reassuring words: *lessons learned . . . never again* . . . And so Windscale is followed by Three Mile Island, Chernobyl and Fukushima.

I've spent a lot of time thinking about the obstacles that seem to be preventing us from building a mass movement for climate action, and trying to answer Pete Postlethwaite's troubling question. Why is it that we seem to be content as a species to spend all our time monitoring our own extinction, rather than taking active steps to avoid it? Certainly, it would mean overcoming the powerful and vested interests of the fossil fuel companies, who increasingly are not simply lobbying government but being given senior roles within it. It would mean making more space in the busy lives of many, who of necessity spend much of their energy and ingenuity just trying to get by.

Crucially, it would also mean challenging the obsession of the media and politicians about 'growth', which is regarded as the overarching objective of the policies of governments the world over. Yet the truth is that economic growth is fast becoming uneconomic: in other words, the cost of clearing up the social and environmental damage caused by the process of growth – running down resources, cutting down trees, polluting the seas, changing the climate – is increasingly outweighing the value which the growth creates.

The level of analysis in political debate and media discussion is breathtakingly low: according to them all growth is good, no matter whether it brings any real benefits or actually makes us worse off. Announcements that the economy has 'grown' are broadcast as if this is unadulterated good news, and the ups and downs of Britain's GDP are reported as avidly as any Premier League football team. In fact, GDP is a poor measure of economic activity, let alone of whether that activity is good for us or not. Like so many indicators, it measures only those things that can be measured, not those things that matter.

As an example, if an adult stays at home to look after an ageing parent, this does not register on measures of GDP. But if that same adult goes out to work, and pays for someone else to look after their parent, then there are two extra wages that can be measured, and it looks as if the economy is that much better off. In fact, nothing has changed, except that more activity is now counting towards GDP. But this tells us nothing about whether, as a nation, we are better off as a result.

In the same way, if you have a beautiful landscape and you build a major new bypass through it, you have a 'gain' from the building of the road, and a 'loss' from the destruction of the landscape. But only the gain from road-building counts towards GDP. So the temptation for decision-makers – who are judged on their economic competence by levels of 'growth' – is to favour the options that will increase GDP, even if the country ends up worse off as a result.

These are just two examples. Economists have hundreds more to show how poor a measure GDP is of the well-being of a country, and how dangerous as a single yardstick for government policy. Academics and institutes such as the New Economics Foundation have mapped out much more effective ways of evaluating the benefits to society of different economic choices. You would be hard-placed to find a competent economist who would defend the pre-eminence that GDP has in popular and political discourse: while Nobel Prize-winners would line up to point out its faults. Unfortunately, 'popular' economics – the kind we are served up by the BBC and the business pages – has not caught up with much of this thinking, and still presents all growth as good.

This is a particular problem when thinking about natural resources. Again, GDP simply cannot take these into account properly. For example, natural gas is a valuable resource and is the raw material for a huge array of products that we have come to depend upon. When it is extracted and used to make something (such as fertilizer or a roll of cling film) or sold as domestic gas for cooking or heating, that will be treated as a gain for the economy. But there is no matching debit to take account of the fact that the gas is an asset which diminishes. So it appears that the country is better off than it actually is.

Again, every competent economist knows this: but politicians have no interest in drawing attention to the fact that our natural resources are being used up, because to do so would bring into question their management of the economy (and as all three main parties are committed to the pro-growth model, none of them wants to expose it even when out of power). The recently established Natural Capital Committee, set up to advise the government on the state of our natural assets like rivers, forests and land, has the potential to challenge this, but as yet there is little evidence that it is having any meaningful impact on government decision-making.

The prevailing economic narrative that 'growth is good' is probably the single biggest obstacle to tackling climate change. It ignores the fundamental paradox of how we are expected to have infinite growth on a planet of finite resources. As economist Kenneth Boulding remarked, 'anyone who believes exponential growth can go on forever in a finite world is either a madman or an economist'. It presupposes that economic growth will make people more happy, when all the evidence is that – once essential needs are met – more of it does not. It divides countries, making people think we need to compete to have the highest rate of growth, and treats economic activity as a kind of international competition, when we should be working together. And if economic growth is your single most important target as a government, then it plays into the hands of those who claim to provide it: to industry, to those who depend on over-stimulating consumer demand, and to the energy companies who are so strongly opposed to any attempts to tackle climate change. They call the shots on whether to curb growth, or protect our natural resources, or favour the manufacturing of carbon-intensive products over alternatives or over providing services such as personal social care. (Why else would we still tax employment and yet give tax breaks for machinery and other capital investment?) It means that all the advances we make in reducing our energy demands – more energy-efficient light bulbs, appliances or industrial processes – are outweighed by the introduction of new products, most of which hardly fill an essential need.

There is no evidence for the possibility of the absolute decoupling of economic growth and environmental degradation. That's why we need a transition to a post-growth world that is benign, sustainable and just, based not only on efficiency, but on *sufficiency*: on having enough.

The way our economy is currently structured means that, unless there is growth, people lose their jobs, the tax base shrinks and politicians struggle to fund the public services we all rely on every day. We need to break that vicious cycle by building a new macro-economic model that is geared not towards growth, but towards achieving the outcomes that are important to society and which can be sustained by the planet's finite carrying capacity. A steady-state economy is one that recognizes that it is a subsystem of the biosphere, and that since the biosphere isn't getting any larger, the subsystem has to remain within limits. An economy, in other words, that does not measure itself in terms of GDP alone, and that does not depend on the endless consumption of finite natural resources at one end, and the production of waste at the other.

That doesn't mean there is no economic activity. The phrase 'dynamic equilibrium' has been coined to try to capture that sense of activity without overall growth. Steady-state behaviour is a system that permits qualitative development, but not aggregate quantitative growth.

So in designing this new economy, we can start with the positive outcomes we want – environmental sustainability, economic fairness, high levels of human well-being – and link those to the relevant determinants within the model, such as aggregate output, income distribution and working hours, and then 'reverse engineer' what this would imply for the levels and types of differing inputs. Overall our politics should be guided by the rules of 'contraction and convergence', meaning that while some levels of consumption will come down, others may rise – especially those of the poor – within an overall framework of ambitious emissions reduction.

In one sense, tackling climate change is very straightforward. The science is robust, we have many of the right technologies, and we understand how human behaviour can be shaped to move away from those forms of economic activity that create the most carbon emissions towards those that create the least, creating hundreds of thousands of jobs in the process. What we lack is the political will and leadership, in spite of the fact that the costs are not huge compared with the costs of inaction. As I said in the Cancún debate, if the world were a bank, the money and political will needed to avert a catastrophe would have been found within days.

This inertia at the top is also undermining the efforts of individuals to do something about their own 'carbon footprint'. Politicians tend to either ignore climate change, or claim that they have it in hand, citing all kinds of distant targets and deadlines as if announcing these is the same as actually reducing the amounts of carbon dioxide and other gases being released. For some, this suits their ideological block on accepting the reality of climate change. For others, it avoids having to admit that they have failed to act, or that their decisions are positively harmful. Labour, for example, is backing the expansion of either Gatwick or Heathrow airports, even though aviation emissions are already one of the most significant and fastest-growing drivers of climate change. Ed Balls said in his 2014 conference speech: 'Whatever the outcome of the Howard Davies review into airport capacity, we must resolve to finally make a decision on airport capacity in London and the south-east – expanding capacity while taking into account the environmental impact. No more kicking into the long grass, but taking the right decisions for Britain's long-term future.'

The words 'taking into account the environmental impact' are, of course, meaningless; either you expand aviation and accept the impact on climate change, or you don't. If capacity at Gatwick or Heathrow is increased, there will be more carbon emissions; and we will either fail to meet our targets by the same amount, or some other part of the economy, or some other group of people, will have to make even greater reductions to make up the difference. (Predictions for carbon emissions already factor in a lot of assumptions about how much more fuel-efficient planes will be in the future, so there's no help to be had there.)

Successive governments have also argued – entirely dishonestly – that we can only act if others do so too. We are told that there is no point acting here in Britain if China is intent on building new coal-fired power stations; and, of course, China could say the same about our ever-rising carbon emissions from aviation, or the fact that their power stations run the factories that make consumer goods for customers in the West. The truth is, if governments in the rich and developed countries really wanted an agreement, then it could be done. We've seen plenty of examples of the developed and developing worlds cooperating for our mutual benefit, in areas such as disease control and agriculture; and in this case, it is the developing nations who have most to gain from early action on climate change, because they are the ones who have the least capacity to deal with the storms, floods, droughts and epidemics that it is bringing in its wake.

Also, it is richer countries such as Britain that have the ability to take the lead; and also the moral responsibility, given that it is our lifestyles, our consumption, that remains by far the largest driver of climate change (for example, where carbon emissions in China come about from manufacturing plastic and electronic goods for Western markets). And we have shown in the past how it can be done. In the 1980s, two climate crises emerged into popular consciousness: climate change, and the hole in the ozone layer. Both were caused by human emissions, and in some cases the same gases were responsible for both (so CFCs, for example, were eating away at the ozone layer and also contributing to the 'greenhouse' effect by trapping the energy from the sun's rays within the atmosphere). Both were, to a large extent, identified by British scientists. Both involved chemicals and processes that were woven into the fabric of modern life: such as coal, oil and gas for climate change, and coolants and aerosol propellants for the ozone layer. Both could therefore only be dealt with by concerted international action. But there the stories diverge.

Within a few years of the discovery of the growing hole in the ozone layer, the world had a binding agreement in place to phase out the chemicals causing the problem: the Montreal

Protocol. It had two crucial features. First, it accepted that developed countries had the greater responsibility for the problem, and the greater capacity to find alternatives to CFCs and other 'ozone-depleting substances'. Therefore less developed countries were given longer to develop alternatives, and also given finance to help make the transition. Second, agreement was reached because a handful of European countries, including Britain, took the lead in committing to rid themselves of ozone-depleting chemicals. They persuaded the rest of the European Union to agree to rapid action; and thereafter the EU could use this leadership to persuade other developed countries such as the United States, and also developing nations, to accept a deal. There was hard bargaining, and the cost was high; but the deal was done. Now, twenty years on, the ozone hole is slowly healing, and we can start to count the benefits, particularly to human health.

But climate change did not follow the same track. The obvious move was to introduce a tax on carbon emissions, but the UK blocked this in the EU in the mid-1990s. Without EU unity, it was hard to put pressure on the United States to do a deal; and without the United States, no international agreement was possible. Instead, from Kyoto on, we have had a succession of deceptions and loopholes: countries commit to doing what they would have done anyway, and agree to meet again a few years down the line in another international circus. Kyoto, Copenhagen, Cancún: in a way, it would have been better if none of these had ever happened, for at least the public would have known that nothing was being done, rather than being reassured with talk of treaties and agreements.

The coverage given to climate change 'sceptics' or 'deniers' reflects the wider reluctance to engage with the reality. Lord Lawson is of course free to set up something called the 'Global Warming Policy Foundation', but the coverage it has received is out of all proportion to its size or role. It does not have a substantial membership (it does not publish figures, but the best guess is that it has around a hundred members). Nor does it represent more than a tiny fraction of the scientific community. Most of all, though, the BBC and others should be cautious of any organization with such an obvious agenda that will not reveal the source of its funding (the 2013 accounts show that it received £12,771 in membership income and £342,530 in anonymous donations). Many of those associated with it (including Owen Paterson, whose first outing after leaving his post was to give a speech to the GWPF) have a track record in attacking climate science or acting as cheerleaders for anti-environmental businesses. And while the GWPF says it exists to educate the public on climate change, its approach is so selective – old tricks like selecting a particular range of years that 'happens' to show annual temperatures staying the same – as to make any 'educational' role laughable.

If climate-change deniers were operating in the same way in challenging the scientific consensus on evolution, they would not receive anything like the same media attention. But then evolution does not pose a threat to 'business as usual', or put at risk the activities and profits of major corporations. It is not so long ago that there was consensus on climate change, in which Conservatives such as Margaret Thatcher and George H. W. Bush realized the danger, and corporations such as BP could accept the need to move 'beyond petroleum' in meeting future energy needs. The threat has not reduced since then; and the robustness of the science is much stronger. What has changed is that energy firms and right-wing politicians have fought a highly effective campaign to turn science into politics, where everything becomes a matter of debate and nothing can be agreed: a situation which benefits those who want things to stay as they are, and who will not have to pay the price of climate change.

We have to recognize the danger; but if we rely on fear alone to bring about change we will fail. Instead, we must offer a message of hope. To start with, this is not beyond our capabilities as a nation or a species to overcome. There is no missing element in the plan that would take us from where we are now to where we have to go: except for the will and the means to put that will into action. The Centre for Alternative Technology's report 'Zero Carbon Britain' has mapped out how by using existing technologies we could eliminate net carbon emissions while maintaining a modern way of living. One plank of this is modelling current patterns of energy supply and demand to show that renewable sources could meet almost all our needs, and synthetic gas from biomass could fuel the existing gas-fired power stations to provide cover for peak loads. Overall, becoming a carbon-neutral country would involve changes in our behaviour, but these are modest compared with the changes that will be forced upon us if we do nothing.

And many changes would be for the better. The same report looked at the impact of switching to a healthier diet with less meat and dairy produce. This would help reduce emissions because it would mean less intensive farming (and fewer livestock producing methane). There would be other benefits too, including on animal welfare. It's an example of how the changes we need to make in response to climate change are ones that would bring us benefits anyway.

The flip side of this is to sublimate the fear of what we would lose if we do not act into a more positive appreciation for what we have now. Thirty years ago the experts were predicting the spread of new diseases that would affect crops and forests. Now those diseases are arriving, and we are already losing millions of trees, with the very existence of the ash and the oak in doubt. We need to channel the same commitment that saw us beat the government over the sell-off of our forests into forcing the government to do more to protect those same woods by acting now. Britain's forests should be a symbol of what we save for ourselves and future generations; and in planting more trees we have a way of removing some of that excess carbon dioxide from the atmosphere and enhancing our landscape.

The threat has been compared to a war: yet our economy is hardly on a 'war footing'. That gap in rhetoric has led some to think the threat is being overblown: if it were that bad, people reasoned, politicians would be introducing energy rationing, or putting up proper flood defences.

Thinking of the climate crisis not as an environment problem alone, but as the greatest threat to our collective security, led me to commission a report that we called the 'New Home Front'. This sought to examine how Britain finally mobilized in response to the overwhelming threat of the Second World War, in order to see what could be learned, positively and negatively, to help with the unprecedented challenges posed by climate change. There are no exact parallels for our current crisis, of course, but the social change and national economic re-engineering at that time approach the scale of what we need in the face of these modern threats. The similarities are striking, in everything from the way we can adapt our diet to feed ourselves more healthily to the way ordinary people demanded rationing as the best way to share the responsibilities of wartime more fairly. And back then, we met the challenge with a remarkable mix of bold leadership, creative flourish, brave social and economic experimentation, occasional ineptitude and failures of planning, coupled with a more impressive, overarching focus and commitment to achieve the objective of winning.

The report struck a chord with people – from deep Greens to readers of the *Daily Telegraph* (and those who are both) – mostly because it set the nebulous menace of climate change in a more familiar context. It also helped that the analysis was so positive: we can win against carbon, if we pull together. It felt right to have emblazoned on the cover of the report the figure of Rosie the Riveter, together with the exhortation that rang so true in the 1940s: *We can do it.*

I believe we can: but it does depend on recognizing the enemy. Climate change is not only about taking a message out to people: it's also about fighting against those who want to confuse, to muddy the waters and prevent us forming a coalition for action.

One of the main drivers of climate change is consumerism: or, as Professor Tim Jackson memorably summarized it, buying things we don't need with money we don't have to create impressions that don't last with people we don't care about. We know this. We want, as individuals and as a society, to live more natural lives, and spend more time on the things that matter: family, friendship, community.

Though climate change keeps me awake, it is also a source of hope. If we are to survive, we will need to re-forge our society; and as we found after the Second World War, with the creations of the NHS and the welfare state, we may find we have been forced into building a better and fairer society. In my maiden speech, I said that climate change would be the great test of that Parliament. It is a test we collectively failed. The Parliament elected in 2015 simply has to do better. Our futures depend on it.

9

Heat, Light and Homes:
How We Could All Have Warm, Affordable Places to Live

> '*To be truly radical is to make hope possible rather than despair convincing.*'
>
> Raymond Williams

There are times in the House of Commons where what is taking place before you is so detached from reality that it can seem like a parallel universe. In the autumn of 2012, I secured an adjournment debate on the important but rather technical issue of the exposure of the financial markets to 'high carbon assets' such as oil and gas. Adjournment debates don't end up in a vote and can't change the law but they can put issues on the agenda. The officials have to draw up a briefing and the minister has to prepare his or her response, so it's a valuable chance to get them thinking about the subject. Usually the government want to take the heat out of these debates with some flannel – *important issue, right it is raised, arguments on both sides, etc., etc.* – and so they lack a little passion.

But not this time. The minister, John Hayes, dived straight in:

> The Honourable Lady made that case – I shall put it as generously as I can – with confidence.

His tone was surprising. After all, I hadn't attacked the government, only raised an emerging issue and given them a chance to set out their thoughts.

> The second misassumption that underpins the Honourable Lady's analysis – I am afraid that I must put it this way; I always try to be generous, as you know, Madam Deputy Speaker . . .

As his speech rolled on, what took me aback was not so much that he disagreed with me, or misrepresented my position, or did not engage with the issues, or was complacent, or disingenuous (though he did or was all these things), it was how he said it.

> I do not want to lecture her – I say this as a paternal bit of advice, really – but a degree of humility is required in these matters . . . Those fundamental misassumptions rather colour her approach to these matters . . . I think, less apologetically – not that I have been particularly apologetic so far . . .

No civil servant would have drafted a speech remotely this rude, patronizing or personal. This was coming from the heart.

> I think that the Honourable Lady is not only outside the mainstream, but, arguably, on the very fringe of the debate. I do not want that to be the case, because, as I have said, I am generous and am approaching the issue as paternally as I can. Dickens wrote about '. . . a heart that never hardens, and a temper that never tires, and a touch that never hurts.' I do not want to hurt the Honourable Lady . . .

That was a relief. But when the debate was over, I tried to think what it was about the subject matter that had so infuriated him.

Perhaps it was the combination of energy and finance. 'High carbon assets' underpin the valuations of the energy and mining companies that make up around a third of the total value of the London Stock Exchange. If those oil and gas reserves were all used, it would create around 2,800 gigatonnes of carbon emissions. But if we are to avoid catastrophic climate change, we have to limit carbon emissions over the next thirty-five years to just 565 gigatonnes. In other words, we have to leave the majority of current carbon 'assets' underground – which means they will lose their value (or, in the jargon of the investment community, will become 'stranded' assets). If not properly planned and managed, that could have a serious impact on the stability of the international financial system. This ought to be an issue where policymakers, environmentalists and the financial sector could have some useful conversations. But on this occasion at least, the minister did not even want to listen.

Like defence, the financial world has more than its fair share of machismo; and you don't have to have been a fan of *Dallas* to recognize the glamour of the oil and gas sector. Politicians of a certain kind love it: they are forever putting on hard hats and staring intently at vast pieces of machinery while men in overalls stand around deferentially for the TV cameras. Big Energy is power; money; influence. The culture is often aggressive, single-minded and 'can-do' (look at Trafigura and their attitude to disposing of hazardous oil by-products). Certainly I've been on the receiving end of more rude, unpleasant or unprofessional behaviour when it comes to energy than all the other issues I've pursued in Parliament combined.

Another characteristic of the topic is the way the cheerleaders for Big Energy play fast and loose with reality. It is just so overwhelmingly frustrating when someone is sitting in front of you reeling off a set of untruths, who then tries to make you sound unreasonable when you drag them back to reality. Only the week before that interview, the government voted against having effective minimum energy standards for social housing from 2015. But on air, the Minister simply would not accept this. I was saying they had, he was saying not, and it risked turning into a Punch and Judy show.

The public would have every reason to be baffled by all this, because demonstrating why the government is being 'economical with the truth' takes time. On another occasion I was interviewed by a BBC journalist who seemed determined to suggest that the public had turned against energy efficiency because 'green levies' were putting up their bills. In fact, there's no real evidence that the public have been put off energy efficiency, and in any case the primary cause for higher energy bills is the rising price of gas. The so-called 'green levies' account for a much smaller amount, and are designed not just to support renewables but crucially to pay for energy efficiency measures in the homes of some of the poorest and most vulnerable people. Of course it doesn't suit this government to admit as much. In years gone by, energy efficiency measures for people who need them most were paid for from general taxation, like the Warm Front scheme. Under this government, it's paid for through a levy on the bills of all consumers, which is unfair, because it doesn't relate to their ability to pay; and divisive, because people don't necessarily understand what the money is used for. But in a radio interview, there's often not enough time to fill in the background in this way. (Journalists are often frustrated by this as well – which is why the legendary BBC reporter John Sergeant called his memoirs *Give Me Ten Seconds*).

These limitations mean that the media can hold politicians to account very effectively; but only some of the time, and only on some kinds of issues. This makes Parliament's scrutiny role so vital. But again, with their current limited powers, and with a culture that turns deceit into an act of loyalty to one's party, MPs can only go so far. Most of what passes for parliamentary scrutiny takes place not on the floor of the House but in committees. Here

MPs have the chance to really dig into the detail of a subject, and to put questions to ministers and even to their civil servants. Even better, you can ask a series of questions to try to unpick the evasions that these witnesses too often throw at you. (All the proceedings are recorded, published, even made available as a TV and online feed and also archived. Unfortunately, given that this is where the truth sometimes slips out, it doesn't always make for riveting viewing and is not vastly popular with the viewing public.)

The hearings held by the Environmental Audit Select Committee over subsidies for nuclear power show the frustrations – and how the truth can still be uncovered. The Liberal Democrats have always been dubious about nuclear power; so the 2010 Coalition Agreement included a compromise with the pro-nuclear Conservatives: new nuclear power stations would only be allowed '. . . provided that they receive no public subsidy'. Now that's pretty clear, you might think. No sign of the hand of Sir Humphrey, wrapping it up in ambiguity. If only politics was always like this, we could have more trust in our politicians.

But by 2013, things had . . . erm . . . *evolved*. The government announced that EDF (formerly *Électricité de France*) would build a new nuclear power station at Hinkley Point in Somerset, partly funded by Chinese investors. And the British government would help out by guaranteeing to buy electricity from the plant for the next thirty-five years. The guaranteed price would be £92.50 per megawatt hour, which is about twice the current price for energy, and would ensure EDF and their backers would make a return of between 10 per cent and 30 per cent on their investment – a potential profit of £1 billion a year. (This is one reason the deal was described as 'economically insane' by City analysts Liberum Capital, who went on to add '. . . we are flabbergasted that the UK government has committed future generations of consumers to the costs that will flow from this deal.' Quite.)

However you look at it, this is a subsidy. EDF were clear that the project would not go ahead without this guarantee. It had to be referred to the European Commission for clearance, because it was classed as a form of 'state aid'; and throughout the process the Commission has called it a subsidy. And the government was offering other subsidies too, including underwriting the costs of dealing with the nuclear waste from the plant. All in all, the European Commission has estimated the subsidy as £17.6 billion (and that excludes the incalculable costs of a nuclear accident at Hinkley).

The government apparently had two choices. It could say that the 2010 pledge had been a mistake and it was, after all, the right thing for Britain to subsidize a new generation of nuclear power stations. Or it could explain what had changed since 2010 to mean the pledge had been right then, but not now.

Instead, they came up with a third approach: claiming that this wasn't in fact a subsidy but a 'market-based support mechanism'. And, anyway, if it was a subsidy – which it wasn't – it would be all right because it was being offered to other energy sources as well. They even tried to claim that the Coalition Agreement only prohibited giving a subsidy – not that this was a subsidy, of course – to nuclear power alone. This was a particularly dishonest line, as this wasn't what the Coalition Agreement said, but rather dreamt up months later. So having begun to weasel out of their original plan, they then implied that the new wording was in the original agreement. Creating this kind of confusion is never accidental. As with the invention of 'market-based support mechanism' as a synonym for subsidy, you can't with the best will in the world think that the ministers, advisers and civil servants actually believe any of this. And if you say things that you know aren't true, then that's lying (or what the coalition might call a 'dishonesty-based perception-changing mechanism'). Not that you can say so. Accusing another MP of lying is 'unparliamentary language', for which you have to apologize, even if you are right.

There is a point to this: if MPs simply found more and more incendiary ways to insult each other, then Parliament would become even more dysfunctional, and the public would be even more put off than now (and that is, just, possible). But it means that when ministers are lying through their teeth you can't say so. It also means the debate appears to be between two competing points of view – not between one side at least trying to say what they think is true, and the other side knowingly saying things that aren't true.

To claim that it's not a subsidy if you give it to more than one type of energy is a complete barbarity of the English language. But this is what the Environmental Audit Select Committee had to listen to, because the 'executive' (that is, the government and civil service) has learned to manage parliamentary committees just as effectively as it manages the media. The techniques are the same as those of the spin doctor: suppression of information, evasion and sometimes, when cornered, outright deceit. It creates a new constitutional problem, for the system depends on the assumption that ministers will at least tell the truth, and nothing but the truth – even if they are not expected to volunteer the whole truth if no one asks them the right question.

The other area where scrutiny can and sometimes does work is in the committee stage of a bill. The full chamber is the place for big, set-piece debates on the principles of legislation, or battles over particularly contentious issues. But when it comes to detailed consideration of the draft legislation, the committee – perhaps fifteen MPs discussing the legislation line by line to tease out the implications and challenge some of the assumptions – is the place. It can be hard going: two sessions or more each week, sometimes going on late into the night, plus studying the papers beforehand and talking to interested groups, campaigners and experts, if you are taking it seriously. But it gives individual MPs who are prepared to put in the work the chance to have a direct impact on legislation. That's why the whips generally try to keep people with too much expertise or independence of mind off these committees. Sarah Wollaston, the Conservative MP for Totnes, tells of how because of her background as a GP, she was keen to sit on the Health and Social Care Bill committee. Instead, the whips offered her a committee looking at double taxation in the Cayman Islands. When she protested that she knew nothing about the subject, the whips said that was all to the good: all they wanted her to do was to vote the right way at the right time.

In my first year, after a protracted tussle, I won a place on the Energy Bill Committee and could work with other backbench MPs and with campaigners and experts outside Parliament, and argue the case for a range of improvements. You can't usually change the overall shape of the legislation – the Energy Act still had many flaws and failings – but I think we helped to avoid it being an awful lot worse: and in Parliament that often counts as a victory.

Sometimes the challenge in dealing with ministers is in the other direction: they seem to agree with you. This can come about when the arguments are clear in one direction and the public are supportive, but the government still don't want to do it. Then the risk is that they accept the principle and pledge to put it into action; yet, somehow, the time is not ripe, the circumstances not propitious, and the expected progress never comes to pass: as with the Green Investment Bank.

Cross-party consensus is rare in the tribal world of Westminster, and so the fact that there was support from all sides for setting up a government-backed bank that would invest in environmentally friendly technologies and projects was encouraging. Its origins lay in businesses and campaigning groups coming together to set up Transform UK. It was exciting enough to have business leaders, Friends of the Earth and the Institution of Civil Engineers all in a room together and talking constructively; and the Green

Investment Bank proposal they launched in 2009 was the right idea at the right time. It would have its core capital provided by the government, but would use this to borrow more funds on its own account, and could also work with partners so that the initial funding could bring in many times the value of investment in green energy. In Germany, the state-owned KfW banking group was already investing heavily in renewable energy projects and could fund many times its core capital. But the UK had no similar state-owned bank that could do the job (in fact, the Royal Bank of Scotland, which had fallen into the government's hands after being baled out during the 2008 financial crisis, was busy lending to oil and gas companies and showed little interest in investing decisively in renewables, and the UK government insisted it would not influence RBS to do otherwise). A new institution was clearly needed. Alistair Darling included plans to set up the GIB in his last budget under Labour. The coalition pledged to carry these forward. So, with all three main parties in support, what could go wrong?

The short answer is, HM Treasury. The senior Treasury officials who advised George Osborne on the proposal had a deep-rooted ideological opposition to allowing any organization not under their direct control to raise money that could be seen as a part of the public debt. Further, they had no interest in the benefits the bank would bring: notably, in helping to stimulate employment at a time when the economy was mired in recession. The primary purpose of the bank was to invest in innovative green projects where there was a lack of support from private markets. But there would also be other benefits. The kinds of projects the bank would support, such as refurbishing housing to reduce the energy bills of residents, could be up and running quickly, and would need the skilled workers who had lost jobs with the downturn in construction. But Osborne would not accept that this would mean less money spent on unemployment benefit and more money coming in to the Treasury through taxes from the extra employment. However much the facts stacked up on one side, Osborne and his officials were sharpening their knives.

Like all practised assassins, they did not move openly. The line they took was that of course they wanted the Green Investment Bank to have the power to borrow – no one was more enthusiastic to allow them to do this than HM Treasury and the Chancellor of the Exchequer – but there was of course a question of *timing*. Would it not be more *prudent* to allow the bank to build up a track record first? Then, in the fullness of time, the bank could be allowed to go to the markets for additional funds. In, say ... five years?

Then the opponents of the bank dreamt up another line: that it would be better if the bank waited to raise funds until the public finances were back in order. They proposed that the borrowing powers should only come into effect once the level of government debt had begun to fall – whenever that might prove to be. The irony here was that it was the very same deflationary policies that Osborne and the Treasury were pursuing, so pushing Britain further into recession, that were reducing the taxes coming in and so making the debt burden higher.

So the bill that came before Parliament had in it all the powers to allow the bank to borrow additional funds for its work; but it also had a clause that meant that these powers would not become law until the government chose to enact them. Was that a defeat? A victory? Or the most frustrating of all: acceptance of the principle, but a failure to act upon it?

This is the central weakness of the government's energy strategy: their acceptance that energy efficiency and renewables are the future; but then a determination to ignore them in favour of supporting big and eye-wateringly expensive solutions such as nuclear power and further exploration for oil and gas. And the clearest demonstration of this is what it means for us in our homes.

This matters not just for the country as a whole but for all of us as individuals. Where we live underpins everything else in our lives. But too much housing is poor quality and expensive because there is not enough of it and because too much of what there is has not been invested in properly. Add to this the cost of trying to heat your home when it lacks proper insulation and may suffer from damp and other problems, and the opportunity to improve people's lives through reform of housing and energy are clear. But while the Energy Bill gave opportunities for progress – some taken, some not – housing has been neglected in this Parliament.

Housing policy is in a mess. It is perhaps being too charitable to call it a 'policy', unless you think that term covers the approach of doing what the house-builders ask and encouraging house-price inflation as an election bribe. We do have a 'housing crisis' in Britain, but it is not the one the government sees, and it certainly will not be helped by the remedies the government peddles. The crisis arises partly because housing is too expensive. For millions of people, whether buying or renting, it takes up far too great a proportion of their income. An average family, on average earnings, cannot reasonably afford to own their own house in most parts of the country, and certainly not in Brighton, where average house prices have reached £350,000. For people starting out in life, it makes the chance of finding a home where they can settle down slim, because in most of the country property to buy is so expensive and very few landlords will offer long-term security of tenure. At the other end of the scale, those who have retired find that they often have so much of their savings tied up in their homes that they are forced to sell or enter into questionable transactions to release equity from their properties to supplement their pension. Many of those encouraged to buy their council homes in the 1980s and 1990s are now being presented with vast bills for repairs and maintenance that they can ill afford.

From the lack of affordable homes to the ease with which some landlords exploit their tenants, the failings of housing policy are self-evident. It is also one of the issues raised most often with me in constituency surgeries, such as cases of people being housed in entirely unsuitable 'emergency' accommodation for years on end. Imagine a single parent trying to bring up twins in a single-room, second-floor flat where the lift does not work, so that a simple task like taking your children to the park or to the shops becomes a nightmare; but where the alternative is to be driven to distraction in what should be a home, but feels like a prison. We should as a country do better than this.

The solutions are equally clear. For example, rogue landlords who abuse their power and provide substandard or unsafe accommodation could be identified and taken out of the system through a national licensing scheme. Letting agencies should be banned from exploiting those seeking accommodation by imposing registration and other fees while they are already taking a cut from the landlord. Deposits should be properly protected for rentals, just as they are when buying a house. The notice period and length of a tenancy could be linked so that the longer you have lived there, the greater your protection from eviction. We should have 'smart' rent controls that protect tenants but also give responsible landlords a fair deal, including incentives to invest in proper maintenance, while so-called 'revenge' evictions should be prohibited. These are very real issues in Brighton, where we have high rents, a disproportionately large private rented sector, our share of rogue landlords, and around 18,000 people on the council's housing waiting list. Solving these is not simply a matter of resources – and can't be blamed solely on austerity – but about political will and ideology.

Beyond this, we also need more homes for people to rent or buy, and therefore a major new affordable house-building programme including lifting the cap on borrowing so that councils can fund the building of new homes, and ensuring that if council housing is ever sold to a sitting tenant, then 100% of the proceeds goes straight back into the building of new social housing.

The market too often delivers unsustainable developments, using up irreplaceable green space or creating unsuitable flats that attract international investors who want to take a punt on Britain's housing casino. Instead, housing associations, local authorities and, increasingly, housing cooperatives should take the lead, with a firm and locally accountable planning system. This would require more money: but investment in social housing would be far better use of the billions put into 'quantitative easing'. It would create or support more jobs. Allied with investment in the existing public housing stock, it would improve the quality of life for millions of people. Communities would be strengthened too. And it would also be far more fair, benefiting those who need it most, not making the very rich even richer.

After consulting local residents and housing organizations, I brought these proposals together in a Housing Charter for Brighton; but I'm convinced that the same approach would make a huge difference in communities across the country. Lack of affordable housing and fuel poverty go hand-in-hand: particularly where a lack of investment in housing makes homes even harder, and more expensive, to heat. This wasted energy is also one of the key issues for our national energy policy: one where I have had to work hard to provide an alternative voice to that of Big Energy.

It's simple logic that the place to start if you want to save energy because of its cost or its environmental impact is to use energy more efficiently. Since the first dramatic rises in energy costs in the 1970s, everything from cars to washing machines have become more energy-efficient. The same is true of newly built houses: or rather, they have the potential to use less energy (and so, like cars and washing machines, become much cheaper to run). In Germany, energy-efficiency standards for new homes mean that they need almost no heating at all: the warmth comes from normal domestic activities such as cooking, with top-up heating in the winter that is hardly more expensive than keeping a single light bulb burning.

But in Britain, we have not adopted these standards. It makes modern homes more expensive to heat than necessary. But worse than that, we have not invested enough in making older houses easier to keep warm. Basics like proper insulation, modern lighting and more efficient boilers can cut bills dramatically. Adding in simple micro-generation measures such as solar panels on communal roofs, public buildings and individual houses (as the Brighton Energy Co-operative are doing so successfully) means that communities and individuals can have some or all their energy for free, or even sell it back to the National Grid. But none of this suits Big Energy. They have no interest in selling us less energy. They like having an energy 'market' in which they can make good, predictable profits on generating electricity in large power stations and then even more money for meeting 'peak' demand.

City financiers don't like energy efficiency or micro-generation either. They can make a single investment in Drax or Kingsnorth or Hinkley: big, visible, national infrastructure; and a good prospect of taking their money out again easily if they want. With the powerful energy and finance lobbies lined up in support of macro-generation – and the supporters of the alternatives both smaller and more fragmented – policy is skewed in their favour.

It also means that the debate over energy is based on false assumptions. Nuclear is sometimes touted as a 'low-carbon' energy source, offering an alternative to the coal and gas power stations that are contributing to climate change. In my view, this was and is misleading: a clumsy attempt to distract attention away from the fact that nuclear is anything but clean, and will do nothing to help with the immediate danger of carbon emissions. We need to act now on climate change. The first priority is to reduce energy consumption through demand-reduction measures and energy efficiency: everything from lagging boilers to ensuring electronic devices switch off automatically when not in use. And we need to promote micro-generation, so that energy is generated from renewable sources close to where it is needed. (At the moment we lose something like 20 per cent of the power generated in major power stations in the electricity lines carrying it across country to the cities where it is used.) There are also huge possibilities in larger-scale renewables, such as tidal generation and offshore wind farms. Together, these provide a faster and safer route to a low-carbon economy than building nuclear power stations. Hinkley C would be the most expensive power station ever built; will generate electricity at twice the current price; and have massive, open-ended liabilities that only the government can cover. It will also take so long to build (even if we assume it does not suffer the years of delays that have affected other nuclear power stations) that it will arrive too late to deliver the carbon reductions we need.

Fortunately, the alternatives can work. There are individuals and community groups around the country who are already generating viable amounts of energy for their own needs and to put back into the national system. It's not yet on the scale of other European countries, particularly Germany, where there are over 600 community generation schemes, compared to 50 in Britain. And that's frustrating, given that the Coalition Agreement pledged to '. . . encourage community-owned renewable energy schemes where local people benefit from the energy produced'. Part of the reason for our poor performance is that we lack the kind of support provided by the KfW bank (the German prototype of what our own Green Investment Bank could have been, had the coalition not lost its nerve). Alan Simpson, the former Labour MP for Nottingham South, has worked with Friends of the Earth to map out how community energy generation could provide 20 per cent of our energy needs by 2020 if the right framework were in place. This would be a far better contribution to energy security than Hinkley C, which will be little more than a very large and expensive hole in the ground in 2020, if it goes ahead at all.

One particularly symbolic example of community generation is at Balcombe, where the village is threatened by fracking. Alongside the protests and activism, a group of local people decided to see if they could generate enough clean energy to power the whole village. 'REPOWERBalcombe' was the outcome: a community social enterprise that aims to generate 100 per cent of Balcombe's energy through the collective funding of local renewable energy sources – starting with solar panels on the roof of a local barn. It undermines the claim that protesters are Nimbys: the people joining REPOWERBalcombe don't want fracking in theirs or anyone else's backyard, and are taking practical steps to show this.

Energy was a frustrating issue in my first term in Parliament. We had the chance to create decent jobs, save energy, help those in fuel poverty and contribute to the fight against climate change. And these chances were largely squandered because of the government's failure to challenge the entrenched power of the big energy companies. But the tide is moving our way. We see that being dependent on imports and coal and gas makes us insecure; and the prospect of being dependent on imports of uranium is not enticing. And so, making it ourselves – whether around our coasts or on our own roofs – looks more and more attractive.

10

A Tale of Two Policies:
How Old-Style Politics Blocks Progress

'Drug policy has been failing for decades. We need fresh thinking and a new approach.'

David Cameron, 2002

'We have a drug policy that is working in Britain.'

David Cameron, 2012

I owe Hannah a lot, and this was the day I hoped to pay some of it back. Hannah is Cath's daughter, and I hate to think of the number of times I've phoned their home during the evenings or at weekends, making or changing arrangements, asking for information or advice. Anyone drawn into the extended family of an MP finds life is disrupted from time to time, and you have to hope, if you are that MP, that they have a high tolerance level and a shared belief. And when there are chances to thank them in a more tangible way, then you take them. So today, I was hoping I could bring Hannah face-to-face with Russell Brand.

We were in Parliament Square, where the Austerity March organized by the People's Assembly was to end in a rally. I was to speak, as was Russell, though there was some anxiety, as we were waiting in the backstage area, that he might not show up. Certainly he was late, but it turned out that was because Russell Brand, bad-boy superstar, had come on his bike, somehow wobbling his way across London and presumably being asked for his autograph at every junction. As usual, he spoke with characteristic honesty and directness. I was particularly struck by the point he made that when he was poor and talked about inequality, he was accused of bitterness and envy; and that now he has some money, and talks about inequality, he's accused of hypocrisy. As he said, it shows inequality 'just ain't wanted on the agenda'.

And when he spoke of how power doesn't lie with those in Parliament – gesturing to the Palace as he did so – but with the audience who had come on the rally, it was clear he'd caught the public mood. The politicians had shown solidarity and common feeling with their friends in the City during the recession, but would deny the same solidarity to the rest of us. We the people had to take back power: that would be real democracy. It chimed with my sense of being in Parliament to try to find a way of opening it up: unlocking the gates from within and letting the people in.

Fortunately, and to Hannah's delight, I was able to engineer the introduction because I'd met him on a couple of occasions before. We'd been working together on another issue, about which he was a self-confessed expert: drugs policy. And he had the ability to engage with a vast swathe of people left cold by the 'business as usual' of politics.

Historically, Brighton and Hove has had more drug-related deaths for its size of population than anywhere else in the country. In 2009, fifty people died from drug-related causes in the city. It led to it being dubbed 'Britain's drug death capital'. When I was elected, I was determined to do all I could to understand the causes and find ways to turn the situation around.

This was also an issue where I would not be constrained by the official line pursued by the three main parties, which has let Brighton and the whole country down so badly. Drugs policy is an area where, for decades, ignorance and a synthetic morality have taken the place of evidence and compassion. The result is an approach – the 'war on drugs' – that has proved costly, unjust and counter-productive, and has lost public support. Two-thirds of people want a rethink on drugs policy, and even a majority of *Sun* readers agree that the 'war on drugs' is not working. But a fear of being portrayed as 'soft on crime' meant that neither Cameron nor Miliband would admit that we need to change course. Only in the last months of the coalition did the Liberal Democrat Norman Baker succeed in putting drugs reform on the agenda of an unwilling Home Office – though he resigned as a Home Office minister shortly afterwards.

It also showed that the idea that politicians are driven by polling and focus groups is not the whole story. There is much more calculation involved. Labour believe that if they argue for any relaxation in the drugs laws, they will be branded as 'soft'. The Conservatives know this, so they don't want to call for reform, because their 'tough' stance gives them a weapon to hold over Labour. And while many Liberal Democrats want reform, their leadership did not make this a priority in the coalition.

The cost of this is huge. In monetary terms alone, the 'war on drugs' costs us something like £16 billion a year. This comes in police and court time, in enforcement and imprisonment, and in treatment. The Home Office estimates that there is around £4 billion of fraud a year committed by people with drug addictions, and about the same amount of burglary; and hard drugs are linked to between one-third and one-half of all 'crimes of acquisition'. As well as an economic cost – one we all pay in higher prices and insurance premiums – there is also a huge social and personal price to be paid: anyone who has had their home broken into knows that the impact is far more than just financial.

But even this underestimates the damage that the misuse of drugs, combined with current drugs policy, does to our society. Those who become addicts have their own lives damaged or destroyed; but they are also sons and daughters, friends and neighbours, parents and work colleagues, and their suffering is shared by their loved ones. There are few families in Britain – certainly few families in Brighton – who have not had some connection at some point with addiction; and it is this human dimension that makes the support for reform so widespread. Once a social issue such as addiction has a human face, then our natural instincts of sympathy come into play: we can no longer think only in clichés. Even an 'evil pusher' may be an addict who has begun to deal because they will do anything to get the money to pay for their next fix. And we may also feel humility, and recognize that if things had been a little different in our own lives, then that might have been us.

There is broad agreement among experts, drug users, their families and friends and even the law-enforcement agencies that criminalizing drug use does little to discourage it: but it certainly creates an opportunity for criminals to make enormous profits. This in turn gives those criminals an incentive to foster demand: if the personal use of drugs were decriminalized, then addiction could be treated as a health issue. Further, over time and subject to proper scrutiny, regulation of the drug market could replace the current free-for-all, driving the criminals and drug cartels out of business. This route offers more hope than trying to cut off supply at source. When troops were sent to Afghanistan in 2001, one key objective was the eradication of illegal opium poppy cultivation. But thirteen years later, the crop was at an all-time high, directly profiting the Taliban among others; and the same pattern of paramilitary intervention has failed repeatedly elsewhere in Asia and Latin America.

Of course, this is a complex subject. There are different kinds of drugs, different routes in and out of addiction. But a starting-point would be for the government to admit that the current policy is not working; causes untold human misery, leaving aside the economic and social cost; and that they must base their policy not on prejudice but evidence. For example, Portugal decriminalized the possession of drugs for personal use and introduced an approach that treated addiction as a health issue, not one deserving of punishment. The number of people taking heroin has since halved, and drug-related deaths have decreased significantly.

When I was elected, Brighton already had many committed professionals who were working as best they could within the current state of the law, and to some extent pushing those boundaries. For example, Graham Bartlett, one of the most enlightened police chiefs in the country, set up 'Operation Reduction' which targeted dealers but helped addicts towards treatment – so radically reducing crime. Brighton was also one of three centres for the Randomised Injectable Opiate Treatment Trial, run by Professor John Strang and his colleagues at King's College, London, which has produced such encouraging results. To have launched a high-profile campaign might have created a backlash and put all that good work at risk. So I began working behind the scenes to bring the health, policing and social care professionals together to see what practical steps we could take that would help this situation. I also went to Portugal to see first-hand (in what has so far been my only overseas trip as an MP, and one I paid for myself) how drugs policy can evolve successfully. And in 2011, I invited 'Safe in the City' to set up an Independent Drugs Commission to investigate what more could be done in Brighton.

'Safe in the City' is the community safety partnership led by Sussex Police and the City Council with partners from the public sector and community and voluntary groups. Its credibility and network of contacts and community forums made it an ideal lead organization, and to their credit they took the task extremely seriously. The Commission consisted of ten people with different perspectives – from the heads of student services at Sussex and Brighton universities to the mother of a recovering addict, and from a popular local crime writer to Tony Blair's former drugs czar – and had experts from the police, council, health and care services and drugs agencies. It also reached out to residents and users, including an event for young people at the prestigious Amex football stadium.

Their conclusions were wide-ranging, informed by the best possible evidence, and full of practical recommendations, such as the need to take account of changing patterns of drug use and reviewing how services for drug addiction and mental health could be brought closer together. Many of these have since been put into effect with some encouraging results. Half the people now leaving treatment are drug-free, compared to a third when the Commission began its work; wider success rates in treating addiction are at 17 per cent compared to the national average of 7 per cent; and drug-related deaths have come down as well. Not all of this is down to the Commission alone, of course, and some of the trends were moving in the right direction already – particularly after Naloxone (a powerful antidote in cases of heroin overdoses) was made more widely available from 2009 onwards. But it is still an achievement, particularly against the background of cuts to local funding and the massive upheaval of the NHS reforms, and a tribute to those involved.

Some of the options that the Commission considered, such as consumption rooms where users could self-administer drugs in a clean and safe environment, off the streets, and with medical help on call, could not be pursued within the current legal framework: changes in national legislation would be needed. This is one reason why I launched a campaign for a review of national drugs laws. (This is still largely based on an Act of Parliament dating from 1971, and since that date no government had carried out a proper assessment of its effectiveness or its value for money.) As part of the campaign, I set up a petition on the No. 10 website to help show that this was an important issue of widespread concern. Soon we had 40,000 people signed up, opening up the prospect of forcing the government to allow a proper debate: there is an understanding that petitions that reach 100,000, and have a sponsoring MP, are likely to be granted parliamentary time.

One of the really satisfying aspects of the campaign was that it involved people who would usually have little or nothing to do with politics. I had been careful not to make it a party political issue, and had support from all sides, including the Lib Dem Julian Huppert and the Tory Zac Goldsmith. This meant people like Richard Branson felt comfortable backing us. With Russell Brand on board, and clearly not 'politics as usual', a lot of those disengaged from the mainstream of political life became supporters and within a few days we had passed the 100,000 target. This in turn gave ammunition to Norman Baker to push forward reform from within; and it meant that my debate, when it finally happened, had MPs from all parties supporting the call for a review of current drugs policy, with the government deciding not to block it. Though we have a long way to go, things are at last moving. It is also heartening that public concern can make a difference; if the evidence is there, a mix of people take up the cause, and there are allies on the inside of government and Parliament.

And this is just the kind of issue that politics should be about. It's serious – lives are at stake – but it isn't easy and there are conflicting interests and points of view to reconcile. Above all, there is inertia: the fact that something is a problem does not mean that everyone wants to try to solve it; and the longer it has been going on, the greater the excuse to push it to one side.

This was certainly the case with another long-overdue reform: the taxation of property. It might seem like a dry, technical matter, a world away from the urgency and human impact of drugs policy. But though it is not exactly a life and death issue, property taxation affects people's lives directly through Council Tax, and indirectly through business rates, which are passed on to consumers in the prices charged for goods and services. Property taxes are used to fund local councils, but over the years this relationship has been eroded and the lack of a proper base for its revenue is one of the ways in which local government has been undermined in recent decades. And the Council Tax, being based on crude and increasingly outdated assessments of the value of properties, creates more and more unfairness.

The one clear set of winners under the current system are landowners. Current taxes fall on the users of the land – the people who live in the houses, or the tenants who occupy the shops, offices and factories – not the owners. And any improvements in the local infrastructure – anything from a new school to an extension to public transport – will increase the value of the land, without the owner making any direct contribution. Winston Churchill put it more poetically:

> Roads are made, streets are made, services are improved, electric light turns night into day, water is brought from reservoirs a hundred miles off in the mountains – all the while the landlord sits still. Every one of those improvements is effected by the labour and cost of other people and the taxpayers. To not one of those improvements does the land monopolist, as a land monopolist, contribute, and yet by every one of them the value of his land is enhanced.

It also has a damaging effect on the way land is used. Under the current system, if you leave land unused, you pay less tax: this is one reason why there is so much derelict land in our towns and cities. It often makes financial sense to sit on unused land, expecting that it will rise in value over time. This in turn drives urban sprawl and puts pressure on the countryside from new development. And it also undermines efforts to build more homes to tackle the housing crisis.

But there is an elegantly fair and simple way of reforming property tax so that the burden falls most on those who can most afford it. It also helps ensure that society gets something back from the windfall profits made by large landowners from property deals. When a local authority grants planning permission for a greenfield site, its value can rise a hundred times over – hence the old saying that the best crop a farmer can grow is a crop of houses – and a land value tax, as well as replacing the unfair Council Tax and business rates, would tax that profit in a manner similar way to the way capital gains tax does.

It works in this way. Instead of taxing the 'improved' value of land, you tax its unimproved value based on its optimum permitted use: that is, not the buildings on top but the value of the actual land beneath. This may seem like a small difference, but the effect is to tie the tax to the owner of the land, not the user. There is then much less incentive to hang on to land as a speculation, and much more reason to let someone do something worthwhile with it, whether that is housing or even a new urban park. The tax is linked to ability to pay, and there is no question of evasion: you can hide cash and similar assets in a Swiss bank account, but not land.

Why, you might ask, do we not hear more about this 'wonder tax' that is cheap and easy to collect and also progressive, in that the richer you are, the more you pay? Well, economists have written about its benefits from Adam Smith onwards, and these have included supporters as varied as Milton Friedman, Henry Marshall, Paul Krugman and Joseph Stiglitz. The old Liberal Party supported a land value tax as far back as before the First World War. The Labour government even managed to introduce it twice: in 1931 and (in a rather different form) in 1947. In both cases it was repealed by incoming Conservative governments.

And this is, of course, the problem. A tax that falls mainly on rich landowners and is almost impossible to evade is not going to be popular with those who fund and support the Conservative Party. And so land value tax joins drugs policy as one of those issues that most politicians consider simply too difficult to take on. Worse, so do their civil servants. And if they think that reform is too difficult, or too controversial, then the chances of an incoming minister pushing them into action are not great: and it is very difficult for MPs to challenge this.

Generally, MPs have very little to do with civil servants. Ministers like to keep it that way, because it helps keep backbenchers in the dark and avoids opening any channels for discussion or briefing that they don't directly control. Their excuse is that it is a constitutional principle that ministers answer to Parliament, not officials, and therefore MPs should deal only with them. Once upon a time, this might have been a reasonable line to take: but ministers are now perfectly willing to blame their officials when things go wrong. So if MPs are to be effective in scrutinizing government, that must now include civil servants.

Select committees are becoming more forceful about calling officials to give evidence, and ministers are less defensive about this, but these are ritualistic, set-piece events. What is still lacking is the right for MPs to meet officials less formally to be briefed on the technical aspects of an issue, which might be anything from occupational pensions to flood prevention. Without that, MPs risk relying on the media, or pressure groups, or (particularly on education) a hazy memory of how things were in their own day. This is one reason why smart MPs make so much use of the House of Commons Library. It produces factual and authoritative briefings on topics that MPs are interested in, and can help MPs to make their own minds up – if they want to.

Civil servants also need to listen more to MPs, in just the same way that they have two-way discussions with businesses, charities, think tanks and pressure groups. The more they are cut off from Parliament, the more the relationship develops into one of conflict, with MPs becoming more confrontational and civil servants more intent on hiding what they are up to. It feeds the 'not invented-here' syndrome, whereby proposals to reform drugs policy or property taxation or anything else are resisted simply because they have come from, or been supported by, MPs.

To make progress on the land value tax, it was essential to make it a live political issue once more. There were groups within the Labour and Liberal Democrat parties pushing the issue, and the Institute of Fiscal Studies had published an important report on it. The next step was to return the issue to the floor of the House, and so I tabled a draft bill – not to introduce LVT, but to require the government to consider the benefits and practicalities of its introduction. This more modest aim reflected the curious situation of one of the key ministers responsible for property taxation, Vince Cable. He was himself a fan of LVT, as his speech to the Liberal Democrat Party Conference in 2010 shows: 'It will be said that in a world of internationally mobile capital and people it is counterproductive to tax personal income and corporate profit to uncompetitive levels. That is right. But a progressive alternative is to shift the tax base to property, and land, which cannot run away, [and] represents in Britain an extreme concentration of wealth.'

As an economist, Vince no doubt appreciated the simplicity of LVT and the way it avoided perverse incentives. And as a politician who perhaps still aspired to become Chancellor of the Exchequer one day – and who surely believed he could do a better job than George Osborne – he could see that taxing rich landowners instead of ordinary householders made political sense. So I arranged to meet him to discuss how we could take this forward.

Unfortunately, as a minister he also had to follow the government line, and the coalition was not in favour of LVT. Surrounded by officials, including one from the Treasury, he switched uneasily between enthusiasm and caution, and made no commitment. In the end, his only frank comment was that 'the politics of it were horrific'. I took this to mean that, as ever in politics, you had to calculate that the losers from any initiative always shouted much louder than the winners, and if the losers were also some of the richest and most powerful people in Britain, the kind of people who lunch with Cabinet ministers and then dine with newspaper owners, then LVT was going to run into some turbulence.

LVT has been nudged up the agenda. We have shown that the Conservative reluctance to pursue it is not rational, but based on the influence of their rich backers. We have reminded people that LVT has worked in other countries, and was once the policy of the two largest progressive parties in Britain. We have also made the link to globalization and the difficulty of taxing the rich – whether companies or individuals – in a world in which technology has raced ahead of regulation, and governments (particularly that of Cameron and Osborne) cannot bring themselves to cooperate on a fair and equitable system for international taxation. But what the campaign still lacks is public resonance: a focus, or an individual, who can convince the majority of people that this really matters.

The difference this can make was clear from my work on drugs reform. When Russell Brand came into Parliament to discuss the campaign, it turned into something of a royal progress, causing disruption and delight in equal measure. Because he was willing to sign the petition, a lot of others did too who might otherwise have thought that anything coming out of Parliament would be a waste of time (though they might have used more colourful language).

Of course, he is nothing if not controversial. When he called on people not to vote, then unsurprisingly I didn't agree with him. The risk of not voting is that it looks too much like apathy. Changing the voting system, for example, so that every vote counts, would encourage more people to take part in elections. But in the absence of this and other political reforms, I believe that it is better to go to the polling station and spoil your ballot paper than not vote at all: at least then you have shown that you still believe in democracy, even if you cannot bring yourself to vote for any of the candidates who are standing in your constituency. But whatever our differences, he was brilliant at making the case for reform. That evening, he was interviewed by Jon Snow on *Channel 4 News*: 'It's a disease that requires therapy and compassion, not to be pushed underground. I'm not talking about a free-for-all – some crazy, whacked-out world where everyone's on drugs. I'm saying drugs should be of pharmaceutical quality, they should be controlled and prescribed, and not part of a huge criminal economy.'

I might not have used exactly those words, but he was right. And whatever else he has said or done, he has succeeded in getting a lot of people thinking and talking about politics. We need that. Our belief that Parliament can be reformed, and politicians respect the views of the public, have taken many knocks in recent years, from the failure to clean up after the expenses scandal to the decision to go to war in Iraq despite over a million people taking to the streets to protest. Yet the public is still making its voice heard: perhaps above all in foreign affairs.

11

Foreign Adventures:
How Arrogance and Deceit Have Brought Death in Their Wake

'Shall we have womanly times, Or shall we die?'
Ian McEwan, 'Or Shall We Die? An Oratorio'

Modern media can make watching the news a deeply painful experience: the broadcasters can, if they choose, give us a ringside seat for repression, conflict and tyranny. Our reaction ought to be 'Is there something we can do?' Anything else would be callous. But in answering that question, we also have to ask 'If we do something, will it make things better?' Not, crucially, make us feel better: but truly improve the situation of those who are suffering.

This is an essential but often unanswered issue in Britain's foreign policy. In Bosnia, Sierra Leone, Kosovo, Afghanistan, Iraq and Libya, the British government of the day decided that military action was better than doing nothing. At other times and in other places – most troublingly, in Rwanda – they did not. The justifications for war have varied: supporting democracy, avoiding a humanitarian crisis, preventing genocide, or the 'war on terror'. Sometimes the justifications changed as the war unfolded. But there was always the suspicion that the real reasons lay elsewhere: being seen to be decisive; supporting the United States come what may; ensuring British businesses would be first in the queue for oil concessions or other deals; international machismo; or playing domestic political games.

After the painful experiences of Afghanistan and Iraq, it seemed that Britain had lost its taste for military intervention. The public were increasingly unconvinced about the reasons for the wars, and began to question whether British involvement was doing anyone any good. And no politician was eager to follow Tony Blair and have their reputation ruined by foreign adventures. Equally, the temptation to bestride the world stage and wield the power of one of the largest military machines seemed to remain terribly tempting. In Libya, David Cameron had initially held back from military action. After the French and Italian governments had taken a more forceful position, he followed them in providing air support to the rebels seeking to overthrow President Gaddafi. But even that modest commitment did not include any clear idea of what would happen if and when Gaddafi was removed.

Then in the summer of 2013 came the appalling chemical attacks on civilians in Syria. Within a few hours, the lines of the debate had been drawn up. Cameron and Miliband might have been sharing the same briefing notes: 'we cannot stand idly by . . .', 'Assad must be brought to justice . . .', and so on: the familiar war-making consensus.

Yet, along with a handful of other MPs, I remained hugely doubtful as to the wisdom of Western intervention. Our history of involvement in Syria, as in the whole Middle East, was too tainted. Bombing is rarely as precise as the military would like to claim. Innocent people were likely to die, creating a legacy of bitterness. Modern warfare uses language that suggests clean and easy solutions: *targeted intervention, surgical strikes*. Patient diplomacy, finding compromises that reduce tension or isolate hardliners, can seem weak in comparison. Measures that fall short of warfare, such as economic sanctions, can cause widespread suffering while leaving a tyrant such as Assad unharmed. And the most honest answer – 'I wouldn't have started from here'

– can sound evasive. But the truth is that most of the problems with intervention by the West are ones of our own making. They are rooted in a mix of economic exploitation, colonialism, arms sales, corruption, self-interested support for repressive regimes, double standards, militarism and previous conflicts, stretching back over many years.

I also knew from experience that much of the media take the view that if you are 'anti-war' then you must have no idea about warfare or its consequences. Much of the discussion intended to 'inform' the public was about the minutiae of warfare – military tactics, and exactly what aircraft or missiles would be used – and was conducted by retired military commanders and by analysts from the many defence think tanks. In fact, there were people – especially retired diplomats – who shared our views. But despite this, what was missing was a proper debate about the impact on Syrian society and Middle East opinion, putting aid workers and development experts alongside diplomats and generals. Then the public could begin to see that the real issue was not how the war would be fought, but what the consequences would be.

This bias towards an exclusively 'military' analysis of international crises has been a source of frustration since I was at university and joined CND. At the time, right-wing governments in the United States and in the UK were deliberately raising tensions with the Soviet Union by siting new nuclear weapons in Europe. This seemed a huge risk: not because I or any of my fellow students had a rosy view of the Soviets, who were invading Afghanistan and intimidating the Solidarity movement in Poland. In a way, it was precisely because the Soviets were paranoid and militaristic that raising the stakes with additional missiles seemed so foolish. As a totalitarian regime, closed to outside influences and convinced that it was threatened from within and without, we saw that the Soviet leadership might use the threat of war to silence internal dissent. In 1982, we had the example of another dictatorship in Argentina doing exactly this and occupying the Falkland Islands. So the case for opposing any escalation in nuclear weapons was partly moral, partly a matter of realpolitik. Although right-wingers were always ready to label CND as naive idealists, I still believe that we were every bit as realistic as the Cold War warriors such as Ronald Reagan and Margaret Thatcher. If anything, it was they who were driven into dangerous acts by ideology.

It was a further irony that those who claimed to believe in freedom so strongly that they were willing to risk the destruction of life on earth to defend it, were also happy to throw aside the principles of transparency, accountability, freedom of speech and freedom of assembly to crush any internal dissent. The peace camps at the bases chosen to house the new generation of missiles, Greenham Common in Berkshire and Molesworth in Cambridgeshire, became points of conflict not because those who came to protest were a physical threat to the country's defences, but because we formed a moral challenge to the government's aggressive stance. The conflict took place not only around the perimeter fences but in the media, with the right-wing press competing to vilify the protesters. This was not really 'free speech', in the sense of a free and equal exchange of ideas, for CND and individual protesters had no platform that could remotely compete with the power of newspapers such as the *Sun* and the *Daily Mail*. Nor was it democratic debate in the sense of an interplay of different or competing policies or values. Instead, the papers concentrated on personal, sometimes rabid, attacks on the peace campaigners themselves. We were closet communists, or anarchists, or dole-claiming, work-shy layabouts. By comparison, the description used by Michael Heseltine, then the Defence Secretary, that CND supporters were 'woolly minds in woolly hats' felt like old-world courtesy. But the aspect of the Greenham Common camp that made editors and commentators splutter the most was that it was a camp of women.

Whatever the recent advances in the position of women in society, there remained no question that war was for men. This was true of the military, where women could not serve on equal terms with men and could not rise to the highest ranks. More troublingly, it was also true of the politicians, think tanks, defence correspondents and newspaper editors: in fact, all those who felt they 'owned' the debate on defence. They seemed to believe that the role of women was to stay by the hearth, content to be defended, and not have any views about what form that defence should take or how the risk of war could be averted. So the idea of women leaving their homes and setting up camps outside military bases was a challenge that struck at least some of these men at a deep, psychological level; which helps to explain the outburst of hostility disproportionate to any threat we in fact posed.

It wasn't only women protesting; it was women protesting *as* women: tying flowers and ribbons into the sinister silver-grey wire of the fences; singing and laughing; making the effort to talk with the police as fellow human beings; the sense of two different value sets coming into conflict in a vivid way. When we formed a human chain to surround the base, someone would squeeze the hand they were holding, and that would go all the way around the perimeter, perhaps a mile or more, and return like a Mexican wave. More than anything, I remember the colourfulness of the protesters, in their clothes and songs, and the grey and bleak drabness of the base: a metaphor for the forces of life and death.

Looking back on these days, it's striking how many of the same issues and prejudices survive. We still have not had a female Secretary of State for Defence, the senior ranks of the military are all still men, and while there have been female heads of both the Security Service and the Secret Intelligence Service, the 'commentariat' for defence and security is resolutely male. More widely, women who challenge the establishment are still at risk of being attacked not for the views they hold, but for holding views in the first place; the subtext being that, by entering a 'male' world, they are in some way betraying themselves or their family. The media are still ready to seek to shape public opinion, rather than educate it, and debate on issues such as nuclear disarmament – when it occurs at all – is portrayed as a question of international status rather than either the ethics of nuclear weapons, or their value as practical tools for keeping international peace. And the mainstream political parties still marginalize pacifism, treating it as freakish or naive, rather than an ideal that we should work towards, even if we may never reach it.

The threat of a full-scale nuclear exchange may be less than it was in the 1980s. Certainly successive governments have wanted to close down any debates on whether we need nuclear weapons, even to the farcical extent of trying to exclude nuclear weapons from the 2010 defence review (the subject of my very first clash with ministers after being elected). But the disappearance of nuclear anxiety from the cultural and political mainstream disguises the perpetual danger posed by these weapons, still sitting dormant but deadly in bunkers and under the ocean. Like a tide that has receded to the horizon, the threat of its return remains. With more nations seeking to obtain or develop nuclear weapons, openly or behind the cover of civil nuclear and space programmes, there is considerable peril in ignoring the problem, or thinking that disarmament or restraint is only for others. The current debate about replacing the Trident missile system is based on the assumption that possessing nuclear missiles makes us safer. The more cogent argument is that our security is better guaranteed by addressing the causes of war: the scramble for natural resources, increasing poverty and inequality, international rivalries, the arms trade, the suppression of democracy and freedom of speech, and so on. The money spent on Trident could do far more good in supporting ways to reduce tensions between nations and combating nuclear proliferation. A commitment not to replace Trident could be a valuable card in persuading others – perhaps even Iran – to back away from developing nuclear weapons of their own without loss of face. And our own credibility on the rule of international law is weakened when we are committed to possessing the ultimate weapons of mass destruction.

The legality of our actions as a nation is not something that should only be of interest to lawyers. The more that Britain acts as a self-appointed world policeman, 'intervening' because we think we are doing the right thing, the more that the international rule of law is undermined and the more we will live in a kind of 'Wild West' world, in which justice is dispensed from the barrel of a gun and we as a nation and as individual citizens are ourselves at risk. And unlike the sheriff in a Hollywood western, we do not mosey into every town to clean it up; only those where it is in our strategic or commercial interests. All too often, we turn out backs and let the bandits run the town.

So it was in Syria. For years, we had backed the regime of Assad. Now, following on from the so-called Arab Spring, the West had decided it was time for him to go. We had encouraged separatists and fermented a civil war; and now Assad or his supporters appeared to have responded in the most callous and inhuman way, by using chemical weapons against the Syrian people. Barack Obama had declared that chemical weapons was a 'red line' for Syria, and their use would provoke a overwhelming response from the United States. David Cameron had pledged his full support to Obama, in effect coummitting British forces to contribute to whatever punishment the United States might choose to deploy in Syria. The US stance was that they would act whatever the United Nations might do or say. If there was a UN Resolution authorizing military action, that was fine; but even if there were not, this would not prevent air strikes or other action.

This was one way in which Syria threatened to become a rerun of the Iraq War of 2003. And it was a contrast with the first Iraq War, back in 1991, where Iraq had occupied Kuwait. Then, whatever your view on the wisdom of this action, the UN had at least provided a legal base for the invasion of Kuwait by a coalition that, although led by the United States, included many other countries, including Arab states such as Saudi Arabia. The 2003 Iraq War had no such authorization – it was illegal, as the advice from lawyers in the Foreign and Commonwealth Office, suppressed at the time, clearly demonstrates. Legality in international affairs matters because, in the years since the Nazi war crimes trials at Nuremberg, the international community has slowly built up a set of principles that govern how states should treat each other; and the scope for action when they do not. This is incomplete, and in many ways unsatisfactory, but it is far better than the dog-eat-dog world that preceded it. There are still bloodstained dictators and war criminals, but some are brought to justice. Countries still go to war, but the response of the international community can sometimes put this right. The UN can be a frustrating forum, and certainly one in need of reform, but we should judge it not by its failures but by the way it sometimes succeeds, against all the odds; and the best way to increase its authority and effectiveness is to use its processes not only when it suits us, but all the time.

Once it was clear that Parliament would be recalled to debate a motion about military intervention, it became apparent that the draft Labour amendment on Syria fell short. Critically, it said that intervention ought to have been 'discussed and voted on' at the UN before British forces went into action: in other words, it deliberately avoided an absolute requirement that the UN Security Council should have 'authorized' action. As in Iraq, this gave too much 'wriggle room' for supporters of an attack to twist some lesser UN resolution and present it as sufficient to allow attacks to go ahead.

But beyond legality, there was also the question of where intervention would lead, and whether it would improve the situation on the ground. Air attacks might provoke the Assad regime to use chemical weapons on a larger scale: and though the responsibility would be his, that would be of little comfort to the civilians who would be affected.

Ed Miliband had asked if I would support his amendment, but though we discussed possible changes to the wording, he didn't want to shift on these points. The deadline for tabling amendments was nearly up (even though the government motion itself hadn't been released – another bizarre parliamentary situation) so I asked my office to draft an amendment of our own, setting out the argument that the case for military action in Syria had not been established and that no formal UN authorization had been given. When the government's motion was finally published late on Wednesday, our amendment was first in the queue. The rumours were that a compromise would emerge to allow Labour to back the government, and that the bombing of Syria would begin that weekend.

This had a nightmarish quality, in part because of the echoes of Iraq. One of my campaigns since being elected had been to ensure that Parliament, not the prime minister, would in future decide whether to commit Britain's military to war. The key was that MPs should have a free vote, rather than being pressured or bullied by their party whips. Then, each and every Member would have to take personal responsibility for a vote for military strikes, and so – hopefully – they would think through the pros and cons rather more carefully and not take the smooth words of the party leaderships at face value. This was the line I had taken during the debate I had finally succeeded in getting held on the tenth anniversary of the Iraq War. But I hadn't thought that the test would come so quickly.

When it finally emerged, the government motion was far less bellicose than anticipated. Though condemning Assad (we could all agree on that), it made clear that Parliament would have another vote before any action. In the few days between the decision to recall Parliament and the publication of the motion for debate, the government had lost their nerve. They had come to see that public opinion – and their own backbenchers – were not in favour of war: or at least, not yet. The government clearly planned to back off and then work hard to build a consensus for military action. And there was always a chance they would fail, or that the United States would not wait for them and would go it alone.

Then I learned that my own amendment, which had the backing of Plaid Cymru and some Labour backbenchers, would not be debated. At the last moment, Labour had produced an 'amendment' that was almost identical to the government's motion, but it was this we would vote on at the end of the evening. No doubt this suited the Government and Opposition front benches, because it helped to stifle any real debate, but it left backbench MPs on all sides annoyed. The Conservative Tracey Crouch was one who said she would have voted for my amendment, if the Speaker had called it, and Jim Fitzpatrick resigned from the Labour front bench because the Miliband motion was so weak. The Parliament has no mechanism to challenge the Speaker's ruling on the choice of amendments. It meant that, as we gathered in the chamber, there was a sense of anticlimax. Everyone was asking why Parliament had been recalled if there was to be no meaningful vote. The general view was that the government had been put, or perhaps put itself, in a ridiculous position.

David Cameron's speech didn't help, being very short – 'Is that it?' whispered my neighbour – and giving little on the legal side or the case for intervention. The debate itself was sterile, with no stand-out speeches, and plenty of those who spoke were clearly trying to work their way through some difficult judgements about morality and international diplomacy without much help from their respective front benches. We had a desultory winding-up speech from Nick Clegg. Either his heart wasn't in it, or he hadn't prepared properly, or both. A simple question, such as Phillip Lee asking if the British base in Cyprus would be used by the Americans, even if the House voted against intervention, left him floored. He hadn't sat through the whole debate and so hadn't tuned in to the mood of the house, and he didn't have the credibility on Foreign Affairs to fall back on, as William Hague would have done. Hague's witty and persuasive style would also have drawn in the Tory backbenchers, but presumably it was seen as more important to bind the Liberal Democrats to the coalition on this divisive issue. In the event, Clegg's performance left the debate flat and the vote was called at 10 p.m.

We milled about, waiting to file through the lobbies, and even at this stage there was no sense of drama. There were a few odd faces in the No lobby, MPs who were usually staunch supporters of the government, but as expected Labour's amendment was lost by a substantial margin: 332 to 220. Then we all trooped out for the next vote, on the government's motion. Again, there were some interesting refuseniks who were voting against the government, but as we filed back into the Chamber once again, and the tellers performed the ritual of walking forward and nodding to the Speaker, everyone assumed the government had won its meaningless vote. And then the result: 272 in favour, 285 against. Somehow, the government had lost.

It was hard to know who was more surprised: David Cameron or Ed Miliband. It was Ed who recovered more swiftly, calling on Cameron to rule out the use of the Royal Prerogative; that is, the prime minister's ability to act without reference to Parliament. Cameron, presumably without thinking it through at all, instead said he ruled out any further action on Syria.

The defeat sent some journalists back to Suez or the Norway debate of May 1940 for their over-excited comparisons; but Cameron's position was never in danger. The greatest impact was in the United States, where Congress now expected to be consulted in the same way by President Obama. That created time for Russia to broker an alternative proposal: the destruction of chemical weapons under international supervision. While this did little to address the civil war itself, it offered a way to deal with the immediate danger of further chemical attacks without the practical and moral risks involved in air strikes. On one level, this was a remarkable achievement for Parliament. But it was clearly unintentional. David Cameron wanted Parliament's endorsement to a blank cheque. He misread his own party, and Ed Miliband too, who shifted his position to avoid signing the Cameron cheque and ended up bringing about Cameron's defeat.

The reputation of both Cameron and Miliband was damaged over Syria. So too was the UK's standing with the United States. The US Secretary of State John Kerry pointedly referred to France, who was joining the air strikes, as America's 'oldest ally'. But to have promised to intervene and then failed to deliver is at least a sign of a prime minister woefully out of touch. Britain as a whole could not see how air strikes would make things in Syria better: but it took a week of bungling for our political leaders to realize it.

So out of this strange affair came two positive outcomes. First, it seemed that Parliament had clawed back some control over the executive and dented the Royal Prerogative. It strengthened the feeling that no government should commit us to war without a vote in Parliament. And yet – how typical – this had come about not through principle or debate, but through sheer incompetence by the country's two leading politicians. Second, the international community had found a peaceful way of ridding a dictator of chemical weapons, and the people of war-torn Syria were at least to be spared that horror in future; and spared, too, the inevitable death and destruction that Western air strikes would have brought in their wake.

The situation in Syria and the wider Middle East remains

desperate. Fuelling violence, whether through air strikes or arms sales or support for governments intent on repression, cannot provide the answer. Anything that creates fear plays into the hands of the extremists; and that includes responding to deliberate attempts to provoke the West into military intervention. As Paul Rogers, professor of Peace Studies at Bradford University, has commented on ISIL's strategy in Syria and Iraq:

> In the longer term, ISIL planners are looking to secure and consolidate an Islamist caliphate stretching across large parts of northern Syria and northwest Iraq. This will require increased support from abroad in the form of financial and material aid as well as the boost in personnel. The greatest help in advancing these aims would be open western military intervention in any form, even if restricted primarily to the use of armed drones.

Instead, we need to promote a regional process, in which those countries with a strategic interest can come together to explore a peaceful settlement that can lead to long-term stability, justice and an end to poverty in the region. That must also include an end to the illegal occupation of Palestine and the implementation of the 'two-state' solution with effective guarantees for Israel's security. We need, in other words, a strategy for bringing the misguided 'War on Terror' to an end, and a vision of a more peaceful and prosperous Middle East in which every nation and tradition can share.

Warfare is not inevitable. The history of Europe since 1945 has shown that nations with a long tradition of enmity and conflict can learn to live together. I don't believe that such a path is closed off to other nations, wherever in the world they are, whatever legacy they hold from conflict, exploitation or civil war. Perhaps there is an element of idealism in this: but the alternative of cynicism will in the long term be more destructive. At the height of the Cold War, this choice was put in stark terms: 'These are the stakes: to make a world in which all of God's children can live, or to go into the dark. We must either love each other, or we must die.'

These were not the words of an idealist, let alone an anti-nuclear campaigner. They were spoken by the man who, for five years, presided over the US involvement in the Vietnam War, President Lyndon Johnson. He understood that security depended on reaching out to other nations and creeds, however difficult that might seem. In our own age, it remains a potent message.

12

A Modest Proposal:
How Women's Voices in Politics
Will Enrich Us All

'*Well-behaved women rarely make history.*'
Laurel Thatcher Ulrich

Until my election to Westminster, the highpoint of my political career, as far as my mother was concerned, was being photographed with Colin Firth, as he presented me with the 'Ethical Politician of the Year' award some years previously. The framed photo has pride of place on top of my parents' TV set, displacing one of me and Richard, my long-suffering husband of almost twenty-five years – an act of betrayal for which he has still not completely forgiven her.

Awards, though, can have their uses, particularly if they help to shape what people think about politics. In my first year I was surprised to receive an invitation to the *Spectator* Political Awards. It was all very 'clubby', with lots of large, confident chaps in good suits, enjoying themselves. (As I recall, Peter Oborne of the *Telegraph* was being so expansive that I ended up with a glass of champagne down my back.) It felt such a traditional event, reflecting the old-fashioned, male-dominated politics that has such deep roots in Parliament. But my prejudices took a knock when they announced the winner of the Newcomer of the Year

Award and I suddenly found myself being presented with a large glass plate by David Cameron. It was probably the first and last time I will ever be photographed standing next to him, both of us with big smiles: a surreal moment.

The plate we now use as a fruit bowl in my Westminster office. That felt like the right home for it, as being effective in Parliament is a team effort, and Cath, Ingrid, Melissa and the others had worked so hard to help me find my feet in the first year. It also showed that the Greens could have an impact not just on issues that were perceived to be 'ethical', but across the whole of the work of Parliament.

But in politics, a higher profile comes at a cost. You become the target for aggression and for malicious rumours, which you often have to ignore because trying to respond simply drags you into pointless exchanges and distracts you from what matters. Some of the allegations that have come my way are so outlandish that they are actually quite comical: my favourite was that my main reason for standing in Brighton was that I wanted to set up a UFO monitoring station in the city. Others may be equally puzzling but have the potential to do more harm. One was the allegation that Richard and I owned four or five houses: as if someone didn't realize that if you move house, you usually sell the one you are moving from. We had lived in Oxford, then in Brussels, and then in Brighton: but we hadn't kept the old houses, like some kind of souvenir. Nor did I have houses in the name of my husband, or my sons, any relative, or my dog. Yet the rumour persisted, because it suited some people to keep it alive, and it suited others to believe it. Like other urban myths – crocodiles in the sewers, or the names of the crew in *Captain Pugwash* – it is just too good not to be true, if you happen to believe that no one who stands for public office can be anything other than a liar and a crook.

But what I have had to put up with is nothing compared with the vile abuse and threats suffered by other women who have chosen to speak up about social issues, such as Mary Beard and Caroline Criado-Perez. This is the extreme end of a trend towards aggression in our political discourse that is extremely troubling. The apparent anonymity of Twitter plays its part; but it doesn't explain why some people should believe that the usual rules of decency and honesty don't apply to politicians or to those merely discussing political and social issues.

Parliament hardly sets a good example. The way that Honourable Members treat women in particular would no longer be accepted in any other workplace. No female MP, however much you might disagree with what they are saying, should have to put up with endless comments about how they look, or be treated as a sex object, or be told to *calm down, dear*. In any other walk of life you'd be up against laws of discrimination and harassment. Here, it's politics, so that's OK.

Westminster remains very male. The 2015 election saw more women elected than ever before: 191 in total. But still over 70 per cent of MPs are male, which leaves Britain well down the international league table of fair representation, not only far below the 'usual suspects' such as Sweden or the Netherlands, but many countries whose parliamentary traditions are far less deep-rooted than ours, such as Mozambique and Serbia. And that matters, because it means that the concerns of half the population are not heard loudly enough. As a result, we get policies that perpetuate women's economic disadvantage, such as the brutal public sector cuts imposed by the current government, which hit women hardest, and the ongoing gender pay gap. Moreover, the issue of equality is a matter of principle. No one should be discriminated against, or excluded from becoming an MP because they're a woman, or black or gay or disabled or transgender or from a working-class background. If Parliament is to represent everyone in society, its own composition needs to reflect that society, not just a subsection of it.

Better female representation would bring many benefits,

including challenging perceptions of what leadership looks like, introducing different expectations, and creating new role models. Clearly, women are not one homogenous group with the same views and preoccupations, but shared experience makes it more likely that women will have some shared priorities. Moreover, diversity is a desirable goal in and of itself. Women and men alike are entitled to a healthy democracy, and it is only through creating a Parliament that better reflects the population that it is designed to serve that this can be achieved.

It doesn't help that Parliament has a macho culture, and an unattractive tolerance of intimidation. When the Labour MP Ian Davidson threatened to give the SNP's Eilidh Whiteford 'a doing' during a session of the Scottish Affairs Select Committee, this wasn't an acceptable way for one professional to speak to another, and his later clarification that he hadn't meant this 'in a sexual way' hardly helped.

Improving the position of women in Parliament is not a priority for some parts of the media. After the reshuffle in 2014, the *Daily Mail* dissected the clothes of the female ministers arriving in Downing Street – from 'catwalk queen' Esther McVey, Minister of State for Employment, to 'mother of the bride' Lady Stowell, Leader of the Lords and Chancellor of the Duchy of Lancaster – as if the previous fifty years had never happened. At least it gave Nick Clegg a chance to provide some light relief when he tweeted a picture of himself in Downing Street with the message: 'What I wore to the office today. Fingers crossed the Mail approves. Hope I don't look too '80s cabin attendant.'

The ways we could tackle this are not radical. A start is to recognize – 'call out' – this kind of sexist abuse for what it is. Then there are simple and proven approaches to supporting women in politics, such as better mentoring programmes and support networks, properly resourced, and affordable childcare, all-women shortlists and a fairer voting system. Changes outside Parliament would also make a difference, including challenging stereotypes, increasing the voices of women in the media, and introducing measures like a requirement for company boards to comprise at least 40 per cent women.

Some of these measures are so obvious, you would think they must already have been introduced – were it not for the inertia created by Parliament's delight in precedent: that is, if you have done something one way and nothing has gone badly wrong, then why change? This was why legislation was always drafted as if talking solely about men, and never women. If it refers to a Secretary of State, then it will always say that 'he' will need to do this, or have the power to do that, and never 'she'. To some, this seems petty: after all, we 'all know what it means'. But to me, what it means is that it remains the assumption in our society that people in power will be men, not women. (The fact that, under the coalition, the majority of Secretaries of State were men hardly justifies this.) Similarly, when legislation refers to senior police officers as 'he', it suggests that this is the reality now, and how our legal and social frameworks and decision-makers want it to remain. So when I was preparing the draft bill on Land Value Tax as part of my work on a Housing Charter I asked for it to say 'he or she' in the appropriate places. When this reached the Table Office, it escalated in a very polite way to the Clerk of Legislation, Simon Patrick. To his credit, when he found there was nothing in precedent to forbid such a formulation, he made no objection and that was how the bill was printed and laid before Parliament. A tiny victory; but it all helps to raise the issue and prepare the ground for change; and as it happens, shortly afterwards the approach was changed in all legislation, so that it avoids the personal pronoun altogether.

There are so many of these kinds of signals embedded in our legislation that perpetuate these kinds of differences. The distinction between civil partnerships and marriage was one, and David Cameron's determination to push through gay marriage in the face of hostility within his party was to his credit (just as the vehemence of that hostility was to the discredit of his party). But even this reform was structured in such a way as to continue another, though more modest, form of discrimination: one highlighted in a petition begun by Ailsa Burkimsher Sadler. The marriage certificate had always required the name of the father of each spouse to be entered, even if he had taken no part in their upbringing; and even more strangely, the name of the mother could not by law be entered either instead or as well. The bill was an opportunity to allow the mother's name to be entered; a small change that would mean a lot to some people, on a day that mattered to them enormously. The only objection the government could come up with was revealing: that it would cost too much to replace all the marriage registers up and down the country. It turned out that these registers rarely lasted more than a few weeks or months before they were filled up, so this was nonsense.

I put down an Early Day Motion that became one of the most-supported of that session. The petition ended up with 70,000 supporters, and the Home Secretary said that she would consider it. In some cases 'consider' means 'pretend to consider it with no intention of changing it': but it can also signal a willingness on the part of government to shift position without the embarrassment of conceding that this is anything to do with the campaign. So though there may be a further delay, I think this campaign battle has now been won.

Another battle, and one with particular resonance for young women growing up in what is in many ways an increasingly hostile and judgemental environment, is typified by Page 3 of the *Sun*. This isn't about banning pornography. It's about challenging its normalization in society, particularly in the context of what claims to be a family newspaper. I'm sure most readers of the *Sun* don't buy it to gaze at a picture of a bare-breasted woman; but the owners of the paper seem to think that the minority who do matter more than the millions of women (and, indeed, men) for whom this treatment is offensive. Simply having the image and its accompanying leery text there in the paper suggests that this is appropriate.

The frustration that Page 3 creates has been channelled with great success in the campaign to remove the *Sun* from university campuses. It is a way of showing that those who have to put up with routine sexism can push back, and not feel they are lone voices. When I secured a debate on media sexism in July 2013, the No More Page 3 campaign provided a natural focus, in part because I was pushing for the *Sun* to be removed from display alongside other daily papers on the parliamentary estate until Page 3 was changed. I also wanted to quote the campaign's founder, Lucy Holmes: 'We are all affected by Page 3 whether we buy it or not, because we all live in a society where the most widely read paper in the country makes "normal" the idea that women are there primarily for men's sexual pleasure.'

I also gave examples of the academic studies linking media sexism, discrimination, exploitation and violence. The campaign against sexism in the media is not about being 'offended' – it is about tackling a continuum in which this casual, everyday sexism creates an environment where violence against women is tolerated or excused. But most of my speech was given over to examples of everyday sexism in the media provided to me by constituents in Brighton who had joined the 'Spot the Sexism' campaign: the objectivization and denigration of women, from pop stars to murder victims; and the limiting of the opportunities and ambitions, particularly of young women.

In order to show my support for the No More Page 3 campaign, it seemed natural enough to wear one of their campaign T-shirts. It created a bit of a stir.

The parliamentary rules on dress code had always seemed a bit of a mystery to me, but they appeared to exercise a number of colleagues. Thomas Docherty, for example, then the Labour MP for Dunfermline and West Fife, appeared to have a problem with women wearing denim in the House, and raised a point of order in the chamber to ask for guidance 'as to what is an appropriate dress code for the mother of Parliaments?'. Clearly a man with too much time on his hands, he'd been fretting at the sight of a 'handful' of female MPs on the Tory and Lib Dem benches – who sit opposite Labour MPs – wearing 'black denim, knee length boots and leather jackets'. No doubt he would have been more at home a few decades earlier: until 1998, MPs wishing to raise a point of order during a vote had to wear a hat – indeed, a collapsible top hat was kept in the chamber in case it was needed. Fortunately Dawn Primarolo, Deputy Speaker at the time, was in no mood to indulge him, and declined to comment on MPs' 'sartorial elegance'.

Scanning the pages of the parliamentary bible *Erskine May* didn't make me any the wiser, although the 2004 edition helpfully states: 'Members are not permitted to wear decorations in the House. The wearing of military insignia or uniforms inside the chamber is not in accordance with the long-established custom of the House.'

On the day, the discomfort of the chair, Jimmy Hood, when he saw the T-shirt soon became apparent. I was scarcely two minutes into my speech; he stood up and interrupted me:

> Mr Jim Hood (in the Chair): *Order. Can I tell the Honourable Member that there are standards of dress that Members must comply with, both in the House and in Westminster Hall? I ask her to respect that and to put her jacket back on, which she was wearing when she came in, please.*
>
> Caroline Lucas: *I will of course comply with your ruling, Mr Hood, but it strikes me as a certain irony that in this place people can get copies of the* Sun. *Perhaps I can even show you what is in the* Sun. *In eight places in this House—*
>
> Mr Jim Hood (in the Chair): *Order. I am not commenting on what the Member may wish to say in the debate; I am only*

addressing the appropriate means of dress. If she does as I asked,
she can carry on with her speech.

Caroline Lucas: *Thank you, Mr Hood. I was simply*
going to say that it strikes me as an irony that this T-shirt is
regarded as an inappropriate thing to be wearing in this House,
whereas, apparently, it is appropriate for this kind of newspaper
to be available to buy in eight different outlets on the Palace of
Westminster Estate. That is why I have written to the Palace
asking for them to be withdrawn, and for them not to be on sale
until page 3 is removed.

Mr Hood's rebuke ensured the debate received far more
coverage than I could have dreamed of. I had, from time to time,
considered whether or not some kind of demonstration within
Parliament would be justified by a particular cause, or set of
circumstances. But I hadn't seen the wearing of a T-shirt as a
particularly controversial act. Nevertheless, the irony of it – being
asked to cover up a T-shirt while debating newspapers selling
images of topless models – was priceless.

When you look at the low number of women in Parliament,
there are two possible responses. The first is to blame women:
they are not up to the job, not interested, too emotional,
lack staying power, keep having babies, and the rest of the
chauvinistic nonsense. The second is to blame the system: there
are assumptions, preconceptions and systematic barriers in the
way of fair representation that need to be dismantled. There are
still some who favour the first response in Parliament (women
as well as men): but their belief that this is the 'natural' state of
affairs becomes less and less credible when you look at how other
countries have moved so much further and faster than the United
Kingdom. Are British women somehow less capable, intelligent, or
motivated than the Dutch, Swedes, Rwandans or Australians? Or
are these countries somehow massively over-promoting women
and discriminating against Dutch or Australian men as they do so?

Of course, anyone who exchanges prejudice for psychology will acknowledge that so much of how we see the world is conditioned by our previous experience, and by what we see around us. Most people, when asked to describe a doctor, will talk about a male doctor: even though within a few years there will be more female doctors in the UK than male (much to the *Daily Mail*'s alarm). The more that people see white, male, middle-class MPs, the more they think those are the necessary attributes. So the people who select the candidates in each constituency will tend to pick those who are also white, male and middle class. Similarly, potential female candidates (consciously or unconsciously) will self-select themselves out of contention. So the defence that 'women don't apply' to be MPs misses the point: to the extent that women don't apply, it's because they don't think they will be chosen (or because they find it difficult to fit with family or other commitments, or don't like the look of Parliament as a place to spend their working life, and so on).

Behind the scenes, this imbalance continues. The majority of special advisers, who often wield more influence than some ministers, are white males. This has a distorting effect on policy: and as a stint as a special adviser is an increasingly common route to becoming an MP, also helps perpetuates that gender imbalance as well. Political journalists, too, are mainly male, forming a chummy homogeneity that reinforces the sense of a 'Whitehall bubble' detached from everyday life.

When it comes to encouraging women to stand, the way politics is presented in the media is unhelpful. The BBC recently ran an advert for their Parliament channel and used clips of Cameron, Clegg, Miliband and Farage to show politics in action. They were, of course, all men; and by excluding Natalie Bennett, Nicola Sturgeon and Leanne Wood (who like Farage were the leaders of national political parties represented in Parliament) they were yet again presenting an all-male club. They would no doubt claim that UKIP have more political resonance than the Greens: but this is only in the BBC's own particular view of politics. Nigel is like them, and talks about the stuff they are interested in; and so the BBC editors think he matters more. The more publicity they have given him over the years, the more UKIP has progressed electorally; and so the BBC can now claim they were 'right' to give him airtime denied to other parties.

This makes female role models so important. As a child, there were individual MPs that I admired from a distance, such as Barbara Castle and Shirley Williams, whose occasional appearances among the serried ranks of pinstriped suits on television caught my eye. The more I learned about politics, the more I was aware of female pioneers who were sanctified by time, such as Jennie Lee. And of course there were the suffragettes. Their story, more than any other, was inspiring. It is also an object lesson in not giving up: histories of the suffragettes often focus only on the last twenty years of their struggle, but women fought for the vote for more than a century. Mary Wollstonecraft was a pivotal figure in the campaign. Her *A Vindication of the Rights of Woman* was published in 1792, but it was another forty years until the first petition for the women's vote was presented to the House of Commons.

Over the course of the next century, campaigners kept up the pressure, often enduring imprisonment and – if they went on hunger strike to protest at the conditions they had to face – the excruciating process of force-feeding too. It was not until 1918 that women over the age of thirty and meeting certain property qualifications were granted the vote, a right finally extended to women on the same terms as men in 1928.

The refusal of the suffragettes to compromise is legendary. One of my favourite letters from the time was sent by Bertha Brewster in 1913 to the *Daily Telegraph*:

> Sir, Everyone seems to agree upon the necessity of putting a stop to Suffragist outrages; but no-one seems

certain how to do so. There are two, and only two, ways in which this can be done. Both will be effectual. 1. Kill every woman in the United Kingdom. 2. Give women the vote.

Yours truly, Bertha Brewster.

Compared with the struggles they faced, ours can pale in significance. Yet there are still battles to be won. As in so many other careers, the current choice for female MPs is whether to take time out to raise a family and therefore accept that we will always risk being years behind our male colleagues in promotion and status; or to attempt to combine politics and family, with the tensions, sacrifices and anxieties that this imposes on all sides; or to put aside the idea of raising a family at all. Some are blessed with very understanding and supportive partners: I could never have pursued a career in politics without Richard, and without a lot of understanding from my children. Others – particularly those early pioneers – had the very considerable financial resources needed to pass on much of the time-consuming tasks of home life to other people. Some women have always known with confidence that they did not wish to have children. But for the majority, the choice has been very hard, and while we might admire those who have managed to combine the two, there can be no criticism of those who choose not to or who have tried and not succeeded. A Parliament is which only 29 per cent of MPs are women is not a sign of progress but of a system that remains unfair, and needlessly so.

This led me to the idea of job-share MPs. It was always a good way to challenge the assumption that politics is different from all other forms of employment and therefore the principles (or even the legal obligations) about equal treatment for men and women shouldn't apply. Margaret Thatcher's time in the top job still feels like a quirk rather than the start of a trend. Since she was elected as leader of the Conservatives, there have been twenty leaders of the three main political parties: all of them male. The same decapitated pyramid extends through cabinets and shadow cabinets, junior ministers, MPs and candidates. I was proud to be the first woman elected in Brighton Pavilion, but still over half of constituencies have never in their history elected a woman MP. It's only when it comes to local constituency parties (where the hard work is done, for little thanks or recognition – a familiar story?) that women have anything like an equal presence.

Job-sharing is a simple way to give parents and other carers more choice or flexibility about resolving these tensions. There's plenty of evidence that the additional commitment and talent that job-sharing brings to any workplace easily outweighs the need for some additional management or coordination. In simple terms, if more people can find their right role in work, and find it easier to reconcile work with other commitments, then we all gain economically and socially. Naturally, each profession and sector has advanced arguments why job-sharing – though highly desirable in theory – would not be practical in their particular area. Doctors, teachers, judges, managers: they have all claimed this and have all been shown to be mistaken.

Of course, MPs are a bit different. You elect an individual as well as the representative of a party; and you expect that individual to make judgements and decisions based on their beliefs and values. So the obvious objection is, what if one half of a job-share MP wanted to vote one way, and the other disagreed? To which the response is first that this is not very likely to happen, as the two people who agree to job-share have a common interest in making it work (or they are both at risk of being thrown out) and will have chosen to work together because they share the same outlook. And if there is a residual risk, there is also the advantage that on significant issues the two job-sharers will have had the chance to discuss the matter between themselves, and so are likely to have come to a more considered and informed judgement.

The idea of elected representatives entering into a job-share was not new: but it had yet to be taken seriously in Parliament. I used my first conference speech after being elected to call for job-sharing MPs and as I expected there were many politicians who rejected it out of hand ('bonkers', 'outrageous', 'sheer lunacy' and so on). But the media coverage gave the idea new momentum. Sarah Wollaston, the Conservative MP who had job-shared for many years as a GP, backed it. Labour's John McDonnell brought forward a Ten Minute Rule Bill. Tim Farron of the Liberal Democrats gave it his support. And though it took three years, Nicky Morgan, the Minister for Women and Equalities, said the government should consider it. We did not see job-share MPs elected in 2015, but their time will surely come.

Again, this isn't simply about justice for the individual, important though that is. Our Parliament is impoverished if people are excluded from participating, particularly if they have experiences that Parliament ought to hear. It would be wrong to consider a politician such as David Blunkett only in the context of his blindness: but equally, Parliament without Blunkett would have been diminished not only because of his personal contribution as a politician and his experience as leader of a major city council, but also because his example challenged people's preconceptions and prejudices. Allowing job-share MPs is just one modest proposal for change, along with family friendly working hours, reformed constituencies that weaken the grip of the selectorate, all-women shortlists, more affordable childcare, and better mentoring and support. The sooner they come, the better off we will all be. Like Shakespeare's sister, we cannot know what we are losing because of prejudice and an unwillingness to change. But we can be certain that loss is a heavy one.

13

Arrest:

How a Peaceful Protester Ended Up in a Police Cell

> *'Hope just means another world might be possible, not promised, not guaranteed. Hope calls for action: action is impossible without hope.'*
> Rebecca Solnit, *Hope in the Dark*

It could be a village fete. There are rugs spread out, and bunting, and several of those open-sided green gazebos you get from garden centres, and people sitting on folding camp-stools, and knowledgeable locals keeping an eye on the Sussex skies for the first sign of rain. Or perhaps a street party, because people have laid picnics on the verge and the road has been closed off and children are running up and down, hardly believing the tarmac is now their football pitch. The backdrop of oak and chestnut in full leaf could not be more English. Only the placards and banners strike the wrong note. For the villagers and visitors gathered together are not here to raise money for the church roof, but to try to stop a plan to drill for gas under their homes and fields.

This is Balcombe. Not quite picture-postcard, but perhaps all the more precious because it is a living community that has expanded over the years without losing its character. There was already industry here when the London to Brighton railway was built on its western edge, and it is not a community of the retired, weekenders or commuters: as you walk the lanes you sense that the residents are as likely to work on the industrial estates of Crawley or around the airport at Gatwick as take the morning trains to London. It has shops, a pub and a village school. It's a place that works, in every sense of the word. And Balcombe does not instinctively turn its back on progress.

So why should so many of the citizens of this Sussex village be so angry? Anyone might be concerned to learn that a company wants to look for oil or gas so close to their homes, but the anger is rooted in more than some local disruption or loss of amenity. It stems from fear. Because when Cuadrilla turned up in Balcombe to drill a test well, it brought home to people two disturbing facts. They couldn't trust them. And they had no power to stop them.

Induced hydraulic fracturing – you can see why the industry shortened it to fracking – means injecting water, sand and chemicals into the ground under high pressure to break up rock formations and so release the oil and gas (or uranium or whatever else you want) trapped within them. It's not a new technique, but its use in more and more ambitious ways in recent years has led to unexpected effects – or rather, effects that the oil and gas companies did not tell anyone that they expected – such as pollution of drinking water with methane and other contaminants. One of the essential problems with fracking is that the chemical brew pumped in to break up the ground doesn't all come back to the surface through the well itself. Some of it can stay underground, or gradually seep off in other directions. As the whole point of the operation is to break up the underlying rocks, it makes it inherently difficult to know quite where it will end up or what harm it might do.

Worse, the 'industry-friendly' approach of US regulators has left it to individual communities or campaigners to establish the truth about fracking. Since the start of widespread fracking in the

United States in the 1980s the energy companies have, in effect, claimed there will be no harm; and then, when that harm is proved, have said that whatever has gone wrong will not happen again.

Fracking also poses a global threat. The more hydrocarbons such as oil, coal and gas we take out of the ground and burn, the more we will change our climate in damaging and potentially catastrophic ways. And hydrocarbons are also a finite resource, and one we are dangerously dependent on in our economy. The faster we consume them, the more we risk price increases and inflation. All this means that anyone with an open mind or a sense of self-preservation would ease up on burning carbon and ensure we leave the vast majority of fossil fuels in the ground.

But fracking is born from the opposite impulse: to use ever-more extreme ways of extracting what hydrocarbons remain, without thought to the damage to the climate or the way it harms our attempts to wean ourselves off oil and gas – or to the additional risks of a particularly dirty kind of production. This was the flip-side of the debate on 'stranded' high-carbon assets: if we are not going to burn all these reserves, then the financial markets need to adjust; but if we are, then we will bring catastrophic climate change upon us.

There is also the local impact. The track record of the energy companies shows how foolish it would be to trust them on fracking. They will suppress inconvenient facts, rubbish and intimidate their opponents, and use their financial muscle to put their messages across forcefully. They will argue up to the limits of the truth, and sometimes far beyond. The best you can say is that such issues are thrashed out in an adversarial system, where they put their case, just as their opponents set out the counter-arguments, with the government as the judge, holding the ring, and public opinion as the jury.

If only.

The idea that fracking could lower gas prices is superficially attractive: after all, fuel poverty is a major concern and higher fuel costs hit the poor harder than the rich. However, there is absolutely no reason to believe that this would happen. Former Treasury economist Lord Stern has called such claims 'baseless economics', and even Cuadrilla's Francis Egan admitted as much himself when he gave evidence to a House of Lords Select Committee.

To the contrary, since UK gas is traded internationally, any shale gas boom in the UK would be unlikely to have an impact on the price of gas. In the United States, where fracking has lowered prices significantly, gas is rarely exported because other markets are too far away. Experts, from the International Energy Agency to Deutsche Bank, have all said different geological, legal and regulatory conditions make it unlikely the US shale gas boom would be repeated in the UK.

And, of course, fuel poverty is not only the result of fuel costing too much, but of people being paid too little – in wages, or pensions, or benefits – to afford their energy bills, or to pay for better insulation or more energy-efficient appliances. People who find it hard to pay for gas or electricity will also find it hard to pay for their weekly shopping, or save up for a holiday or a new coat, or pay their rent or mortgage payments or Council Tax or bus and train fares and all the rest. Energy costs in the UK are not particularly high, compared with many other European countries. But our stock of housing is in poor condition, and therefore harder and more expensive to heat, than in much of the rest of Europe. Also, Britain has wide divisions between those comfortably off at the top and the majority of people who live modestly or even struggle to get by. So when electricity and gas prices soar, it has a huge impact on people's lives.

Many people remember that the energy supply companies used to be in public hands. Then, if the price of fuel went up, you would know that it wasn't to increase the bonuses for the bosses or the dividends to the shareholders: and if there were profits, they went back to the Treasury and everyone benefited. But then the electricity and gas boards were privatized by the Conservatives, and we were left with a dysfunctional 'market' for gas and electricity that gives the big six energy companies every opportunity to exploit their customers with unjustified price hikes. Labour, for all their recent noise, did nothing during their thirteen years in power to reverse this or to control the energy companies effectively. A temporary freeze on energy prices, as they have proposed, is not enough. We need decentralized and community energy, and suppliers who treat their customers fairly either because they have an interest in doing so – for example, cooperatives or small businesses rooted in their local communities – or because they are effectively regulated. And we need investment in making homes easier to heat and other forms of energy efficiency.

So the cost of energy is not like the cost of other essentials such as potatoes, butter or rice. People see it as linked to decisions taken by the government. If prices go up, those in power get the blame – so the temptation is for those in power to favour the energy companies with subsidies in the hope that they will pass some of that cash on to consumers. Further, the production and sale of energy is in the hands of a small number of large firms, which have close links to government and to the major banks and investment firms. Add to this the income the government receives from taxing oil and gas and you can see why so many politicians instinctively feel that what is good for the sector is good for the country, ignoring the plight of those who struggle with ever-rising energy bills.

But gas prices remain on an upward curve in Europe. Within that curve, there is a great deal of volatility. This makes customers and voters unhappy, and puts profit margins under scrutiny. No wonder the energy firms and the government like the look of fracking. All this means that the government is in no sense an impartial judge or honest broker. It wants it to happen. It will do everything it can to facilitate it, and to overcome any opposition.

The 'adversarial' system for policymaking in Britain is already skewed in favour of business and against local communities. Big business stands to make vast profits from building and running new infrastructure and from exploiting natural resources. They can afford the lawyers and lobbyists, can splash money on lavish adverts and on 'community engagement', and pay for so-called independent research that supports their case. Ordinary people cannot match this. Often they cannot even enter the ring, because of the threat of having to pick up the costs of the other side. If the business loses, then the costs are spread across their shareholders or their customers. If their opponents lose, they could face personal bankruptcy and the loss of their home.

When the government supports one side, then the unfairness of this adversarial approach is redoubled. The government can set national policy, which can then be used in court to trump the views of local people, or even their elected representatives. If a local authority turns down a development, the government can overrule them. And for councils already facing cuts in funding, the prospect of fighting a protracted legal case against developers with apparently limitless financial resources can be intimidating. It is often easier to cave in, hoping to receive some crumbs of 'community enhancements' instead. Some councils even welcome controversial developments, because the cash that the developers offer to sweeten the deal can be used to lower Council Tax or to spend on vote-winning initiatives far away from the community that is to suffer.

In short, the system is loaded in favour of big business, from the policy decisions at the top, influenced by lobbyists and political donations, to the way the courts can be used to intimidate or silence local activists.

I don't think most people in Britain see our country this way. Most of us would like to believe that the government is trying to do the right thing, and that if there is a dispute between developers and the local community, the courts will give them a fair hearing. So it is often a deeply unpleasant shock when people first come up against the power of big business interests.

It happened to the village of Kings Cliffe, when the nuclear industry was looking for somewhere to dump its radioactive waste. There was a hazardous-waste site on the edge of the village, and its owners saw that they could make good money by taking in the nuclear waste that no one else wanted. Now you might think that disposing of nuclear waste would be the kind of problem that government scientists would look at carefully, taking into account the local geology, the risks to drinking water and wildlife, and the distance the waste would have to travel before being disposed of. You might think the government would then consult on some suitable sites, and then – having taken the tough decision in the national interest – would do everything they could to reassure and if necessary compensate local people.

What actually happened was that the government, who wanted to expand nuclear power but had no idea what to do with the waste, seized on the offer from the waste-disposal firm and wrote the policy to fit. No matter that the waste would have to travel over a hundred miles. No matter that there was no rail link, so it would all have to go by truck. No matter that the local geology was wrong. And it certainly did not matter that local people were utterly opposed, as were the parish and district councils. The government, in the shape of Eric Pickles, could call in the decision of the local authority, overturn it, and ensure the dumping of nuclear waste could go ahead regardless.

When you witness such events up close, the frustration of seeing the wrong decision imposed for the wrong reasons is overlaid by sadness that people's belief in the way their own country is really run can be shattered. They end up angry, disillusioned, and cynical. Sometimes they fight on for justice, or try to stop it happening to others. Sometimes they withdraw altogether, and decide – perhaps reasonably – that from now on they will just look out for themselves and those close to them. Their civic spirit is crushed.

So, to Balcombe. The village first heard that it had been chosen as a site for test drilling in 2012, and the parish council organized a referendum of local residents, and of those who responded, 82 per cent were opposed to the plans. Nevertheless, in July 2013 the government issued a permit to allow drilling to go ahead. One resident spoke of her shock that the views of the community could be so casually ignored. Another pointed out how close the well was to Ardingly reservoir, which supplies customers of South East Water with drinking water. These fears and frustrations meant that villagers were determined to protest as the Cuadrilla trucks rolled in.

They were not alone. Many veterans of previous environmental campaigns came to join them, setting up camp along the grass verges. Many others, new to protest, came to make their voices heard too. It was an impressive sight. My first visit, on a rainy Monday in August, found them damp but upbeat – already planning workshops and debates to raise more awareness about the threats from fracking. Their mood was captured on a Radio 4 programme called *Summer Nights*, chaired by Evan Davis, and including environmentalists Mark Lynas and Solitaire Townsend, along with Matthew Sinclair of the TaxPayers' Alliance and myself, talking about the future of the environment movement. One of the callers was a Balcombe resident who described the journey she had made from a couple of months ago, when she'd never heard of fracking and never been part of any kind of protest. The more she found out about it, the more concerned she had become, and so she'd gone along to some of the workshops that the environmental activists camping at Balcombe were holding – not just about fracking but about climate change and energy policy more generally. She had clearly not expected to be so impressed by the knowledge of the campaigners, nor to be welcomed so warmly. Hearing her speak with such enthusiasm and excitement about what she had discovered, it was almost like a door had opened onto another world, as a result of what was taking place on her doorstep.

I went to Balcombe again for Solidarity Sunday. There was a family march from the station to the fracking site, with old people and young people and kids running around. Seeing the villagers mingling with the people who were camped outside the site and those who had come for the day from other communities around the country – Devon, the North, Oxford – it felt like the carnival had come to town, and people perhaps with very different background and outlooks were coming together because of a shared concern. The decision of the Reclaim the Power climate camp to change their plans and relocate to Balcombe meant that numbers swelled still further. A slightly surreal moment came when, as one of the speakers, I was invited to climb onto the back of a giant, and distinctly dodgy-looking, plastic turtle, in order to be seen and to make myself heard.

I was back in Balcombe the following day. It felt even more of a family affair for me because my twenty-year-old son, Theo, arrived during the afternoon and joined in the protests. There were tents, bunting, music and home-cooked food, but an underlying purpose too. The protests had succeeded in making Cuadrilla back off a little, and they had announced that they would be suspending operations in Balcombe for a time. This in itself was an achievement, because it showed that public anger was sufficient to give the company pause for thought. But it also meant that the day's protest had a ritual feel to it. We blocked the driveway up to the Cuadrilla site, but as they were not planning to use it anyway, this was more symbolic than anything.

I joined a dozen or so others sitting in a circle on the drive. The police looked on tolerantly. From time to time the journalists would come over and dip down to interview us – the BBC, the *Telegraph* and so on. And around us the carnival carried on:

lots of music, drums, people dressed up, colour, food. Here was a demonstration that crossed the boundaries of class and of generation.

The police lines had been friendly, or neutral, but not aggressive. We were on a turning off the road which ran up to the gate to the Cuadrilla site, and as no one was planning to go in or out of the site, we were – after five hours – starting to think we should call it a day. Better to end the sit-in together than have people dribbling off because they had to get back to their families or catch a train. But as we were discussing in our ring whether, come five o'clock, we should get up, make a statement and go, the police came for us.

Theo was the first to be pulled out. The police were using a new technique of targeting pressure points behind the ear to subdue the people they were grabbing. It was clearly very painful, and very upsetting to witness. Without thinking, I found myself crying out: 'That's my son.' I'd not anticipated how distressing it would be to see him treated so violently. It was a moment when the clash of responsibilities – campaigner, politician, mother – suddenly became very real.

We were put into vans, driven off to the police station in Crawley, booked and put in the cells. It all took an age, right into the evening, but to be fair to the police it was mainly because of the procedures put in place to ensure that those under arrest are properly protected, and to ensure the police themselves have some protection from false allegations of mistreatment. Again, in a further reverse of mood, the police were friendly, even funny, about my being in their care. They asked if I was a vegetarian or vegan, and proudly announced that they had three choices: vegetable curry, vegetable chilli or potato wedges with baked beans. Having made my choice, the guy who delivered it through the hatch into the cell said apologetically: 'I'm sorry it tastes disgusting, but it's the cuts, you know.'

That made me smile. It also reminded me that my arrest wasn't really part of a clash between demonstrators and the police. It was about an unrepresentative government using force to coerce a local community into accepting something it did not want; and to suppress protests that reflected the concerns of a wide section of the public. Once again, the trail led back to Parliament.

PART THREE

A Better Way

At Brighton Pride, 13 August 2011

14

A Parliament that Works:
How We Can Start to Make Parliament Serve the People

> *'If one walks around this place, one sees statues of people, not one of them believed in democracy, votes for women, or anything else. We have to be sure we are in a workshop, not a museum.'*

> Tony Benn

It is the stuff of nightmares. You are standing in front of a hostile crowd of people, and you have forgotten what you are supposed to say. Your mind locks up, and all you can do is wish that the ground would swallow you up. And while it is bad enough as a dream, the reality, with the knowledge that you are also on television, and that Hansard will be recording your shame for posterity, is even worse.

It happened a few weeks after my election. I'd been heavily involved in trying to change the legislation on academy schools to provide some accountability and had put down a mass of amendments. This meant I had to rise in the chamber to make my case for each one, as well as intervene on (which is really interrupting) other speakers to respond to their points. But in one such intervention I tripped up on the convention that you can only describe another Member as 'he' or 'she' (or 'the honourable member' or some similar circumlocution), and never as 'you', and as a result I completely lost my flow. I was left standing there; and could do nothing else but say that I was sorry but I had forgotten my point. With that, I sat down, utterly mortified. I was already imagining how it would sound on *Today in Parliament*.

A little later the longstanding Tory backbencher Michael Fabricant darted over to the Opposition benches and, in a low whisper, told me not to worry, that it happened to everyone (even Winston Churchill, apparently – not someone I am often compared with) and that I should stand up again and intervene as soon as I could. In the event, the media didn't think it mattered, and Hansard covered up my blushes with some dots. And like falling off a bike or a horse for the first time, it was almost a relief to have screwed up when intervening: I knew it wouldn't be the last time.

Even so, it was a chastening experience, and taught me the value of arming oneself with even the briefest of notes before rising to speak. It also showed that Parliament is at its best when we treat each other as humans, not enemies; and that you can find humanity and goodwill in the most unlikely places. That reassurance has stood me in good stead in perhaps the most difficult task I've faced as an MP: trying to reform Parliament itself.

The history of parliamentary reform is long and chequered, from the Putney debates of the seventeenth century to the Great Reform Act of 1832. Sometimes the pressure for reform has been sufficient to overcome the entrenched interests within Parliament; at other times, such as with the Chartist movement, peaceful protest has been greeted with violence and repression. Progress has come when reformers inside Parliament have forged an alliance with mass public protest outside, as with female suffrage. But in its absence, as with Lords reform, the forces of conservatism can easily delay reform for a century or more.

Building on work done in the previous parliament by the

Wright Committee (named after its chair, Tony Wright), I began not with such grand causes but with some practical and, I hoped, non-controversial ways to make the place function more effectively. For example, Parliament currently has very weak powers to scrutinize the executive (the government and civil service) compared to, say, under the US Constitution. But the chances of winning more powers in the face of resistance from government seemed remote. So instead I looked at how the effectiveness of existing powers of scrutiny and challenge could be increased. I had seen first-hand over Iraq and on voting reform that efforts to challenge the government by tabling amendments could be thwarted by the Speaker deciding there was not time to vote on those amendments. Very well: let's speed up the voting system so we can include more – and more radical – amendments.

The obvious way to do this would be to allow MPs to vote electronically, rather than by shuffling through two wooden doors to the 'Aye' and 'No' lobbies. Like many other simple reforms, it was a proposal that has been discussed for years. Other Parliaments have shown the way: the French National Assembly, Scottish Parliament and Welsh Assembly use electronic voting, as does the European Parliament.

The arguments put up against electronic voting were fairly fatuous. One claim was that it would make MPs less likely to attend debates if they didn't have to vote straight afterwards: but electronic voting would make no difference. Often the benches are almost empty during a debate while the lobbies are crammed with MPs during the following vote. In the same way, opponents claimed it would make MPs lazy (no, really) and mean they would not bother thinking about the issues they were voting upon. Again, the reality was that MPs often had no clue about the substance of the debate on which they voted; and in any case were told how to vote by the whips. They also complained that backbenchers would miss the chance to lobby ministers as they milled around to vote. In fact, one way of organizing electronic voting would be for MPs to gather in the chamber at one point during the day and take a series of votes in a few minutes; so they could still buttonhole ministers or indulge in some gossip.

Against the background of public disillusionment with Parliament, I ploughed on with these reform proposals, including making contact with one of the companies which provide this kind of equipment. They reassured me that there were plenty of ways that genuine concerns could be overcome. For example, you could set the voting pads so they could only be used by MPs themselves using fingerprint or iris-reading technology – and so exclude the risk that some MPs might ask their researchers to vote for them and then bunk off or pass out through alcoholic excess. I was surprised by how well they had anticipated the likely objections – reasonable and otherwise – and they explained that ten years previously they had gone through a similar process: on that occasion it had been Margaret Beckett who had been pushing for reform. Now, she was one of those who had come out against any significant change; and had even gone so far as to take me to one side and tell me not to be in such a hurry to change things in Parliament '. . . because I'd get used to it'.

MPs spend about 250 hours over the course of an average Parliament just running around the building and queuing to vote. Electronic voting would save at least £30,000 a year in the direct costs of this wasted time. Add in the cost of keeping Parliament going during all this – everything from the security staff to the lighting and heating – and you have every reason to think the costs of the equipment (something like £400,000) would soon be paid back. There would also be gains in efficiency from MPs being able to plan their days better and know where they will be at any time. (And there would be less of the inevitable discourtesy to our constituents and other visitors – it looks very rude to keep having to rush out in the middle of meetings to vote.) Perhaps most importantly, it would do away with the argument that issues of public concern – such as whether our troops should stay in Afghanistan or not – cannot be debated because it would take too long to put it to a vote afterwards. To hold six votes in the European Parliament takes one and a half minutes: holding six votes in the Westminster Parliament takes one and a half hours.

With another reform close to my heart, I had a different kind of precedent: Richard Taylor. He had a degree from Cambridge University, studied medicine at Imperial College, London, and after a successful career he became a consultant physician at Kidderminster Hospital in Worcestershire. Just the kind of intelligent person, with a record of public service, that we would want to see in Parliament. What set him apart was that by 2001 he'd had enough of politics as usual. The A & E department at his local hospital in Kidderminster was threatened with closure, and he felt the views of his fellow citizens and patients were not being listened to. So he stood for Parliament. And won.

As an independent MP, Dr Taylor soon came up against all the absurdities of Parliament. One of these was particularly irksome: there is no way to record an abstention. You either vote Aye, or No, or you don't vote at all. For anyone of intelligence, this is a frustrating situation. A proposal may have some good elements in it; it may be basically right but need more work; there can be a hundred reasons for not wanting to support a measure without being actively hostile: and in most other settings (indeed, most other parliaments) you can record this position through an abstention. But not in Westminster. And of course, if you don't vote, it looks like you could not be bothered to turn up: with every likelihood that your political opponents will draw this to the attention of your local newspaper and your constituents, without bothering to explain why you did not vote.

There is one way to buck the system: to vote twice, once in each lobby. Then your vote is discarded, and those in the know can see the position you wanted to take. But for Dr Taylor, this was double-edged: at least one hostile newspaper portrayed him as so dim or confused that he didn't even know how to vote.

So onto my list of reforms went the option of abstention; and the linked idea of allowing MPs to record formally in a short paragraph the reasons why they voted, which their constituents could read. For now, the public have to make do with Hansard or with websites like 'theyworkforyou.com': but these only record how you voted, not why; and legislation is often so complex that it can be hard to know whether your MP was voting the way you would have wanted, or not.

This was one reason why I also wanted to see the introduction of a formal explanation for each amendment on which MPs were expected to vote. Obviously, the more that MPs can attend debates and hear for themselves, the better. But many debates in Parliament have only a handful of Members present. This isn't necessarily idleness: MPs will also have committees to attend while the chamber is sitting, and many other worthwhile calls on their time. But it makes it essential that MPs have a clear statement on the issues at stake: otherwise they will rely on the sheets provided by their party whips telling them which way to vote (but not why). Explanatory notes are produced for every bill; but not for amendments to those bills; so their production would be straightforward. Once again, the real barrier is that it would put a little more power in the hands of backbench MPs; and reduce the power of the whips. I have seen MPs being forcefully pushed into the Aye or No lobby by the whips, even as they are remonstrating that they did not want to vote that way. So naturally the whips ensured that a majority of MPs turned up at the vote to block making explanatory notes mandatory. There had been around twenty MPs in the chamber for the debate itself: but the vote was 23 in favour of my amendment and 142 against. (One wonders, in the absence of an explanatory note for the amendment, if they all knew what they were voting on.)

Backbenchers would also have a stronger hand if the ability of the government or of cliques of MPs to block Private Members' Bills were curtailed. These bills are the only chance that MPs who are not part of the government have to advance proposals for new legislation. One way to secure a PMB is through the annual ballot that determines the order in which backbench MPs can bring forward their chosen bills. (You can also table a Ten Minute Rule Bill or a Presentation Bill, though these are far less likely to make it through the labyrinth of parliamentary procedure to become law.) Over the years, some very important legislation has come about through this route, either directly – such as the abolition of the death penalty in 1965 or the outlawing of female genital mutilation in 2003 – or by drawing attention to the issue at stake. But it is terribly easy to stop these bills in their tracks. They need at least a hundred MPs to move to a vote if they are to proceed to the committee stage and be seriously considered; but they are debated on Fridays, when MPs are traditionally in their constituencies, and so individual MPs who are hostile to the principle of the bill, or who have been asked to block it by the government, can intervene to waste time and ensure that, by the time the vote comes, most of the MPs have gone home and there are not enough left to reach the hundred required.

The Sustainable Livestock Bill is a typical example. It was introduced by the Labour MP Robert Flello, who had come second in the PMB ballot, and would have reduced our dependence on animal feed grown in South America (on land taken from the Amazon rainforest). But Jacob Rees-Mogg, the Conservative MP for North-East Somerset, didn't like it and so popped up in a series of wrecking interventions and then made his own long, rambling and irrelevant speech that ranged from sewage to Agincourt by way of P. G. Wodehouse. He was abetted by Christopher Chope among others, and even the government minister Jim Paice was ready to waste everyone's time with a long and dreary response claiming that the bill was not needed because some kind of nebulous 'partnership' with the farming industry would achieve the same thing. All this took from 9.30 in the morning until 2 p.m. in the afternoon – all this for a five-clause bill and on the question whether it should be given more detailed scrutiny. In the end, the proposal to move to a vote was won by 62 to 29 but the 100-MP rule for Private Members' Bills (no such rule applies to government-backed legislation) meant that it was killed off. As were several other bills that followed: for those, because there was no time for debate or for a vote, it only needed a single MP to object to stop them progressing to a second reading. Hansard does not record whether on this occasion it was Mr Chope, his partner-in-obstruction Mr Bone or Mr Rees-Mogg or someone else: only that the block was made.

What is most unpleasant about these kinds of farce is the pleasure the 'filibusters' take in making a mockery of democracy in this way. If they argued over the legislation on its merits, it would be easier to accept the outcome. But they have no need to make any sensible or convincing arguments: they can block it even if every other MP knows they are wrong. These outmoded parliamentary procedures has given them a heady dose of power; and like the small-minded abuses of petty power that they themselves constantly perceive in the civil service, local government and European Commission, they delight in thwarting the good intentions of others.

It would not take much to end this situation. Each PMB could be given a set amount of time for its first reading, such as a maximum of three hours, after which a vote would be taken. Interventions from MPs could be limited to six minutes. The Speaker could be harder on time-wasting and on irrelevant points of order and other interruptions. If PMBs were dealt with properly, then MPs would then be more likely to attend and vote; and more likely to reflect the views and priorities of their constituents, not only their own priorities (or prejudices).

These were some of the proposals I set out in a report on

'The Case for Parliamentary Reform' which I published in November 2010. I concentrated on practical issues, including reform of working hours to encourage more people with caring responsibilities to become MPs; more transparency on the selection of those who can speak in a debate; and a systematic overhaul of parliamentary language to make it more accessible to the public. My intention was to bring them together and give them some urgency, taking advantage of new evidence I had collected and the fresh perspectives of the new intake of MPs.

The Speaker, John Bercow, was supportive of several of the proposals. The media, too, was surprisingly interested, given the dry subject-matter and the recent revelations about MP expenses: setting a limit on PMB debates could hardly compete with moats, duck-houses and pornographic films. But when the BBC came to talk to me about the report, it so happened – truly not my work – that there was a vote in the middle of the interview. The journalist gamely ran alongside me as we jogged towards the lobby, bells clanging in the background, and the soundtrack must have given the listeners of Radio 4 more of an impression of the ludicrous nature of the way we run our national affairs than any number of sound-bites I might have dreamt up.

I was glad to be part of the reform process, and to be connected with other like-minded MPs from all parties, for example in the Parliament First group, headed up by Labour's former Environment Minister Michael Meacher. It also helped show that the Speaker was not pursuing change for the sake of it, but responding to real issues and the concerns of a sizeable segment – perhaps now even a majority – of MPs. Bercow was on the receiving end of a hard-edged campaign mounted mainly by reactionary Conservative members who were said to feel aggrieved that he had 'betrayed his Conservative roots' but perhaps simply didn't like what he was doing. If anything, this intensified as time went by; and he found those opposed to his changes to procedures were allied with those who were against his attempts to modernize the way the parliamentary estate and services were run – coming to a head over the appointment of an Australian woman (the horror of it) as the next Clerk (in effect, the chief executive of Parliament).

A Speaker can't be above criticism. I had found some of John Bercow's decisions exasperating, particularly in blocking more radical amendments in favour of Labour's more mainstream alternatives such as those on Iraq, which were often hard to tell apart from the Conservative texts they were supposed to be changing. But he has been a force for good in bringing in some useful reforms and in making the existing procedures work a little more fairly and sensibly. You can at least now carry your baby with you through the lobbies, though the ban on breastfeeding in the chamber remains. One of the many Westminster bars has been replaced by a nursery. Backbenchers have a little more say over the time allocated for debates. Ministers are now more frequently summoned to answer urgent questions of the House. And he has resisted those wanting to turn the clock back on MPs' expenses.

Even his manner has helped keep up the morale of those who want change. I have seen him struggle to keep a straight face during a particularly ludicrous speech, and somehow the idea that the Speaker could see the absurdity of what was taking place was reassuring: an acknowledgement that we live in a looking-glass Parliament. This approach may not have won him many friends among the old guard; but they were never likely to back his vision of opening up Parliament to greater scrutiny and efficiency, and making it more responsive to the public. But perhaps because he was fighting a war of attrition with those against change, his reforms have sometimes lacked ambition against the scale of the challenge of rebuilding public trust. Some of the absurdities of Parliament do not matter that much. It may be ridiculous that MPs cannot resign, and instead must apply for the post of Crown Steward and Bailiff of the three Chiltern Hundreds of Stoke, Desborough and Burnham, which as a paid Office of the

Crown means immediate disqualification from sitting as a MP; but the only harm it does is to add to the general bafflement and alienation that many people feel towards the institution. But other things matter a great deal.

Although electronic voting has won some support, we could take it much further. MPs already have many of the documents they need, such as those for select committees, available electronically on an iPad, so there's less need to carry bundles of papers around. If this were extended to all debates and legislation, and Parliament becomes paper-free, it becomes mobile too. There's no need for it always to meet in the Palace of Westminster. In years gone by, Parliament might assemble in Oxford, York, Bristol or Winchester. In the future, if the will were there, Parliament could meet in a theatre, or conference centre, or sports hall: anywhere that got MPs out of Westminster and back into their own communities. They wouldn't need to bring their researchers and advisers with them, so they'd have more time to talk to local people and hear their concerns. Just think how much we'd all gain if MPs were reconnected in this way. Less reliance on statistics and reports about crime or housing or fisheries; more on MPs seeing for themselves and hearing from the people directly affected. The cost would be a fraction of the annual budget of Parliament, or of the huge redevelopment planned to start in 2020. We could still keep Parliament as a base; but we would no longer be trapped within its crumbling walls.

Redeveloping Parliament is also a chance to reshape the way we govern ourselves. In the Netherlands, the new Parliament building has glass walls so that the public can look in on their representatives – a symbolic way of reminding their MPs why they are there and who they are supposed to serve. In Berlin, the rebuilt German Parliament goes further: there, citizens look down on the proceedings from a high walkway. Parliament doesn't have to be a divisive, raucous place. A new building could foster more thoughtful exchanges, more collaborative working;

and give people much more of a sense of participation. The existing chamber is full of history: it could be kept as part of a museum of democracy, or used for occasional debates, much like Westminster Hall is now. But moving Parliament out of the current precincts of the Palace – perhaps out of London altogether – could help to support a parallel change in the balance of power between London and its elites and the rest of Britain. The drive for Scottish independence has shown once more that the current concentration of power in one part of the country is unhealthy. So too has our over-reliance on financial services within the economy, the rise in anti-metropolitan feeling that has boosted UKIP, and the way structural unemployment and other problems facing parts of the North of England in particular simply do not figure in the priorities set from London.

As well as reshaping our physical estate, we should find new ways for Parliament to engage with citizens through digital democracy, which could include more online debates and question-and-answer sessions, a higher status for online petitions (it cannot be right that when over a hundred thousand people sign an e-petition and win a debate in Parliament, the government can simply ignore the result), and presenting Hansard, the TV feed and other content so that the media and citizen journalists can find new ways to show what happens in Parliament to their audiences. The Speaker's Commission on Digital Democracy has mapped out some of the opportunities, but even a reforming Speaker can only go so far; and if the bulk of MPs are either resistant or do not think it is a priority, then progress will remain slow. We have already seen this with the right of recall: the idea that each Member should be subject to recall (in effect, being forced to stand down or to run again in a by-election) if they lose the confidence of a sizeable section of their electorate, for example because of unacceptable behaviour. We have seen plenty of examples of MPs who have betrayed the trust put in them, by everything from fiddling expenses to drunken brawls, yet thought they could carry on representing their constituents. The system relies on them 'doing the decent thing' and resigning; but not all MPs are 'decent'. And while the right of recall has wide public support, and the apparent backing of the main parties, it is yet to be implemented. Instead, the government has proposed that the recall of one of their colleagues would only be allowed in very narrow circumstances: if the House of Commons authorities suspend them for at least twenty-one sitting days, or if they are convicted of an offence and receive a sentence of twelve months or more. That defeats the whole point of the process, which is to give the public the ultimate power of censure over their elected representatives: and instead of reassuring us that Parliament can reform itself, risks making people's disillusionment all the more complete. When an amendment was tabled to restore the right of voters to decide whether, and on what issue, to recall an MP, the Labour front bench were noticeable by their absence. But this was also a failure of Parliament as a whole. As Zac Goldsmith, who had tabled the amendment, said: 'Do we trust our voters to hold us to account or not?' The answer, it seems, is not. And rebuilding public trust is now harder than ever.

One measure of this challenge is the annual survey of public perceptions of Parliament commissioned by the Hansard Society – an independent charity that champions parliamentary democracy around the world. Over the last ten years or so it has charted the decline of Parliament's standing with the British public in forensic detail, through surveys of public opinion and through dispassionate analysis. It leaves little to doubt. People think MPs are in it for themselves, cannot be trusted, and do not understand ordinary people. Belief that our parliamentary system is 'fit for purpose' has fallen, so that only a quarter of people in Britain think it works well or only needs minor improvements, and three-quarters think it needs a lot or a great deal of improvement. Perhaps most telling is a map showing satisfaction with the current political system being strongest in the south-east of England and lowest in Scotland. More widely, the Hansard analysis supports the feeling that the further you are from London, the less trusted and relevant Parliament seems, and the less it works in your favour. We can hardly expect to continue as a united country unless these feelings are remedied.

There is a further reason for radical change in the way Parliament works and where it meets. The culture of Parliament is as decrepit and in need of serious renovation as the physical buildings, with their crumbling foundations and pockets of asbestos. The expenses scandal showed how MPs considered themselves to be entitled to take freebies and benefits that they would never have dreamed allowing the rest of us. The mindset of someone who could order the latest 42-inch flat-screen television and charge it to the taxpayer, while at the same time voting for curbing benefit payments to those in dire poverty, is indicative of an organization dangerously out of touch. When MPs attempted to justify these actions, they had two main defences. The first was that they were underpaid: but they are already paid two or (in the case of ministers) three or four times what everyone else earns on average. Even then, thinking you are underpaid is not a reason to make unjustified claims or play the system to make tens of thousands of pounds in mortgage payments. The second excuse was that 'they were all at it': in other words, that new MPs saw that their colleagues were making these claims and decided to help themselves as well. Again, this is unjustifiable: surely the one attribute you would expect in an MP is that they should be able to make their own minds up, not simply follow the herd.

The way some MPs have exploited the system of internships is an example of this debased political culture. Internships should not be a system to extract unpaid labour from young people anxious to gain the experience they need to get their first job. The rules on paying internships and on the National Minimum Wage are clear; but a number of MPs have broken these rules, and then been surprised that anyone should challenge them. This sense of being above the law is still widespread. They also tolerate a culture of bullying and sexism that would not be acceptable in any other organization, particularly one funded by the taxpayer.

Changing the culture of Parliament will take time. It may also be a race between the new MPs who see what has to change, and those same MPs being absorbed into the existing culture. I've met many people whose judgement or fundamental decency seems to have been undermined by the corroding atmosphere of modern politics. In choosing the following example, I wouldn't name the minister involved because it wasn't about them as an individual, but the system they work within. It came about because one of my constituents, who worked in IT and had a lot of experience of ways people with disabilities could be given the right support to pursue their careers, suggested that he come and meet the minister and pass on what he had learned. On the day, we met up at the Department for Work and Pensions, where there is a cafe in the foyer. I was concerned by how anxious my constituent was. It wasn't only the extra stress of adjusting to a new setting that can affect anyone with severe disabilities – he was in a wheelchair, with a full-time assistant, and communicated using 'eyechat' (the kind of computer-generated communication tool you use your eyes to direct). It was the importance of the meeting itself. This was his chance to speak directly to one of a handful of people in Britain who actually decide how people with disabilities should be treated. If he could convince the minister to think again about some of the excesses of the 'back to work' scheme, it could improve the lives of hundreds, perhaps thousands, of people. But he knew he only had one shot at it.

In the event, he need not have worried. Even before he said his piece, the minister had arranged a photo-call for us all: 'one for the newsletter' was the cheery cry, as if this evidence of being seen to listen was the real reason for agreeing to the meeting. Even more bizarrely we were asked to pose within an ornate but empty picture frame. With this out of the way, the minister seemed to listen attentively enough, but it was hard not to feel that my constituent was being managed. And when afterwards I wrote on his behalf to follow up on the points he'd made, all we got back was an official reply listing all the same old stuff: schemes that simply didn't provide the kind of support that my constituent knew would work.

The corrupting influence can also affect the hundreds of researchers and interns who pass through Westminster in the course of a parliamentary term. These will often become the decision-makers and thought-leaders of the future as they pursue their careers in the media, public affairs or politics: and Parliament provides just the wrong kind of education in cynicism and deceit. On one occasion, I had come from a debate on the impact of the Bedroom Tax on vulnerable families and overheard two young researchers talking dismissively about MPs 'giving their bleeding heart charity cases'. If people working in Parliament can feel that way about the poor and vulnerable, it's hard to see how we can move towards a more compassionate and less punishing approach to poverty and inequality.

The culture of Parliament and politics also needs to change for the sake of those within it. That makes it all the more important to change who gets elected to Parliament.

15

A Valuable Prize:
How the Mechanics of Elections Push Voters Out of the Picture

'The world continues to offer glittering prizes to those who have stout hearts and sharp swords.'

F. E. Smith

Some odd people have been elected to Parliament down the years. Some who have served a term of five years without ever speaking. Others who have been drunk and disorderly, who started fights and had to be ejected from the chamber – pioneers of antisocial behaviour long before the term was coined. Even in the last hundred years, MPs have taken bribes, sold honours, been imprisoned for treasonable dealings with the Nazis, and faked their own death by leaving their clothes on a beach. You might think that being elected to Parliament is not such a big deal. But there is a catch: first you have to join one of the established political parties.

For decades, the hard political truth was that no one was ever elected to Parliament in England in a straight fight with the three main parties. For most of that time English politics was a duopoly: you were Labour or Conservative. The Liberals hung on to a few precarious seats in what London commentators dismissed as the Celtic Fringe, but otherwise neither minor parties such as the

Communists, the Referendum Party or the National Front, nor Independent candidates, had broken through. In 1997, Martin Bell won in Tatton as an Independent, and in 2001 Dr Richard Taylor won in the Wyre Valley, but in both cases one of the main parties had stood down to give them a clear run at the sitting MP. George Galloway won Bow in 2005, but he had already served as an MP: and Respect's most talented leader, Salma Yaqoob, came frustratingly close to being elected in 2005 and 2010, but could not manage the additional few percentage points to defeat the Labour incumbent.

So for most people who want to represent their community, or to have a political career with the chance to wield power as a minister, the choice has always been Conservative, Labour or, perhaps, the Liberal Democrats. And the goal is a safe seat: that is, the nomination to represent your chosen party in a constituency where there is a good prospect of being elected and, most importantly, re-elected after that. No one wants to be a single-term MP.

Of the 650 seats in Parliament, only around 100 at most are likely to change hands in any one election. There are some seats that have not changed for decades, and perhaps never will: Beaconsfield, Mole Valley, Windsor or Hertsmere for the Conservatives; Bootle, Glenrothes, East Ham and Jarrow for Labour. Seats where, barring a political earthquake, the sitting MP will be returned; where, in the old saying, they don't count the votes, but weigh them.

In these seats, it is not the electorate who choose the MP, but the selectorate: that is, those in the local party who choose the candidate, who is bound to go on to become the elected MP. Normally this means the members of the constituency party, though naturally the longest-serving and hardest-working usually have a particular influence; as do the elected officers – the chair, treasurer, and so on – and the election agent. It's not always clear what they want (though we can work out from the statistics of who is selected that they are generally less keen on women, on people in their twenties or over fifty, on people from minority backgrounds or with disabilities, or people whose job involves working with their hands). One plus, though, is wealth. The more that you can devote yourself to campaigning in the years running up to the election, the better the chance of winning: so candidates who have enough wealth not to have to worry about paying the bills tend to go down well. Another is connections: these might be local, through hard work on councils, voluntary bodies, and so on; or national, such as having worked for an MP.

As selection for a winnable seat is a very valuable prize, it's common for the party leaders to influence the outcome, perhaps using it to reward loyal service as a special adviser. But it increasingly comes with a price tag attached. Prospective parliamentary candidates are expected to campaign hard for months or even years in the run-up to the election itself, and this is hard to combine with a full-time job. This is why having already made money, or having wealth in the family, can be an advantage in proving to constituency parties that you can put in the hours. It's one reason why the background of MPs is becoming more narrow, and less egalitarian: fewer coming to Parliament with a background in manual labour, for example, and more who have worked in politics as special advisers or lobbyists. The widespread belief among MPs that £67,000 a year is not a living wage shows how the selection process is biased towards the rich.

Once selected, our aspirant MP still has work to do. However safe the seat, they will be expected to keep the local party alive and busy, if only to avoid the internal disputes that can arise in a moribund party with too little to do. They will also be expected to campaign in neighbouring seats where there is a real battle to be fought. These local campaigns form the other side of politics, away from the TV channels and national debates, the *Newsnight* studios and the massive advertising budgets of the main parties. Parliamentary seats can still be won and lost by going and talking to people. But with something like 70,000 voters in each constituency, that's no small task.

The mainstream political parties have over generations developed ways of tackling this. The main one is called the canvass, and involves knocking on doors to find out which candidate the residents plan to vote for. Then comes some surprising calculation. They don't then attempt to persuade those backing one of the other parties to change their minds: this would take too long, and probably not show much of a return. Nor do they waste time with their own voters: they can be taken for granted. They certainly don't spend time with those who don't intend to vote at all: you'd have all the work of persuading them to vote; and then they might end up voting for the other lot. And so by far the greatest effort goes on targeting those who have not yet made up their minds: the floating voter.

(If you're one of those people who really don't like being canvassed, you might think you've spotted the answer: say you never, ever, vote, and they won't bother you again. Unfortunately, political parties are given lists of voters by their local authority, and these mark whether or not each resident voted at the last election or not – though not, of course, who they voted for – so the canvasser will know you are not telling the truth.)

As well as trying to swing the floating voters their way, the parties also want to identify their own supporters so they can make sure that they are properly registered and actually go to the polls on election day. This is what they call 'getting out the vote', and also explains why there will be people from each party standing outside the polling booth, asking if they can look at your polling card, ticking your number off on a clipboard, and then using that to eliminate all their known supporters who have voted. Later in the day, they can chase up their voters who have yet to vote, and persuade them to make the trip down to the polling station.

An inspiring candidate, a well-organized local machine, and committed activists can make a difference to the result. Many seats buck the national trend in general elections, reflecting local issues, campaigns and candidates. But one factor connects the local and the national in politics: the way the main parties conspire to keep out any new challengers.

It will always be a problem that the rules of politics are written by those who are in charge. The Electoral Commission, for example, can make recommendations: but if the main parties don't want to follow them, they will not happen. The Commission, like the media regulator Ofcom, which oversees political coverage in the broadcast media, is independent: but both are funded by government, their members are appointed by government; and they live and breathe the same political atmosphere, with members drawn firmly from the mainstream. The typical board member is a middle-aged, white male – just like politicians themselves. A few years back, when the Electoral Commission was perhaps becoming a little too independent, it was given three new 'political' commissioners: one from each of the main parties.

One 'barrier to entry' is the deposit that each candidate has to put up to stand in a national election. For the general election, this is £500 per candidate; and unless you get 5 per cent of the vote in that constituency, the deposit is not returned. So for the main parties, who rarely lose their deposits, this is not an issue. But for smaller parties, the cost of fielding candidates across the whole country becomes prohibitive. A new party might want to put up 650 candidates, but would face the risk of losing £325,000 in deposits. This is a huge deterrent, given how hard it is to raise funds from the general public or from your membership. (Of course, if you have rich backers – as with UKIP – the problem goes away.) One alternative is to concentrate your resources on a few seats: but then, the main parties reject you as a fringe grouping; and the broadcasters will not give you a slot for a party political broadcast – perhaps your one chance to reach a wide audience. Marginalization becomes self-fulfilling.

The Electoral Commission have recommended that the deposit system be scrapped and replaced by something more effective, such as requiring a higher number of signatures endorsing each candidate, which would discourage 'frivolous' candidates without excluding genuine political parties. MPs – surprise, surprise – decided to stick with the current system; and the Electoral Commission can only advise, not insist.

The broadcasters also contribute to this 'closed shop' by favouring the existing parties in the airtime they are given and in the assumption that their discourse – that is, what traditional politicians think is important and how they talk about these issues – is what 'really matters'. Journalists and editors love to cover politics as a 'two-horse race': who is ahead in the polls, who is up and down, and so on. A new party might be interesting if it fits into that narrative – for example, when UKIP had only very modest support it was still given a lot of coverage because of the theory that even a small proportion of voters switching away from the Conservatives in marginal seats could cost them the election.

Journalists have prejudices and preconceptions just like the rest of us. (I gave the example in chapter 11 of how much of the media seem to think that the military is serious and peace campaigners are fringe, even though the military themselves acknowledge that winning the peace is what really matters.) To journalists, what happens in London often matters more than events in the rest of the country (London being where most journalists live). Their coverage often suggests that only big business can create jobs (small firms don't put out press releases or brief journalists on the 'new jobs' created by an out-of-town shopping development). It also suggests that what happens to house prices is more interesting than anything in the social or private rented sector (perhaps because few journalists rent their homes). And so political coverage concentrates on the issues in the 'middle': just like the political parties, the priorities of people in marginal seats get more media attention than fishing in the West Country or upland farming in Cumbria.

A further source of inertia is party funding. The individuals and organizations who make the largest political donations often want or expect something in return, and they will therefore seek to influence those with power or who are part of the political elite. Those donations help the established parties to dominate election campaigns: not through the weight of their arguments but the weight of the number of leaflets they shove through people's doors, and the chance they have to bulk-buy every poster site or newspaper advert.

It all adds up to a cartel in which the three main parties conspire to write the rules to exclude new voices. And just as business monopolies are bad because they stifle innovation and diversity, so this political monopoly leaves many people disenfranchised.

All this made the achievement of the Brighton and Hove Green Party in the General Election of 2005, raising their share of the vote to 22 per cent, all the more impressive. Given that we were then usually at around 3 per cent nationally in the polls, it showed how well they had reached out to people who wouldn't think of themselves as 'Greens', but shared our way of seeing the world, and thought that our policies should be given a try. This increase was even more extraordinary because the three main parties – all active in Brighton – missed no opportunity to claim that a Green vote was a wasted vote, and would let in 'the others' (whether that was the Tories, Labour or the Lib Dems depended on which leaflet had been pushed through your letter-box). This wasn't tactical voting – putting up with second-best to avoid getting something you really don't like. This was people voting with their convictions: believing that you should not compromise, but should vote for what you believe in.

We had an excellent candidate, Keith Taylor, and a lot of extremely able and dedicated activists who had worked over years, and against all the odds, to gain the trust of local people and win seat after seat on the local council. Pete West was the first, elected in St Peter's and North Laine ward in 1996, and he was joined in 1999 by Rik Child and by Keith. By showing we could beat the other parties at a local level, the idea of winning in the Westminster election became a little less far-fetched. And we had shown they could get things done. Local residents could see that Green activists were not in it for the money or the glory or to kick-start their political careers, but because they believed in something and wanted to serve their community. And they had shown a steely side in fighting for the best interests of the city.

But though 22 per cent was an outstanding performance, it was still a long way from winning. And, in the same way that the more you compress a spring, the more effort it takes, so winning the extra votes would get harder and harder. For the Green Party in Brighton and Hove, the nightmare was that they would come agonizingly close, but miss out – perhaps by only a few hundred votes.

Here, the strength of a strong local candidate can also be their weakness. The more you are rooted in your own community, the less likely it is that you will have a national profile. In any constituency, there are plenty of residents who don't have much contact with local politics. For one thing, they often don't vote. Typical turnout in a national election is around 60 per cent to 70 per cent, while for local elections this can drop to 30 per cent or less. If you don't have children at a local school, or don't make much use of services such as home help or residential care, or libraries, or aren't caught up in a planning dispute or local campaign, then local politics can simply pass you by. And for those who vote nationally but not locally, it is national issues – and also national personalities – that count. It's easy to be a good local candidate for the Conservatives and Labour, knowing that your party has plenty of national profile. But nationally the Greens didn't get anything like the same airtime as the others

– part of the reason why electing a Green MP would make such a difference. But for now, to win in Brighton, the argument went, would need a candidate who would not only engage with those who had an interest in local politics, but who also had a national profile.

When I was asked by some of the local activists to consider standing in Brighton, it was one of the hardest decisions of my life – not least because I knew how difficult it would be for Keith, who is a friend and someone I'd worked with closely for many years. I knew Brighton well – as an MEP, my constituency covered the city – and knew that if we moved home we would soon settle in, but I wondered if putting my family through that kind of wrench was too much to ask. We talked about it a good deal. I could see the opportunities: the chance to have a Green voice in Parliament at last, to be able to hold the government to account on its environmental record, to promote urgent action on everything from energy policy to inequality – as well as the chance to demonstrate that Green politicians work enormously hard for their constituents. At the same time, the campaign would mean even more time away from my family, and I think part of me wanted them to persuade me not to do it. But they were immensely supportive, and in the end, after many sleepless nights, I decided to stand.

I knew from the start that winning would need a huge effort over many months: putting out community newsletters to show what we were doing; constituency work, listening to people's concerns and trying to help solve their problems; and lots and lots of face-to-face conversations, on doorsteps, to introduce ourselves and explain why we deserved their trust.

Just like the other parties, we planned to canvass the entire constituency. But if canvassing is only about harvesting votes, it loses its reality. Every conversation has to be two-way: you want to say to people why you'd like their support, but you also have to listen to their own concerns, understand what they think matters. And people were already disenchanted enough with politics without our adding to it.

The crude reality of modern politics is that, to the main parties, most people's votes don't count, because they live in constituencies where the result is a foregone conclusion, or because they don't usually vote, or have fairly fixed convictions. In their unguarded moments, the strategists for the main parties will admit that they only really care about floating voters in marginal constituencies – perhaps 500,000 out of the total electorate of 46 million.

This makes the way we vote an essential issue in reforming politics. The principles of a reformed voting system are clear. It should ensure every vote counts, so it is the electorate, not the selectorate, who matter most. It should allow new parties to emerge, and give independents a chance of being elected. It should not leave MPs entirely at the mercy of their party leadership, because this limits them in taking their own line over what they believe their constituents want. It should ensure some link between the MP and his or her constituency, including a strong dose of accountability. And it should mean that the share of seats in Parliament reflects the broad views of the electorate. In my view, a system does not have to be 'purely' proportional. Proportionality should be one of the main considerations, but others, such as the constituency link and the openness to independents, matter too. There are voting systems that can do both: what we need is not so much Proportional Representation as Fair Representation, of which proportionality is part; but for now, PR is the label we are stuck with for electoral reform.

One of the problems with voting reform is that there is too much choice – too many systems that could provide a fairer outcome – and many people are understandably left cold by talk of transferable votes and second choices and D'Hondt systems. It's much less of a problem when people actually use these alternatives. Anyone who has cast a vote in the European

Parliament elections, or in national elections in Scotland, Wales or Northern Ireland, has mastered one or other form of Proportional Representation. But when it came to the coalition's pledge for a referendum on the voting system, it created an opening for those determined that there should be no change. After all, the best way to stop people demanding a truly fair voting system was not to ask them in the first place.

The Coalition Agreement signed by the Conservatives and Liberal Democrats in May 2010 pledged a referendum on voting reform. But the only option they planned to offer was the Alternative Vote. Without getting tied up in the technicalities, you rank the candidates in order of preference. If no candidate ends up with an outright majority on the first round, the candidate with the least votes is eliminated and his or her votes are redistributed to whoever was ranked second on each vote. This carries on until one candidate has more than 50 per cent of all the votes cast: they are the winner. This system has advantages and drawbacks, but it is not a proportional system: in fact, you can end up with an even more disproportionate outcome than under First Past the Post. But more importantly, it is only one option. In Britain, we already use a range of voting systems, including the Additional Member and the Single Transferable Vote. Again, they have pros and cons. Even with First Past the Post, it makes a difference if you have single members per constituency (as with Westminster elections) or multiple members (as with local elections in England, where you can have two or three councillors elected in each ward, which can be more proportional than single constituencies).

So we ended up in a bizarre situation. The government was holding a referendum on AV, even though the Conservatives wanted to stick with FPTP and the Liberal Democrat manifesto called for the introduction of the Single Transferable Vote. Meanwhile Labour, who did pledge to introduce AV in their manifesto, did not back the 'Yes' campaign in the referendum, leaving it up to individual MPs to decide which side to support.

(The majority backed 'No'.) And worst of all, although the only reason for having a referendum was to give the people a voice, the people were given no choice on which system they preferred.

In response, I tabled an amendment to the Referendum Bill with support from right across the political spectrum, from those I'd worked with before, such as Austin Mitchell, to some I had hardly spoken to until the issue came up. Chief among these was Douglas Carswell, the (then) Conservative Member for Clacton. We didn't see eye to eye on much else politically, but Douglas had consistently fought for genuine democratic reform and I was more than happy that we should collaborate on this issue. It involved some clandestine conversations in the Westminster corridors, and a few raised eyebrows as other Members wondered what on earth we could be conspiring about; but the result was an amendment that any supporter of electoral reform – or, just as importantly, any MP who actually believed in letting the public have their say – would want to support.

It was based on a referendum held in New Zealand. There, the first question had been whether to stay with the existing FPTP system or switch to a new system (85 per cent of voters opted for change). The second question was, if there was a change, which system should replace FPTP (and the Mixed Member Proportional system was chosen by 70 per cent of voters). It showed that voters could cope with the idea of selecting from a list of options: something that the leaders of the main parties seemed to think was beyond the wit of British voters.

When it came to the debate, I was supported with interventions from Labour, Conservative and SNP members. The government response was revealing. At first, Mark Harper claimed that he agreed with me that '... the public, not the politicians, should choose the voting system. We are going to give that choice to the public ...' Quizzed on what he meant by that, he came out with a truly bizarre argument:

The Honourable Lady has chosen a selection of things to put in front of the public in her amendment; it is just a different choice from that proposed by the government. It is no more or less the choice of the public.

He then went on to claim that if you were going to give the public a real choice, you would have a hundred options on the ballot paper (a really fatuous debating-point). When Angus MacNeil of the SNP reminded him that the four options in my amendment were those already in use in different elections in the UK, he changed tack again:

The Honourable Lady and those on the government benches are doing the same thing; we are putting to the House amendments that we think will get support. If she wishes to test hers and we test ours, we will see which of us has made the right judgement about which will get the support of the majority of Members in this House.

Having no other arguments, Mark Harper revealed the foundation of his position: whatever the strength of the arguments, he would have more MPs whipped through his lobby that we would, and would therefore defeat the amendment. This was the end of the so-called debate. Not Parliament's finest hour.

The referendum campaign itself never came alive in the public's mind: there was not the same passion and commitment, the sense of people reconnecting with politics, that we saw later with the Scottish referendum: perhaps because no one really believed that AV would make a difference to people's lives or help clean up politics in the way that PR could. The Green Party had voted to support the Yes campaign on the basis that the AV system was slightly less bad than First Past the Post, and there would not be a 'none of the above' option on the ballot paper. I spoke at several Yes events, alongside Ed Miliband and others, and it was good to find that we could work effectively across party boundaries. This wasn't just the friendliness you experience behind the scenes in the TV studios, where politicians, either from courtesy or solidarity, usually make an effort to be pleasant to their opponents. They were genuinely pleased that the Greens were helping them present this complex and arcane voting procedure, particularly to a younger and more progressive audience. As one of them said, we sprinkled a bit of freshness onto what otherwise looked a rather tired campaign. But there was never any great optimism that the Yes campaign would win. The referendum brought out all the problems and fears of change; and the benefits of change were just not great enough to overcome people's inertia.

Because my amendment was rejected, we have still not been given a choice on fair representation. The referendum did not settle it for good (and had the Conservative and Labour supporters of FPTP really trusted the people, they would have allowed my amendment to go through). And the underlying need for change remains. Take local government, where the FPTP system means that all the seats on a council can be taken by one party, when that party has much less than 50 per cent of the votes cast (which with low turnout can mean they have the active backing of only 10–15 per cent of residents). Without opposition councillors, local government simply cannot function. The scrutiny committees that are supposed to hold the executive to account depend on having dissenting voices: but in places such as Newham (all 60 seats held by Labour) and Knowsley (all 63 seats held by Labour) all the councillors are in the same party as the executive they are suppose to oversee. It is asking a lot of individual councillors to make this work; and in places such as Rotherham we've seen what happens where scrutiny breaks down.

Fairer voting systems also give more people the chance to contribute, both to local parties and independents. Not everyone who has something to offer their community also wants to align themselves to a specific party. Some of those who now sit as non-aligned 'crossbenchers' in the House of Lords, often bringing a wealth of experience and good judgement, would make excellent Independent MPs, but the current voting system excludes them from a realistic chance of being elected.

However agreeable some Members may find Parliament as a club, it desperately needs to be opened up so that every part of our country has a chance to contribute to debate and decision-making. And this approach would make politics less confrontational too. The more that politicians are willing to work with each other, issue by issue, the better. This is particularly important if the progressive forces in politics, by which I mean those promoting policies such as the redistribution of wealth and greater equality, are to work more closely together. Our electoral system is a barrier to cooperation between progressives, whether they are in the Lib Dems, the Nationalist parties, the Greens or Labour. Electoral reform would not only increase the prospect of a renewal of our political system, it would also help progressive politics become a more powerful force for good. With the Labour Party in its current state, that cannot come soon enough.

16

The Progressives:
How Those Who Want a Fairer Society Could Work Together

Deeds not words.

Slogan of the Women's Social and
Political Union

The lion's den: Labour Party Conference. It's an odd feeling to be surrounded by thousands of Labour activists, and by the legions of lobbyists and public affairs professionals who are conspicuous by their absence at my own party conferences. I can see people giving me a second glance, patently wondering what I am doing there; and I begin to feel like a spy. But I am here by rights: invited to speak at a Compass debate on pluralism in politics.

I was delighted to receive the invitation. I had something I wanted to say about working with Labour; and it was also a positive sign that Compass, a leading think tank with deep roots in Labour, was prepared to ask a Green along to such an event. Neal Lawson, its chair, was trying to make the party less inward-looking. In his view, Labour was essential to the creation of a Good Society; but it could never create it alone. That was why he and Compass wanted to reach out to alternative voices; and why I was there.

Thinking about what I wanted to say became a wider

reflection on Labour, and what it meant to me. You can't be involved in politics – particularly progressive politics – without having complex feelings about Labour. Its history is rooted in the same streams of radicalism and challenge to the established order stretching back to people like William Morris and Octavia Hill that still inspire the Green movement today. It has some immense achievements to its credit: not least the National Health Service. And it remains the vehicle by which many millions of people do what they can – as voters, as activists, as politicians – to serve their communities and to try to make our country a better place to live.

Yet there is also a history of betrayal, of failure and of loss of nerve. Time and again – 1931, 1950, 1997, 2008 – Labour have been in power, yet been seduced by the bankers and financiers, or backed down in the face of their threats. Where communities and whole cities have pinned their faith in Labour, it has led to cronyism and corruption and the local equivalent of one-party states. And when Margaret Thatcher challenged the post-war social democratic consensus, New Labour responded by adopting her agenda wholesale: competition, privatization, and the dominance of market forces. Tony Blair gave Labour three victories; but hollowed out those victories through the betrayal of Labour's true values.

Labour also failed to come to terms with the new progressive thinking that emerged in the 1960s, inspired by feminism, social reform and environmentalism. In a way, Labour was a victim of its own success. In 1945, the creation of the welfare state had benefited union members and the wider public alike. But by the 1960s, their interests were starting to diverge. Inflation was on the rise; but while unions could protect their members by negotiating pay increases, others were not so lucky. Inflation hurt those on low and fixed incomes the most: those in low-paid, non-unionized jobs such as the garment trade; those reliant on support from the state, including mothers receiving

Child Benefit; and most of all, pensioners. The efforts of the union leaders to protect their members were portrayed in the media as greed, and this claim resonated with those who didn't have the power to turn off the lights or bring the country to a halt.

That the 'brothers' were almost all men, and represented mainly men in sectors such as engineering, coal-mining and transport, was no coincidence; nor was the fact that those who lost out the most from their actions tended to be women. Many in Labour and in the unions could not grasp why women would want or need rights of their own. In their world, the husband would go out to work while their wives cooked and cleaned and looked after the children. If the unions could get more money for the men, that meant more money put on the table for 'their' women – and so everyone won. Many could not see, or chose not to see, that this unequal relationship had to change; or that widows, pensioners, single mothers or wives whose husbands kept the extra cash for themselves would see their income eroded by inflation. It wasn't that what the unions were doing was wrong. Far from it. The unions were and remain an essential part of the protection that individuals need in the workplace, and we all benefit from their campaigning work, whether or not we are members. It was that they did not go far enough in embracing the feminist agenda.

Instead of acting as the shock troops of reform, some of the 'old guard' of union leaders played a more reactionary role, opposing equality for women in the workplace, just as they dragged their feet on giving equal opportunities to those from ethnic minorities. They argued that it was right for women to be paid less than men for the same work, because men would have a family to keep and women would not (and helped maintain this by ensuring that women who married or had children had to give up their jobs).

Labour's slowness in responding to these changes in the

wider world had many consequences. One was that it opened up political space for the Liberals. It was they, not Labour, who made the running in the 1960s and 1970s on social reform and equality, despite only having a handful of MPs. Legalizing abortion; decriminalizing homosexuality; sex and race equality; all were promoted by Liberals or by future Liberals such as Roy Jenkins and Anthony Lester.

Another consequence was that reforms to improve the position of women in society were both slow and inadequate. Even Tony Blair's administration, which saw more women than ever in Parliament, did not complete the job of female emancipation, as I have explored in chapter 12. The gap in earnings between men and women remains painfully wide; boardrooms remain painfully male (and white and public school-educated); and the chance to put right the legacy of discrimination was ducked. After thirteen years of Labour government, there are still thousands of women who do not receive the pension they deserve because of the way they were discriminated against during their working lives.

Much the same happened with the other great ideological shift of the second half of the twentieth century: environmentalism. When Labour was founded, pollution was a local problem for workers and communities blighted by the emissions from the mines and factories around which they lived and where they worked. As well as legislation to control industrial pollution, Labour believed in the need for the workers to have access to the countryside, and brought in the first National Parks alongside the rest of the welfare state. But they still relied on economic growth as the key to the betterment of those they represented. Growth put money in the pockets of the workers. And growth also made political and social reform that much easier. If there were a larger cake to carve up, then it would be easier to persuade others to take a smaller proportion, because they would still be getting more on their plate than before. So the long decades of economic growth after the Second World War apparently benefited everyone: people could feel better off without the need to challenge the power of those at the top.

But that economic growth was built on sand: figuratively, because it depended on exploiting resources that were finite; and literally, because the most fundamental of all those resources lay beneath the sands of Arabia. Oil was vital to Western economies and so the West used every neocolonial trick to keep the price down. But from the 1970s, the oil producers turned the tables and began to exploit their power. Meanwhile other signs that the planet was reaching the limits of its ability to sustain the pressure of economic growth were emerging. Loss of habitats, species threatened by pesticides and industrial residues, overfishing, desertification, and the build-up of poisonous chemicals and radioactive substances in water, soil and air. And in every country, those threats bore most heavily on the poor and the vulnerable.

Labour's reaction was to ignore those problems that arose from industry. The unions' most persuasive argument was that if Britain legislated to reduce pollution, then the factories would be closed and production would start up somewhere else, without the same protections – meaning no benefit to the environment, but the loss of jobs and money. Even now, at Heathrow, Labour supports expansion, despite the harm this will do to local communities and to the global environment. Similarly, Labour's championing of nuclear power – against the wishes of many of its members – reflects the power of the engineering unions, representing the interests of their members. We need to be honest about these failings, even though they in no sense outweigh the hugely valuable overall contribution that unions make to civil society, such as the way the Public and Commercial Services Union, UNITE, the Fire Brigade Union and many others have worked to highlight the dangers of climate change and the opportunities to create a million green jobs.

The tension between radicalism and conservatism remains. In the Labour leadership campaign of 2010, Ed and David Miliband ran on similar platforms, which was unsurprising, and not just because of their shared upbringing: both served as special advisers, MPs and ministers under Blair and Brown. Ed was seen as marginally more radical; but the key difference was that David won more support from Labour Party members, and Ed from the unions. This renewed the sense – picked up avidly by some Tory MPs and right-wing papers whose own record on openness and democracy was patchy, to say the least – that the unions wielded unfair power within the Labour Party. Surely, they said, those same union leaders would expect something in return: was it right that one section of society should have such privileged influence over a party leader and potential prime minister? Of course, those same MPs and newspapers did not express the same concerns about the influence of the City or property speculators over the Tory leader.

Party funding is one of the most depressing aspects of our current political malaise. As we've seen, the Tories will not give up their big donors without ensuring Labour gives up the substantial support it receives from the unions. And this keeps politics out of the hands of ordinary people and in the hands of the donors and those they favour. Given that most of the money raised goes on intensive campaigning that is targeted in just a handful of constituencies and which no one would mind seeing the back of anyway, this failure is hard to justify.

The problem has become more acute as party democracy has declined. Labour members did not want to delay the intro-duction of controls on tobacco advertising in 1997, but this was a decision taken by Tony Blair, not by the membership. Once you have concentrated power in the hands of a small circle at the top of a party, then donors have someone they can cut a deal with. Contrast this with the Green Party. Our donors know that they cannot change policy, because every one of our policies is set by conference, where every member has an equal say, not by the party leaders. Nor could a donor expect a seat in the Lords in return for their gift: our nominations for the Lords are decided by a ballot of all the party members. So even with the current broken system of party funding, the incentive for 'cash for access' or for selling peerages could be ended if the main parties gave up their rights of patronage and gave power back to their members. Instead, big donors not only risk discrediting the political system; they also take power and influence away from ordinary members and from the voters.

To his credit, Ed Miliband inched towards some kind of reform. So too have some union leaders, who perhaps see they would have more influence if they were not so clearly tied to one party – just like the RSPB can campaign effectively for birds, whoever is in power. But even more fundamental would be reform of the voting system. In that way, every party would understand that it could be challenged and would work all the harder to reach out to the communities it seeks to serve and represent. Voting reform at national level has been knocked off the national agenda for now. But PR at local level offers a way to revitalize local democracy and political participation.

Despite this spotted record, Labour retains an armlock on progressive politics; one they are most unwilling to let go. Labour grew at the expense of its big brother of the nineteenth century, the Liberal Party, which nurtured and supported its younger sibling, including standing aside in favour of Labour candidates in working-class seats. If Labour remembers nothing else from its early days, it has remembered that lesson; and is ruthless in ensuring that no new party emerges on the left to rival its dominance. Many within Labour have long opposed any reform of the voting system because to do so invites the emergence of new parties. Many loathe the Liberal Democrats far more than they do the Conservatives, because the Lib Dems cannot be written off as toffs or bosses. Indeed, before they joined the coalition, the Lib Dems were often more progressive than Labour and could challenge Labour in its self-perceived heartlands: cities such as Sheffield and Liverpool. And Labour's hatred of the Scottish and Welsh nationalists is legendary. This more than any other factor scuppered any faint hope of an alternative to the Conservative–Lib Dem coalition in 2010. Labour simply could not stomach any talk of aligning themselves with the SNP.

The Greens have been on the receiving end of some of this venom. On one level it is 'hard-nosed politics'. Labour's motto seems to be that if you want to avoid a potential challenger taking root, hit them hard and fast. In Islington in 2010, on the night I was elected in Brighton, Labour brought in activists from across London and beyond not to win a Westminster seat but to try to remove a Green local councillor who had been doing too good a job of holding Labour to account. And in Brighton in 2015 I was number 19 on the Labour list of target seats. You might have thought that taking seats from the Tories would be more of a priority: but Labour decided that 'taking back their seat' in Brighton Pavilion mattered more than, say, challenging Eric Pickles, Nick Clegg or Danny Alexander, or gaining Hove or Brighton Kemptown from the Tories.

One theme that runs through this is the sense of Labour having a natural right to represent 'ordinary' or 'working' people. I don't recall any of my Green colleagues talking about 'our people': but it's a phrase I hear again and again from Labour politicians. And the danger is that you start to take people for granted. There is little or no accountability, or diversity of view, or scope for dissent. Power ends up in the hands of a very few people. Of course, this isn't the only strand of thought in Labour. Many activists, supporters, even elected members are open to working outside the formal structures of the party. Compass, for example, went out on a limb to open up not just its debates but, more recently, its membership to non-Labour people, including those from other progressive parties, and the results have been stimulating and productive. And where Labour politicians have an independent mandate, free from the dead hand of party HQ, then alliances across party boundaries can be fruitful. In London, for example, the Green group on the Greater London Assembly were able both to work with Ken Livingstone as Mayor and hold him to account. He was prepared to criticize the Greens, but also to collaborate – for example, picking up the idea of a cycle hire scheme from the Green member of the London Assembly Jenny Jones and getting Transport for London to turn it into a reality (though it was his successor who gained the credit for what became known as Boris Bikes).

But Labour remains the vehicle by which millions of people in Britain try to build a better future. It cannot be ignored, or written off. For the foreseeable future, any progressive coalition, any plan to improve the way Britain is governed, any attempt to build a just society where everyone is treated fairly and given an equal chance in life, has to include the Labour Party. But to bring about that coalition, one thing has to change: Labour must accept it does not have and should not want a monopoly on progressive politics. Politics has to reflect the diversity of our country. We are not divided into 'bad' Tories and 'good' Labour. No one party can represent every strand of opinion; the last thing we need is a progressive monolith, particularly on the current Labour model. It means too much centralization of power, demands too many compromises, and excludes too many people.

To the Compass audience, I set out an alternative. Tony Blair had talked of a 'big tent' in which progressives could gather; but that model was discredited. Instead, we should picture a campsite upon which different parties and tendencies could pitch their tents, maintaining their separate identities but also adding up to something greater than their individual parts. We are some way off this; but I am encouraged by the fact that most ordinary supporters would like to see more collaboration: or to put it another way, for us to spend our energies working against the common threat. For them, partisanship is an indulgence they cannot afford.

My great hope in Brighton has been that I might break down some of the party political divisions that meant we could not get the best deal for the city. When we all worked together, we were clearly much stronger. An example was the Royal Sussex Hospital, which desperately needed rebuilding. Some of the buildings dated back before the time of Florence Nightingale, and the journey from A & E to the Barry Building was partly in the open, making it impossible in rain or in high winds. But however good the case, it required the agreement of the Department of Health and HM Treasury, and this was at a time when the prevailing belief at the Treasury that private finance was the best way to fund hospital construction was at last being challenged. In the event, the unlocking of the funding was a cross-party affair. The decision to fund the project directly from taxation was made by the Labour government. Planning permission for the construction to go ahead was granted by the Green administration on Brighton and Hove Council. And the final go-ahead came from the coalition. But the shine was taken off this achievement when one of the local MPs started to try to claim all the credit. For anyone who knew the truth, this seemed only to confirm their worst fears about politicians.

This is not only an issue in Westminster. As an MEP, I made several efforts – as did the Liberal Democrats – to try to get a forum where the eleven MEPs in the south-east constituency could work together. You could see from the letters I was receiving that people didn't know who to approach, and often they would write to all of us. It would have been so refreshing for the constituent if we had worked together on a reply. These weren't party political issues, and we could have demonstrated there was a group of MEPs working together in their interests, and we could have spent more time on each reply. But somehow that forum was asking too much of traditional politicians.

Perhaps because I am currently the only Green MP, when I give talks to schools or community groups I'm often asked if I work together with other parties. And people are really pleased when I can say that it has been possible to make alliances with Labour's Jeremy Corbyn on anti-nuclear issues or the Conservative Sarah Wollaston on parliamentary reform. And sometimes we get it to work. Another important issue in Brighton was better broadband connection, which was crucial if we were to attract and retain the high-tech businesses that were helping to bring good jobs and investment to the city. The government had opened a competition for cities to bid for funding, but Brighton was too small to qualify.

I spoke to Phil Jones of Wired Sussex about how we could get the decision overturned, and from this came the idea of a campaign: 'Let Brighton Bid'. The *Argus* backed the initiative, and the other parties gave it wholehearted support, and we even forged an alliance with Cambridge and Sunderland, cities which had also lost out, to put pressure on the government. The Green Council led the bid, local businesses pitched to the minister, Ed Vaizey, and in the end we won. That wasn't the end of the story, as the national scheme was delayed over state aid clearance: but making sure that Brighton and Hove had a chance to share in the roll-out of ultra-fast broadband, helping businesses improve their work and bring the reality of the 'silicon beach' slogan a step closer, was a satisfying moment.

Perhaps the more that politicians experience the positive side of collaboration, the easier it will be to work together. Certainly we need to try. The era of two-party politics is dead. The public are electing multi-party administrations, in local authorities, the London Assembly, in the European Parliament and now, at last, in Westminster. They have set the challenge: we have to respond and find ways to work together. And for the progressive wing of politics, this challenge is all the more sharp. In 2015, the progressive parties working independently, and often in competition, could not find a way to defeat the parties that favoured the elitists and reactionaries. Perhaps the voters are telling us that it is time we found ways to work more closely together.

17

Sovereignty:
How Real Power Can Be Returned to the People

> *'Lasting peace can be based only on a genuine understanding of the relationships between people and planet.'*

> Jonathon Porritt

In October 2013, when on a trade mission to China, George Osborne announced that Chinese investors were to take a major stake in the new nuclear power station to be built at Hinkley in Somerset. He went on to say that he would welcome the Chinese owning nuclear power stations in Britain outright. This was delivered is his usual breezy style, and because he didn't seem to think it was important, it took a while for the implications to sink in back in Britain. But it created a certain amount of astonishment not just among environmentalists (or the people of Somerset) but also among security analysts. The Chinese state is the main source of cyber-attacks on the UK: probing our defences, you might say. Their main areas of interest are commercial or industrial intelligence – in other words, stealing technology or gaining access to financial or business information – and our 'critical national infrastructure'. The latter covers anything that is vital for keeping our modern society functioning, from the water supply to the mobile phone network, and right up there in the list of key infrastructure is nuclear power.

The risk posed by cyber-attacks on nuclear power plants sounds like a Tom Clancy thriller: computer experts on the other side of the world hacking in to the control systems of a nuclear reactor and either putting it out of action or causing it to overheat and explode. But however lurid it sounds, it is technically feasible, as the US and Israeli cyber-warriors showed when they used a cyber-attack to wreck Iran's nuclear reprocessing plant in 2009. Britain takes cyber-security very seriously. As well as hacking into other people's systems, GCHQ has a whole division called CESG (the Communications-Electronics Security Group) given over to helping protect us from similar attacks. It works very closely with the utilities and energy companies; but when those companies are owned by a potentially hostile power, how secure will the technology and control systems be?

There is a more prosaic risk to foreign investment. Where our 'critical national infrastructure' is owned by British firms, we have some extra leverage to ensure they obey the law and take some account of the national interest. But when those firms are based outside the UK, there's a greater risk they will take decisions that mean we lose out; and if they break the law, we may find it difficult to prosecute them or gain any redress for the damage they might cause. It is hardly ideal that the three biggest players in Britain's energy 'market' are French, German and Spanish: not because they are any more or less ethical, but because they don't have to pay so much attention to our national interests, and because it complicates attempts to oversee them. As well as the power and influence they wield directly, they can also call on their governments to back them up (just as our government will tour the world 'backing' British firms).

This is the complex world of sovereignty: that is, the extent to which we as a nation or a country have control over our own destiny. The debate over sovereignty is often seen as the preserve of the old-guard right-wingers, nationalists or xenophobes. But wrapped up in it are issues that affect us all, such as the relationship between the people and Parliament and between the nations of the United Kingdom; and how we pool our sovereignty with others through international treaties and institutions. The North Atlantic Treaty Organization is an example of the latter. The United Kingdom is a member of NATO, and this commits us (among other things) to going to war in the event of an attack on any one of NATO's twenty-eight member states. This is an absolute commitment: no ifs and buts, no 'well, we're not sure' or 'subject to a vote in the House of Commons'. (It is similar to the commitment that the British government made to Poland in the spring of 1939 and which became the formal reason for declaring war on Germany later that year.)

This is, by any measure, a considerable limit on our freedom as a country to make our own decisions. If, say, Serbia invaded Albania, or Syria attacked Turkey, then we would be duty-bound to go to Albania's or Turkey's defence. It is also one that most people in Britain know very little about. NATO is currently preparing for three new member states: Bosnia and Herzegovina, Macedonia, and Montenegro. This will bring the same obligations of mutual defence, but there has been little or no debate on this in Britain, even though the civil war in Ukraine has shown that peace in Europe cannot be taken for granted. Nor can we expect much parliamentary scrutiny: the last round of enlargement in 1997 was debated in the House of Commons for a little over an hour; and there was no vote, as the main parties were all in support.

Compare this to the debate on membership of the European Union. There the shouts of 'loss of sovereignty' are endless, even though, unlike NATO, the people (or at least those of voting age in 1975) had the chance to vote on whether we wanted to belong or not (we voted 67 per cent to 33 per cent to stay in). Those who are against our membership also complain about a democratic deficit (that is, a lack of direct accountability to the voter). Certainly the EU needs to become more transparent and accountable: but at least the EU has the European Parliament which is directly elected and which can and does block legislation and scrutinize spending, while NATO has no similar voice for ordinary people.

And if you were truly worried about 'sovereignty', what about the World Trade Organization? It sets the rules that govern world trade, and so prevents, for example, our insisting that other countries adopt decent standards for the protection of the health of workers making goods imported to the UK, or to limit the levels of pollution. We lose because multinationals can get away with closing their factories here and moving the work to factories where laws are lax (or not enforced). Those countries lose because their workers are exploited and their environment is trashed. The only ones who really gain are those who run the companies.

It is the WTO which stands in the way of making sure multinationals such as Apple pay a fair amount of tax in the countries where they operate. Without it, a country could insist that a manufacturer pays their taxes or face restrictions on their right to import; but the WTO bans this (just as it bans almost all unilateral action, whatever the ethical, social or environmental justification). By insisting that all such controls are agreed multilaterally – that is, most or all nations agreeing to the same restrictions – they make such controls incredibly difficult to introduce. Think of the difficulty of securing a unanimous decision in the UN Security Council, with its fifteen members. As a result, the WTO is often weak or even hostile towards social welfare, development, or the environment.

Over the years the WTO has been able to force upon Britain a lot of unwelcome rules. We were told we could not ban the importation of fur from animals caught using leg-hold traps, despite the cruelty involved; or support banana farmers in the

Caribbean, despite the importance of the UK market to growers in the Windward Islands. We were told that we would have to eat genetically modified crops whether we wanted to or not; and that we could do nothing about the United States and Canada using controversial growth hormones in beef. Often the WTO will not just stop you keeping products out of your country, it will even stop you labelling them, so that consumers cannot make their own choices. Even introducing a label such as 'dolphin-friendly' ended up as a WTO dispute. But despite all these attacks on our sovereignty, the British people have never had a chance to vote on membership of the WTO; there is no WTO parliament to give us a voice; and WTO measures do not have to be debated, let alone voted on, in the UK Parliament. That makes it even more difficult to challenge the focus and direction of the WTO, and to start a debate about replacing its goal of ever-more open markets, in ever-more ruthless competition with each other, with an alternative based on the renewal of sustainable national and local economies worldwide, under the revised rules of a General Agreement on Sustainable Trade.

These institutions matter. Whether or not we want to be members, it is important for us to have some ability to scrutinize them; but even here we have far less right to know what is done on our behalf in the WTO or in NATO compared with the European Union. The European Parliament can question officials, call witnesses and demand to see evidence to hold the Commission to account, just as the UK Parliament is supposed to do; and we have the right to bring cases before the European Court of Justice. There is no equivalent for NATO or the WTO.

So we have the odd situation where a whole political party, UKIP, has emerged which devotes itself to attacking the EU over sovereignty, but which shows no such concerns about the loss of sovereignty to NATO and the WTO. The explanation can be found in UKIP's manifesto. It is not really about sovereignty: it is about removing an alternative source of power. The EU is responsible for a lot of things that UKIP leader Nigel Farage doesn't like, such as environmental regulation, the protection of workers, consumer protection and, yes, health and safety. In the European Parliament, UKIP MEPs regularly vote against such measures, for example against requiring the cabs of trucks to have better standards of visibility to reduce the numbers of cyclists killed in traffic accidents each year. In the same way, UKIP hates the European Court of Human Rights because it would prefer to roll back the clock to a time before such rights had been codified: when you could cheerfully discriminate against people without worrying you'd be in trouble. UKIP's domestic agenda centres on scrapping the ban on hunting and allowing people to smoke in public places; doubling prison places; cutting public spending, except for a 40 per cent increase in the defence budget; and supporting grammar schools. Most revealing are their plans to give the rich and businesses substantial tax cuts, which may help explain why rich business people put so much money into UKIP. And, of course, immigration.

UKIP will deny that its appeal depends on immigration. But until it seized on this issue, rather than EU membership, it had little popular support. This isn't surprising. The EU doesn't seem to be of much day-to-day importance for most people. After all, it's very rare to come into direct contact with the European Union. Britain is not patrolled by EU inspectors, and the threats to the British way of life that are supposed to emerge from Brussels are illusory. For all the scaremongering of UKIP, the *Sunday Telegraph* and the rest, you can still go into a pub and buy a pint of beer; you can still eat a traditional British banger. When rules are introduced to grade the curliness of cucumbers and bananas, it is usually our own supermarket chains who are pressing for them, not the European Commission. And we are not the only country who enforces the rules: our record on compliance is in fact much worse than many others. (We are the country who once tried to avoid paying to clean up the sewage in our seas by claiming that Blackpool wasn't covered by the Bathing Waters Directive because not many people went swimming there.)

It suits national governments to blame the EU for anything unpopular, while taking the credit for anything good. As a result, over the years, support for the EU has been eroded. As an MEP, I was confronted almost daily by the fact that the original 'big idea' – to bring peace to post-war Europe by bringing its nations closer together – is no longer enough to sustain public support for the EU. And thanks to the bureaucratic and remote way in which it works, many people are no longer sure what the EU is *for*. So the challenge now is to make those institutions more democratic and accountable – and to develop a more compelling vision of the EU's role and purpose.

The EU has the potential to do much more to spread peace and make our economies more sustainable, and to promote democracy and human rights, at home and throughout the world. But to achieve that, it needs urgently to change direction, away from an obsessive focus on competition and free trade and towards a re-localization of our economies, placing genuine cooperation and environmental sustainability at its heart. The EU's leaders have become fixated on 'economism': the idea that the overriding goals of European integration are purely economic, and its progress should be measured in terms of economic growth and the removal of internal trade barriers alone. A new big idea, based on placing sustainability, social justice and peace at the heart of the EU, could revitalize the EU institutions and re-inspire the public.

One way to create the space for the debate about the future of the union, and ensure that the goals of the European project really are in the best interests of its citizens, would be to hold a referendum. That's why, in October 2011, I joined 110 other MPs in supporting the Conservative David Nuttall in his bid to bring forward the date of an EU referendum, so that it had to happen by May 2013. I also tabled an amendment to his motion, calling on the government to use the intervening eighteen months to build support for radical reform of the EU, increasing its transparency and accountability, refocusing its objectives on cooperation and environmental sustainability rather than competition and free trade, and enabling member states to exercise greater control over their own economies.

As predicted, however, Nuttall's attempt was unsuccessful. Many of those who voted against were simply afraid of giving people a say on the EU, for fear their answer would be no. Closing down debate, however, is likely to lead only to increased hostility to an EU project that many feel is being foisted upon them.

Those of us who passionately believe in the importance of the EU, notwithstanding its many flaws, shouldn't shy away from the referendum and the debate: rather, we should have the courage of our convictions, and make the case for a reformed EU loudly and clearly. At the top of that agenda for reform should be the threat to sovereignty posed by corporate power. Significantly, this is a threat that neither the Conservatives nor UKIP seem much bothered about, and one that was illustrated most recently in the proposals for an EU–US Transatlantic Trade and Investment Partnership, or TTIP, which would allow corporations to sue sovereign governments in so-called arbitration tribunals on the grounds that their profits are threatened by government policies. Democratically agreed regulations to protect the environment, for example, or food safety or privacy could be deemed 'barriers to trade' and be subject to attack. Even more worryingly, TTIP further opens up public services to private companies motivated primarily by profit rather than people's needs.

This is hardly surprising, given the list of 'stakeholders' invited by the European Commission to help shape the TTIP agreement. Thanks to perseverance from the Corporate Europe Observatory, the Commission has been forced to acknowledge that, of 130 meetings on the agreement, at least 119 were with big corporations or their lobbyists, providing yet further evidence of how far the EU is currently prioritizing corporate interests above the public good. But right-wing opposition to the EU has never been a simple argument about sovereignty. When David Cameron famously used his veto over a German-led agreement to save the euro at the end of 2011, it was not the national interest he was safeguarding, but the City's.

Moreover, many of those who want us to leave have an agenda of their own. They dislike the way the EU puts some constraints on their absolute power. Rupert Murdoch, for example, long feared that while British governments would give him everything he wanted on media ownership, the EU might question whether it is right for one man to control a group of newspapers and also the main satellite broadcasting channel. Murdoch, as a free-market zealot who is also a US citizen, has never warmed to the consensual, social-democratic model that prevails in most of Europe. Nor have his newspapers.

Just as ministers generally resent having an alternative source of power in Brussels, so they cannot tolerate councils in Britain having powers of their own. The extent to which Eric Pickles micromanages local government is absurd. Their obligations are set out in tedious detail in the mass of legislation, directions, circulars and guidance that flows from his department every year. They are weighed down with a massive, bureaucratic reporting regime. And they have been stripped of any meaningful powers to set their own budgets. This leaves local authorities in an impossible position. They have more responsibilities than ever, with none of the power.

The degradation of local government in England is almost complete. Fewer and fewer people vote in local elections, because with all the decisions taken in Westminster and Whitehall, there seems less and less point. Then the same Westminster politicians who have caused the problem by stripping local government of effective powers, turn round and say that local government lacks a popular mandate. Compare this to the revitalization of politics through devolution: but many in Parliament are not keen to see local councils regaining some of their authority and self-confidence. Only the constitutional implications of devo-max in Scotland have opened up a debate on genuine devolution of power within England.

To me, sovereignty looks rather different from how it does to Nigel Farage, or David Cameron, or even Ed Miliband or Nick Clegg. It is about whether the people have power, and pass it to their elected representatives; or whether those representatives have usurped power, and use it to keep the people in their place. And it is about the terms on which we share sovereignty with other nations, through international organizations or treaties, to deal with global issues such as the environment, trade and security; and what we get in return.

Take the extradition treaty we signed with the United States, which means that you can be sent to the US to stand trial, despite the fact that the alleged crime has been committed in Britain. Even if the legal systems were the same, it would be more difficult for the defendant to mount their case when they, their witnesses and their legal team were thousands of miles from home. But of course the US system is nothing like that in the UK. Nor do we have capital punishment, which can add a terrible burden of fear to the accused, and be used to intimidate a defendant into admitting their guilt in return for a lesser sentence. For all these reasons, the treaty was wrong, and the more people heard about it, the less they liked it.

Two cases highlighted the pernicious nature of this treaty. Babar Ahmad was suspected of terrorist activities carried out in the UK. The Crown Prosecution Service did not have sufficient evidence to mount a prosecution; but he could still be extradited to the United States to be tried for the same offences. Gary McKinnon was an alleged hacker whom the US wanted to try and imprison because he had succeeded in breaking into various super-secure computer systems. His case was taken up by the media and there was some hope that Babar Ahmad and others facing the same jeopardy might benefit from the heightened coverage, so that they would either be released or face a British court and jury. But the Home Secretary, Theresa May – and sadly I cannot think this was accidental – allowed Babar Ahmad's extradition to go through, and only afterwards announced a review of the treaty. I was delighted that in October 2012 Gary McKinnon's extradition was quashed, but this was little consolation to Babar Ahmad. Two weeks before, he had been handed over to US marshals at RAF Mildenhall in Suffolk, along with fellow detainee Syed Talha Ahsan, and flown to a maximum security prison in the United States, where he would be held in solitary confinement.

It hadn't helped that those who could have spoken out in his defence – or at least, called for him to have a fair trial in the UK – did not do so. The *Daily Mail*, which had rightly challenged the justice of allowing Gary McKinnon to be extradited, did not appear to feel the same outrage over Babar Ahmad or Talha Ahsan. Not all the celebrities who took up Gary McKinnon's cause supported the rights of the two other men. And the praise heaped on Home Secretary Theresa May, particularly her supposed sensitivity to Gary's Asperger's syndrome, was poignant: Talha Ahsan also suffers from Asperger's.

The support of national newspapers or those with a public profile is all the more important because of the way government can be so intimidating – deliberately so – even to those who have gained some position or status. I was one of a group of MPs who went to the Foreign and Commonwealth Office to argue the case for Shaker Aamer, who is the last British resident being held in the US detention centre in Guantánamo Bay in Cuba. He has been imprisoned for ten years without trial, without even being charged, and has also been the victim of horrific torture. Strangely, in 2007 the US government admitted it had no evidence against him and cleared him for transfer from Guantánamo and in the same year the UK government requested his repatriation to

Britain. Yet it seems impossible for him or his lawyers to turn these announcements into his actual release, leaving him in a surreal legal limbo: exactly the kind of extrajudicial imprisonment from which the right of habeas corpus – that is, that a prisoner must be either charged or released – is supposed to protect us. Jane Ellison, his MP, was leading the delegation and apparently as fired up as the rest of us about this injustice when we met in advance of the meeting. But by the time we had walked through the vast stone gateway of the Foreign Office, been conducted through endless corridors of stone and marble, past the portraits of former Foreign Secretaries who had wielded power over a quarter of the world, bending emperors and maharajahs to their will, the mood of the party had subtly changed. So when we were finally ushered into the presence of William Hague, subsiding onto deep and comfortable sofas, it was as if we were in the presence of the Great and Mighty Oz. We knew it was all a sham; but still, the sense of great power and weighty responsibility was palpable. Hague's smooth diplomatese was deeply disconcerting: we were there to talk not about an abstract issue but a man who had been kept in prison without trial for years on end. And what he could not do was explain why he couldn't simply ask David Cameron to pick up the telephone to Barack Obama and sort it out.

The image of an individual pitted against the power of the British state, and behind it the United States, is a deeply troubling one. It is not about whether the individuals concerned are innocent or guilty, but about ensuring that everyone is treated fairly and equally. Of course, this means that human rights will end up protecting some people we might dislike or condemn – that's the point. If we reserve rights for people we like, they are not human rights: that is, rights that we accord in full to each and every human. And what is most surprising about the right-wing attacks on human rights, and particularly the International Convention and the European Court of Human Rights, is that they are based on principles taken from our own Common Law

that can be traced back to Magna Carta. And those who want
Britain to stop recognizing international law and human rights
usually want to do away with our rights in Britain too. They may
talk of replacing the ECHR and the Human Rights Act with a
British Bill of Rights; but what they are doing is undermining
the fundamental principles that have protected us for centuries.
In the last few years, we have lost the right to silence; the right
to be tried in open court, not behind closed doors; the right to
see the evidence being used against you and to cross-examine
witnesses; and even the oldest of them all, habeas corpus, has been
compromised. Under the Terrorism Prevention and Investigation
Measures [TPIMs] Act you can be confined to your own house,
your visitors controlled and your phone calls restricted. (It is not
so long ago that, in the British mind, house arrest was something
you found in dictatorships and banana republics.) And habeas
corpus was not much use to the British men held for months or
years without trial in Guantánamo Bay, with the agreement of
successive British governments.

These rights have been thrown away because none of the main
parties want to appear 'weak' on crime or terrorism. It is as if the
police or security services only need to say 'terrorist' to be given
every power they can imagine. And when both the Conservative
and Labour leadership are in favour, there is little opportunity for
serious debate or scrutiny. This reached its nadir with the Data
Retention and Investigatory Powers Act, which was backed by
Labour before the draft bill had even been published, and was
rushed through the Commons in a day. MPs such as Labour's
Tom Watson and the Conservative David Davis were among
those who also tried to raise serious concerns, but our efforts
to ensure that the legislation was sensible and proportionate
were thwarted: the government and opposition whips worked to
ensure that it was voted through without proper debate.

DRIP is an appropriate acronym for this Act because it is
exactly this slow, drip-by-drip erosion of our liberties that is so

dangerous. There is little risk of anyone seizing power, declaring martial law or suspending the constitution in Britain; instead, through a hundred lesser acts, the state takes more and more power to itself, and our protections become steadily weaker. We are comforted by being told that these are a response to an extraordinary situation; but we have seen time and time again that powers given supposedly to fight terrorism are soon used by the police for far less significant threats, such as checking up on whether people have claimed the right benefits or tax rebates, or even spying on protesters or campaigners. This is why it is so crucial that our fundamental rights are kept separate from Parliament and government, with independent judges to decide upon them. It is the only way to guarantee that our rights as citizens stay in our own hands, and that we only concede them on our own terms.

Seen in this way, sovereignty is about how we as individuals, communities and as nations govern ourselves: what we retain as our essential rights; and where we pool sovereignty so that we can, working together, be stronger than our individual parts. This was at the heart of the debate in Scotland on independence, although it took until the last few weeks of the campaign for this theme to emerge clearly. In the 1980s Scotland came to be ruled by a Conservative government for which few Scots had voted. That government revelled in rejecting the idea of consensus and believed that the possession of a working majority in Westminster entitled it to do as it pleased. That was followed by a Labour government that pursued the same agenda on privatization, welfare reform, taxation and deregulation; an agenda that commanded very little support among the people of Scotland.

The Scottish independence vote has opened up a wider constitutional debate, one that is surely beyond Parliament to resolve. Within hours of the Scottish vote being announced, the Conservatives and Labour were confronting one another about the link between more devolution of powers to Scotland

and whether Scottish MPs could vote on 'English' issues. The politicians have shown that they cannot bring in this kind of change alone. Inevitably, everything reverts to party politics and self-interest. But the experience in other countries is that attempts to reshape the constitution without involving politicians fails as well. That is why I support the idea of a constitutional convention, where the people would be represented alongside the politicians, and would together try to set out a new constitutional settlement. On a practical level, working with civil society, representatives from charities and businesses, local communities and faith groups, trades unions, professional bodies and constitutional experts would bring a wealth of experience and allow politicians to be more open and creative. And a constitutional convention would help ensure that change is not made, or blocked, in the interests of the political class.

The sovereignty of the people sounds so abstract, and it is rare that, except perhaps at election time, we think in those terms. Yet the fundamental problem with Parliament is that those within it believe they are sovereign; they are the ultimate source of power and authority; and they are then tempted to misuse it, selling it to sectional interests, lobbyists, big business and the rest. We now have the chance to reassert the sovereignty of the people by demanding a people's assembly to reshape the constitution. We saw after 2010 that even the expenses scandal was not enough to ensure that Parliament would bring in genuine and far-reaching reform. We can't let that happen again.

18

Trial:
How We Still Have the Right to Protest – for Now

> *'You are charged that on 19th August 2013 at*
> *Balcombe in the County of West Sussex you took part*
> *in a public assembly and knowingly failed to comply*
> *with a condition imposed under Section 14 of the*
> *Public Order Act 1986, namely to assemble within a*
> *designated area so as not to be part of a public assembly*
> *across the entrance of the Cuadrilla site.'*
>
> R v. *Lucas*

On the night of my arrest, I was released in the early hours and reunited with my family in the car park outside Crawley police station. Theo was none the worse for his experience, and the next day he was back at the camp in Balcombe. Isaac had thoughtfully brought me what he knew I would want most of all at that moment: a small bottle of tonic water, thoughtfully diluted with gin. But as Richard drove us home to Brighton, I did wonder what further worry I had brought upon my long-suffering family.

First, there was the reaction in the media. I was up early, catching up on constituency work and mildly apprehensive about how my arrest would be covered. Was I standing up for what I believed in? Earning my salary? Or was I bringing the law into disrepute, and setting the wrong example?

It also called into question my role in Parliament. If I had to go out and get arrested to make my case, did that mean I wasn't achieving anything as an MP? I felt strongly that I had done the right thing. It wasn't only about fracking, either. The right to protest is incredibly important; but it doesn't always feel that way if you don't happen to have a cause to protest about. Then, it's easy to form the impression that the protesters are in the minority, or asking for something unreasonable, or intent on causing trouble. Certainly that was the underlying view of many of the police officers I met, for whom (perhaps understandably) protests were either a bloody nuisance or a welcome chance to top up their overtime. It was also the view of many journalists, who might welcome demos as a source of news, but were also predisposed to play up the threat: a few wild-eyed anarchists out to bring down society were more newsworthy than thousands of ordinary people juggling banners and thermos flasks while trying to keep one eye on their kids and the other on the threat of rain.

So I had a strong 'morning after' feeling. I felt I'd done the right thing in standing alongside the villagers in Balcombe. But I might still be in a lot of trouble, not just with the police and the courts, but with the media, the public and my own constituents. And then I was invited onto LBC's *Nick Ferrari Show*. Someone once said that LBC is the radio station for London's taxi drivers, and certainly there's a lot of 'give and take' in its debates and phone-ins. But I couldn't duck this.

Nick began ominously:

'We've had callers phoning in since seven o'clock talking about this very issue. And I have to tell you, Caroline, that 90 per cent of people . . .'

He paused for effect, and my heart sank, jumping ahead to complete the sentence: *90 per cent of people think you're a stain on the reputation of Parliament.*

'. . . absolutely support what you've done.'

Suddenly, I was flooded with relief. It wasn't about avoiding a tough interview. It was because most of those callers probably wouldn't have a strong view either way about fracking. If they were backing me, it was because they liked the idea of a Member of Parliament getting out there and standing up for what they believed in: even if it meant getting arrested. It is easy to talk about how, if you trust people, they will repay that trust a hundred-fold. But to have it happen to you, live on radio, is deeply heartening.

This, though, wasn't the end of the story. The public were supportive, and my constituents were fantastic. It was probably the one thing I did or said that got the most obvious 'thumbs up' from people on the streets or buses of Brighton. But there were also the police and the courts to face: which meant months of knowing that at some point I and my four co-defendants would have to go in front of a judge and account for our actions.

Fortunately we had a brilliant legal team, who were able to turn our instinctive feeling that the police had exceeded their powers into a series of telling legal points. These weren't 'technicalities': it is a critical part of our civil liberties that the police should work within the legal framework set by Parliament. That framework includes a lot of necessary protections. For example, Parliament may give the police powers to declare that a demonstration cannot be held at a particular time and place, to avoid the risk of serious disorder. This is a significant reduction in our freedom to protest, and so it is right that there should be safeguards to ensure that this power is used wisely and in the manner that Parliament intended. In this case, Parliament had decided that the power must be time-limited; it must be based on reasonable grounds; it must be issued only by a senior police officer who is actually there on the ground, seeing for herself or himself; and it must be communicated properly to those gathering to protest.

That day, we might not have been able to quote Section 14 of the Public Order Act 1986, but we knew that what we were doing was peaceful, and that we were not blocking the highway or otherwise creating a situation that needed anyone to be moved on, let alone arrested. We also believed that there was no alternative if we were to raise our concerns about fracking and climate change effectively. It wasn't a decision I took lightly, but I had received hundreds of letters from constituents concerned about fracking and Balcombe. On their behalf, and because the campaign to prevent climate change has been incredibly important to me throughout my political life, I had done everything I could in Parliament to pursue the issue: tabling motions, holding debates, putting questions to ministers. But it was also important for me to join protesters making the case outside Parliament.

Then there was the question of why we were arrested in the first place. The police had come in for a lot of criticism for not being harder on the protesters, and maybe this influenced their judgement. In their defence, the police pointed to the expected arrival of more climate protesters in the following days, and maybe they just wanted to 'nip trouble in the bud'. But our case remained that, whatever the future might have held, the police are simply not allowed to arrest people because they want to; but only because Parliament has given them the power to do so. And in our case, they had no right to do this.

There was a second strand to our defence: that what we were doing was necessary to prevent another and more serious crime. Cuadrilla's drilling at Balcombe was intended to open up a whole new fossil fuel industry that would inevitably create more carbon emissions, undermine investment in renewable energy and drive further climate chaos. You couldn't directly link fracking to individual deaths, any more than you can directly say that an individual died of lung cancer because they smoked. What you can do is show that rising carbon emissions will lead to catastrophic events, just as a rise in smoking will lead to more people dying of lung cancer. A variation on this argument had been run in the defence of six Greenpeace activists who had broken into the Kingsnorth power station and painted a slogan on a chimney (which the owners, E.ON, claimed cost £30,000 to remove). There, the activists argued that the damage to property was necessary to prevent greater damage to property arising from climate change. This was the defence of 'lawful excuse': much as you could claim it was a lawful excuse to break a window if it was to rescue a child from a burning building. The jury accepted this defence and the 'Kingsnorth Six' were acquitted. (To E.ON's fury – they were soon lobbying the then Secretary of State for Energy and Climate Change, Ed Miliband, for tougher sentences against climate protesters. What he said in reply is not known.)

In our case, there hadn't been any damage at all, though the potential damage from fracking was just as serious as from the coal-fired power station at Kingsnorth. The problem, was that the case would be tried not in front of a jury but by a judge sitting alone. Judges are not all the same, but there are more conservative judges than radical ones. Here I mean 'conservative' not politically but in the sense of not wanting to 'create' law by taking account of new circumstances such as the mounting evidence of the dangers of climate change; and also in the sense of leaning towards the establishment, particularly property-owners and the police. So running this defence in our case had risks: not only that the judge would reject it, but also that this would undermine what had been achieved – by a jury of ordinary people – at the Kingsnorth trial.

The trial was delayed again and again, but in the end the day came and we assembled at the Magistrate's Court in Brighton one bright and breezy March morning. This is a dreary and rather run-down building just round the corner from the Pavilion, but there was at least a cheering crowd (cheering us in, and cheering us up) at the entrance; and plenty of well-wishers in the court itself. That was doubly welcome because however much I believed in the legitimacy of what we had done, and took real comfort from the commitment and integrity of my four fellow-defendants – Josef Dobraszczyk, Ruth Jarman, Sheila Menon and Ruth Potts – , there is still something intimidating about being on trial.

The proceedings are frustratingly slow, with delays for legal arguments, or while waiting for witnesses to appear, or just struggling with the fact that the courts have almost no technology to speed up the process. Even the examination of witnesses takes two or three times as long as it needs to, with endless pauses to wait for the stenographer to catch up. To add to the boredom, the dock is cold and uncomfortable. I felt I could sense the misery and desperation of the hundreds of accused people who had been there before me – as if their suffering had seeped into the fabric of the building.

For those of my readers who have not been put on trial, I can also report that the judge becomes a figure of fascination. He or she will not usually say very much; but it's so tempting to try to read a lot into the few questions or comments they make, and their overall demeanour. Are they nodding along to a favourable witness? Do they seem frustrated with the arguments being made by the prosecuting counsel? It mattered all the more because Judge Pattinson did not have the semi-anonymity that the traditional judge's wig and robe provide: he was sitting in a grey suit on most days. And there was no jury there as a source of robust good sense if he took at face value what the police witnesses were saying.

The evidence, such as it was, took days to get through. We watched hours of tapes made by the police of the protests, including our arrests, and I had the unpleasant experience of reliving the moment when they dragged Theo away. We had some of the same police officers explaining their decisions, and the senior officers in particular used a strange form of management-speak to do so. But it was hard to guess what the judge made of it all. Most of the time he sat with his chin resting on one hand, seemingly detached.

In the end, it was a relief to be called from the dock to the witness stand. Though personally there was much more at stake, it was a less intimidating experience than intervening in Parliament or appearing on *Question Time*. I suppose if I had been trying to hide something, it would have been much worse. But all I had to do was go through the events of the day, making clear that I did not want to be arrested; I did not know I was going to be arrested; and I did not know that the police wanted me to move to a specific area away from the Cuadrilla site.

The worst moment was listening to the judgment. You can't ask people to take a stand if you are not prepared to do the same, and as I believed the Balcombe protesters were right to draw attention to the criminal folly of fracking, I had to be there too. It had been such a relief that public opinion was largely in support, but a 'guilty' verdict would still be a blow. Looming large now, in a way it had not before the trial, was my own sense of honesty. My evidence had, to put it politely, differed from that given by some of the police officers. To be found guilty might in some way suggest I had given false testimony.

The judge gave nothing away as he took his seat, and his carefully crafted words created something of a roller-coaster between hope and fear. Sometimes they seemed to be pointing our way:

'The prosecution bring the charges. They must prove all the elements of both offences beyond reasonable doubt . . .'

But at other times it felt as if a note of hostility was creeping in:

'This is not a trial about the rights and wrongs of the process of extraction of shale gas by fragmentation of rock (known as "fracking") which was the subject of the defendants' protest.'

He then moved to the Section 14 offence: that is, not moving to a designated area when told to do so by the police. For each of the defendants in turn, he summarized the police evidence and their account; and in each case, he found that they had not been properly informed about where they had to move to, and each was found not-guilty on this count. And I began to allow myself some hope too, for the judge was also clear that much of the police evidence was suspect.

'My finding is that the DVD evidence did not corroborate PC Dudson's evidence; on the contrary, it cast doubt upon it . . .'

'PC Harris's evidence of warning, caution, arrest and description of Miss Jarman were all shown to be inaccurate and unreliable . . .'

'Again, there was a discrepancy between evidence given orally and what I saw and heard on the DVD.'

It was encouraging; but I was the only one of the five of us who had given a statement to the police on the night I was arrested (not because I had forgotten the lessons learned from watching *Inspector Morse*, but because I felt I owed it to my constituents to be absolutely transparent about the situation). They were relying on this as evidence that I deliberately ignored their warnings to move away. I had told them I had been handed a notice by a police officer, but this had been quite incomprehensible to me and in any case it had disappeared shortly afterwards when someone began to unfurl a banner. Would that one statement convict me? Now it was my turn to find out.

'In her police interview, Miss Lucas accepted that she knew of the fact of the notice but not of its contents. In evidence, she accepted that she had briefly scanned it, found it to be incomprehensible and then put it to one side . . .'

It boils down to whether the judge prefers my evidence or that of the police.

'. . . I find Miss Lucas Not Guilty of the Section 14 offence.'

Halfway there; but any elation is immediately suppressed. There is still the charge of obstructing the highway; and the judge is still speaking. Tantalizingly, he is giving a further finding on the first half of the charge, and whether the police followed the rules properly in authorizing and preparing the notice served on us.

'I find that Deputy Chief Constable York was not authorized to make a notice in the particular facts of the case.'

He then questions whether the Deputy Chief Constable had reasonable grounds for anticipating serious disorder; and criticized the notice itself, noting in passing that the 'map' of the area was in fact upside down.

'My finding is that the conditions are lacking in clarity and that the map is inadequate ... In fact, I have such concerns about the notice on the particular facts of the case that I find it to be invalid.'

This is strong stuff. The police should not have issued the notice in the first place; and it was not a valid notice. We are acquitted three times over. But only on this charge: still the second charge is to come.

'All the defendants accept that they were sitting on the ground of the driveway to the Cuadrilla site. They accept that this was a highway. I must decide whether I am sure that this was an offence contrary to section 137 Highways Act (1980). The test I must apply is whether what the defendants were doing was unreasonable ...'

He deals briskly with some irrelevant issues. The prosecution had accepted that we had not in fact obstructed any vehicles through our protest; but had suggested that we might have prevented emergency vehicles from accessing. The idea that we would have continued to sit in the driveway had a fire engine or ambulance needed to go onto the site is plainly ridiculous; and the judge is not impressed. And now, as if seeing the finishing line after this lengthy case, he speeds up.

'Reminding myself of the standard of proof and the legal test for obstruction of the highway, my decision is that I do not find that there was an "obstruction" in law in this case. The obstruction was temporary in nature. No vehicle was obstructed. The road to the north was closed in any event and the defendants were in the driveway as opposed to the main carriageway.

'Therefore, on these facts, I am not satisfied to the criminal standard that any of the defendants is guilty of this offence and I formally find each one Not Guilty.'

And that's it. All of us, cleared on all counts. There are cheers, hugs, a few tears, and soon we're outside the courthouse thanking our amazing supporters who have been outside all along and explaining to the media what this means. There's the satisfaction of the acknowledgement that we were entitled to stand our ground and not be moved on by the police. We had the right to be there; they did not have the power to break up our protest or to arrest us. More importantly, the senior officers involved had attempted to 'extend' the powers that Parliament had granted them: and the gentle rap on the knuckles from the judge would hopefully remind them to take more care in future.

Most of all, though, I was relieved it was over.

Brighton had provided some uncharacteristically grey weather for us as we stood together on the steps of the courthouse to make a statement:

> We were peacefully protesting outside Cuadrilla's site in Balcombe to highlight the environmental impact of fracking, particularly its role in accelerating climate change.
>
> We are very pleased that the court upheld our right to peacefully protest against fracking. Protest is the lifeblood of democracy. We are deeply concerned that the right to protest is being eroded and undermined, with legitimate protest criminalized by oppressive policing in an attempt to silence dissent. This judgment is right but is not a cause for celebration. We will continue to campaign to end fracking and only celebrate when our world is on the path of a clean energy future.
>
> I know that this is very important to a large number of my constituents, because so many of them have written to me about the environmental risks posed by fracking, and the urgency of tackling climate change.
>
> All five of us would like to thank all of the supporters who have turned up to support us today and thank the

thousands of people who have sent letters, emails and tweets to express their support. The action we took was for all of our futures.

That wasn't the end of it all. The media interest was immense. But I could put the trial behind me and concentrate on what was to come, feeling inspired that justice had been done, and determined to fight on through the next election and beyond to represent that cause and the values that had been put at stake.

19

Into the Unknown:
How the Next Parliament Will
Shape Our Futures

> '*Another world is not just possible, she is on her way.*
> *On a quiet day, I can hear her breathing.*'
> Arundhati Roy

I stood in line behind the Speaker's chair and waited, while we went through the 'Chope and Bone Show': that is, the tabling of bills proposed by Mr Christopher Chope, the Honourable Member for Christchurch, and supported by Mr Peter Bone, the Honourable Member for Wellingborough. Soon the list is underway. The Illegal Immigrants (Criminal Sanctions) Bill. The Benefit Entitlement (Restriction) Bill. The Convicted Prisoners Voting Bill. The Asylum (Time Limit) Bill. This litany of obsessions and mean-spiritedness would be almost comical if it weren't for the thought that Chope and Bone have an audience here and in the country. The Working Time Directive (Limitation) Bill. The Employment Rights Bill (and just to be clear, that's the rights of employers, not employees). The Bat Habitats Regulation Bill. (What have the bats done to Messrs Chope and Bone?) The Overseas Voters Bill (which would help those living overseas to vote – fine in itself, but one feels it may have occurred to C and B that many of them will vote Conservative, and some even for their own peculiar brand of Conservatism).

Then, to change the mood a little, we have some bills tabled by Bone and supported by Chope. The British Bill of Rights and Withdrawal from the European Convention on Human Rights Bill. The Department of Energy and Climate Change (Abolition) Bill (presumably, as climate change sceptics, they object to the name). The Foreign National Offenders (Exclusion from the United Kingdom) Bill. Then there's one I rather like – The Hospital Car Parking Charges (Abolition) Bill – because although I'm no great fan of cars, we shouldn't fund the NHS by hitting patients and visitors with these charges. But after this startling lurch into making people's lives better, they get back on track with the BBC Privatisation Bill.

By the end of all this, I feel quite proud of my own modest proposals. The Railways Bill, for example, would mean bringing rail franchises back into public hands as they come up for renewal: a way to end the chaos and waste of rail privatization without the need to pay anyone any compensation. The Public Services (Ownership and User Involvement) Bill is the one I've been working on closely with We Own It as a way to ensure that public sector and not-for-profit providers can take on more public services, and also provide greater transparency and accountability when services are operated by private companies. There's also a bill to make it mandatory to teach personal, social, health and economic education in schools – incredible that the government has not already done this, given how crucial it is for helping young people make sense of the world they are to live in; and another on research into reducing the cost and improving the quality of housing in the private rented sector, and encouraging more council house-building as well, which developed the principles set out in my Housing Charter for Brighton. Every one of these has wide public support, addresses a real need and – perhaps most critically – is not trying to stir up envy or hatred against other groups.

As with austerity, there's something rather distasteful about two men who have done well out of life being so fixated on such a dreary list of obsessions. There's also a hint of paranoia in their vision of a Britain ground into the dirt by health and safety inspectors and European Commission bureaucrats, and in their determination to pursue measures that would cause misery to some of the most vulnerable people in Britain. What they offer is a bitter, negative view of ourselves and of our future. And what I have tried to represent in Parliament is the opposite: one that recognizes the difficulties ahead, but is rooted in my faith in my fellow citizens to make the right decisions.

Somewhere in his autobiography, the Labour politician Denis Healey talked about how, whenever he felt fed up with his life in politics, or uncertain about what he could achieve, he would wander into the chamber to look at the massed ranks of Tory MPs, and the sight of the alternative would rekindle his commitment to the fight. My own feelings are not quite that tribal, but I can sympathize with the sentiment. And it made the prospect of the 2015 general election all the more daunting. I had seen the Conservatives up close for five years. Their ranks include some decent and thoughtful people, and traditional Conservatism contains some valuable principles, such as the liberty of the individual and the obligation of those who have done well to help out those who have not. But David Cameron's brand of Conservatism was essentially small-minded and divisive. The prospect of five more years of the Conservative-led coalition, or even a Tory government with an outright majority, was terrifying.

In part, this was because all the faults of our political system bring out the worst in Conservatism. The electoral system means that there are hundreds of safe seats where it is local party activists, not the wider constituency, who in effect select the MP, and so Tory MPs are often much more extreme than their electorate. Then there is the influence of big business and the media, manipulating public opinion or buying influence, pushing the centre of British politics to the right. The 2015 Conservative manifesto, in its ruthless targeting of the sick, the poor and the vulnerable, its tax breaks for the rich, its attacks on treasured institutions such as the BBC and NHS, and its authoritarian and illiberal tendencies, went far beyond anything Margaret Thatcher ever dreamed of. And at its heart was the promise to make a further £12 billion in cuts to the social security budget, without any clue as to where the cuts would fall or the impact on individuals or on society.

This made the need for a strong, progressive alternative all the more vital. Yet Labour failed to challenge the way the Conservatives and their allies had set the terms of the debate on the economy, taxation, welfare, or immigration. Critically, and unaccountably, they did not counter the myth that the recession was caused by overspending under Blair and Brown, rather than the international financial crisis. Instead, Labour continued to be dragged to the right, and its programme was in so many ways a limp imitation of that of the Conservatives, down to their selling campaign mugs with 'Controls on Immigration' blazoned on the side.

The Scottish Nationalists showed that progressive politics could work; but rather than reaching out to the SNP, Labour followed the Tory line that the SNP were a threat to the constitution. Meanwhile the Liberal Democrats were due to pay the price for betraying the trust of their voters by joining the coalition with such enthusiasm in 2010. Perhaps the result should not have been such a surprise, after all.

If you are a candidate, the general election plays out on two levels. There is the national campaign in the media, with opinion polls, TV debates and the rest; and there is your own campaign on the streets and at hustings in church halls and community centres, meeting voters, answering their questions, and if you are the sitting MP, being held to account. Seeking re-election is always going to be a very personal test: would the people of

Brighton think I'd done a good job for them? Would they be swayed by the national scene, where the polls were saying Labour and the Tories were neck and neck, to vote tactically? And would Labour's decision to target Brighton Pavilion, making us number 19 on their hit list, pay off?

In the event, that background made victory all the more sweet: I was returned with a majority up from just over 1,000 in 2010 to nearly 8,000. But what made me most proud was that the people of Brighton had embraced a truly radical and progressive platform. I had stood on a manifesto that had not been trimmed to make me more electable: it set out increased taxes for the rich, unilateral nuclear disarmament, more generous social security payments, comprehensive education, expanding human rights, no to fracking and new runways, treating migrants and refugees fairly, rolling back the privatization of the NHS, reducing the prison population, nationalizing the railways and a dozen other principles that Labour had jettisoned. And the people of Brighton are not so very different from the rest of the country. It was affirming to know that these policies and values, if expressed with conviction and honesty, will strike a chord with the wider public.

Politics is and should be about competing visions of how we as citizens work together to promote well-being, share resources, resolve conflicts, solve common problems and create opportunities. My political priorities are that we face up to the reality of our situation regarding the climate and natural resources, and move to a more sustainable way of living, where our quality of life does not depend on the exploitation of other people here or in other countries, or the squandering of precious natural resources, or irreparable damage to our common inheritance. But beyond this is a far more positive vision. If we can free ourselves from illusions such as seeing economic growth and consumerism as the root of human happiness, then we can reshape our society so that it becomes more nurturing, more supportive, and more sharing:

one where our wealth is seen in what we share, in friendships, in freedom and in opportunity; and where our own success does not have to be seen in terms of the failure of others. I know we can do it, because I see parts of this better world every day of my life: in the way people put themselves out for others, give their time and money, and work together for the common good. We all have selfish impulses, but politics should not pander to these.

In politics, when you strip away the rhetoric and dogma, the media-driven anxieties, the artificial divisions and the rest of it, you are left with people's essential decency. Our world is so large and complex. It can be hard for individuals to find the right way to their own truths. The natural reaction is to deal with abstracts – 'asylum-seekers', or 'scroungers', or 'addicts'. But when people actually meet a refugee, hear their stories, their ambitions, their gratitude to Britain for providing a place of refuge, they no longer want them out. They are more likely – in that typical British way – to start a petition to allow them to stay. When your own job is at risk, when you know people who want to work but can't find any, or who are sick or disabled and trying to lead a decent life on the meanest pittance the state can devise – then the myth of the army of scroungers soon evaporates. And when a drug addict is also a brother or sister or child, then the 'just say no' rhetoric, the punishments and degradations, no longer make any sense: addiction is seen as a medical issue, treatment not a reward for bad behaviour but a way of helping a fellow human back to the life they want to lead.

This gives me hope for the next five years. The Conservatives have a majority in the House, but they won it on a flawed electoral system, with only 37 per cent of the vote. They lack a genuine mandate for radical measures. On a practical level, their small majority places yet more responsibility on individual Conservative MPs to decide whether specific proposals are in the interests of their constituents or the country; and in some cases, whether they can be justified on moral grounds. On issues such as climate change, civil liberties and HS2, there is every sign that unease may turn to rebellion. This may encourage David Cameron not to rely only on the coercion and cajoling of the whips, but to adopt a more consensual, genuinely 'one-nation' approach to governing.

Nothing illustrates this challenge better than constitutional reform. As prime minister, he has the chance, and the duty, to reach a fair deal with the SNP on Scotland's future. But if this leaves the rest of the British constitution in its current dilapidated and regressive state, then such a settlement will not last. The question of how England should legislate on devolved matters needs to be answered: but this has to include all the political parties in Britain, not be imposed by a narrow Tory majority. And as we move closer to a federal structure, so other changes and safeguards must follow.

We face some huge decisions over the next few years; on the constitution; on Europe; on public services and on climate change. But these decisions will be taken in a Parliament that does not come close to reflecting the values, principles or priorities of the electorate. The Liberal Democrats, Greens and UKIP together won 25 per cent of the votes and ended up with just 1.5 per cent of the seats. Then there are the millions who chose not to vote at all, leaving the Conservatives with a majority in the Commons despite having won the backing of only 24 per cent of the electorate. Our archaic and divisive voting system leaves millions disenfranchised and creates artificial divides between nations, and is self-evidently unfit for multi-party politics. The House of Lords also needs to be reformed. Here the lack of representation is even worse than in the Commons: the Liberal Democrats won just 7 per cent of the vote but have 100 seats in the Lords, while UKIP has only 3; and 76 per cent of peers are men.

And while Parliament remains essentially unreformed, and still firmly in the hands of a narrow and self-interested elite, the sense of change that built up during the last five years will not go away. More MPs are prepared to work together across political boundaries. The power of the whips has weakened. And the 56 Scottish Nationalist MPs, elected on a platform of rejecting austerity, gives progressive politics a significant and much-needed boost. The next five years will not be easy, and the responsibility of doing what we can to protect the vulnerable from the excesses of cuts to social security and public services is a heavy one.

Being the MP for Brighton Pavilion is, in that overused phrase, a privilege. Not the petty privileges of the police saluting you at the gates of Westminster or having tea on the Terrace; but to be trusted to speak out on behalf of a whole community. It has shown me that, whatever impression might be left by some of our national newspapers or the debates in Parliament, we have within us much more virtue than vice. Every day, in Brighton and beyond, I see examples of decency, compassion, and thoughtfulness, and meet people who will do everything they can for others. And to represent such people is the greatest job in the world. Throughout the campaign I said that if I were re-elected I would do the same again: to fight for their interests as best I can, and campaign for a Parliament that works for them, not for a self-interested elite. And now, at the start of a new parliamentary term, that fight begins once more.

Arrest at Balcombe, 19 August 2013

Acquitted at Brighton with fellow defendants Sheila Menon (left) and
Ruth Potts (centre), 17 April 2014

Notes

Preface

xii   *requiring a deposit of £500*   The deposit is the amount – currently £500 for each constituency – that you have to pay to stand, whether as an individual or an established political party. If you reach 5 per cent of the votes cast, it is returned to you.

1. The Shock of the Old

3   *Over two hundred first-time MPs are directed*   I have tried to avoid clogging the book up with explanations of how Parliament works. The Parliament website www.parliament.uk has some excellent resources and fact-sheets on procedure and on history, including an online exhibition about the suffragettes. This book isn't a diary, so if you want more of a sense of what day-to-day life in Parliament is like, you could try Chris Mullin. His three sets of diaries are *A View from the Foothills*, *Decline and Fall* and *A Walk-On Part*. There are also the wonderful diaries kept by Tony Benn and – quite a contrast – those of the Conservative Trade Minister Alan Clark.

2. Coalition and Opposition

13   *When the forms of an old culture*   Rudolf Bahro was an academic, a dissident in the former German Democratic Republic, and one of the founders of the German Green Party.

14   *The whole affair involved many different companies*   The Trafigura story has been covered extensively in the media, and the company emails I have quoted were published on the *Guardian* website on 16 September 2009.

17   *In the event, my first words*   My maiden speech is in Hansard (27 May 2010, column 369; for no obvious reason Hansard is divided into columns not pages) and Mike McCarthy's piece on it was published by the *Independent* on 28 May 2010. My first intervention, earlier that day, is also in Hansard (27 May 2010, column 319).

19   *control orders* These were replaced by a new kind of legal control called a 'TPIM', which is discussed further in Chapter 17 (p. 248).

21   *teasing the Lib Dems about how the Coalition Agreement* The Coalition Agreement was published on 20 May 2010 and is available from www.gov.uk.

3. Austerity

27   *Over half went to Oxford or Cambridge* Channel 4's excellent 'Factcheck' blog published more on the background of MPs on 11 July 2013. The title was 'Factcheck – who runs the country'.

27   *the total wealth of the current cabinet* For more on the wealth of the cabinet, see the article 'Exclusive: Cabinet is Worth £70 million' by Christopher Hope in the *Telegraph* on 27 May 2012.

29   *cutting public spending actually made public debt* For more on the paradox that cutting public spending can increase public debt, see Chick and Pettifor: 'The Economic Consequences of Mr Osborne', available as a download from www.debtonation.org (the file name is Fiscal-Consolidation1.pdf).

32   *'Around one million people have been stuck . . .'* On Iain Duncan Smith's various claims, the 'one million claimants' claim is in the Department of Work and Pensions policy paper 'Social Justice: transforming lives – one year on' (Cm 8606 page 5 – 'Cm' is short for 'Command', which is the term used for official publications such as Green and White Papers), available as a free download from gov.uk (or you can buy a printed copy for £16 – don't be surprised if your local library can't afford a copy); and critiqued in the *Economist* (25 April 2013) and on Fullfacts.org (24 April 2013).

34   *the ONS does not produce statistics on private sector rents* On the ONS 5 per cent private rent claim see Hansard, 9 November 2010, column 167 and *Inside Housing*, 16 November 2010.

34   *Andrew Dilnot, later confirmed* Andrew Dilnot's comment on Iain Duncan Smith's presentation of welfare reform statistics is contained in a letter to Nicola Smith of the Trades Union Congress available from the website of the Statistics Authority.

34   *Iain Duncan Smith had to admit in a letter* The letter from Iain Duncan Smith to Paul Goggins MP (reference POS(1)10734/255) is reproduced in full in the 'Report into the Abuse of Statistics by the Department of Work and Pensions' produced by DPAC (Disabled People Against Cuts) in June 2013. This also includes further examples of misleading claims.

35   *For example, that hotbed of Marxist revolution* The wider issue of how welfare has been 'framed' is explored in a report by the Joint Public

Issues Team of the Baptist, Methodist and United Reformed churches 'The Lies We Tell Ourselves: ending comfortable myths about poverty', published in 2013.

37 *Atos was given a contract* Atos: the examples come from constituency case work in Brighton Pavilion.

38 *And there was money for Academies and Free Schools* The cost of the Free Schools programme is set out in a report by the National Audit Office.

40 *sales of champagne in the restaurants and bars* The information on champagne sales in Parliament comes from a Freedom of Information request from 2014 available on the www.parliament.uk website.

40 *A start would be to collect the tax* For a great summary of how HMRC doesn't collect all the tax due, see the article by Rajeev Syal in the *Guardian* on 11 October 2013. There is more detail in the December 2013 report of the Public Accounts Committee and in the work of Tax Research UK.

43 *a share of the national debt of over £40,000* The calculation that national debt now stands at £40,000 per household comes from an article by Hugo Duncan and Ed Monk in thisismoney.co.uk, published on 25 January 2011.

4. National Ill-Health

45 *Deregulation is a transfer* George Monbiot's quote comes from an article in the *Guardian* on 13 July 2010.

46 *over 50 per cent of GPs* The GP voting intention poll comes from *Pulse*, 6 November 2009.

47 *'From each according to their ability . . .'* The quote is originally from *The Organisation of Work* by Louis Blanc, 1839.

49 *In the next three years, South Eastern Trains* Performance data for public sector South Eastern Trains and East Coast are set out in the National Rail Passenger Survey available from PassengerFocus. In the autumn of 2014 East Coast had one of the highest levels of overall passenger satisfaction; Southeastern (private sector) the worst.

51 *which costs us around a billion a year* For more on the rail franchise costs see 'Rebuilding Rail: Final Report' published in June 2012 and available from transportforqualityoflife.com.

83 *and this is reflected in their Public Service Users Bill* For the Public Service Users Bill: see weownit.org.uk

5. A Voice for the Environment

57 *'The badgers have moved . . .'* There are so many thought-provoking quotes I could have made about the environment, and I have given

examples of some of the writers and thinkers who have inspired me
over the years; but somehow Owen Paterson's words from a BBC
interview on 9 October 2013 were irresistible.

61   *but the costs were at least £7 million*   The costs of the badger cull come
from a House of Commons Library note (SN06837) available from
parliament.uk.

61   *People get very emotional about this subject*   Owen Paterson's speech to
the Conservative Party Conference was reported widely, including
in Adam Vaughan's article in the *Guardian* on 30 September 2013.
Paterson was commenting on the IPCC's Working Group I's findings,
published as the Summary for Policymakers on 27 September 2013.

62   *the most credible estimate is that mean atmospheric temperature rose*   On
global temperatures and the question of whether climate change has
'stalled', the key is to distinguish between atmospheric temperatures
(which you can argue either did not rise or did so only very
slightly during those years – it doesn't matter much which) and the
temperature of the planet as a whole, including the oceans. The latter
is a much better guide to long-term trends, and this showed no let-
up in climate change during these years. For more on the 'cherry-
picking' of data see the post of 4 March 2014 on skepticalscience.com
titled 'What has global warming done since 1998?'. If you want to
look at one of the key documents for the 'stalled' debate try 'Coverage
bias in the HadCRUT4 temperature series and its impact on recent
temperature trends', Kevin Cowtan and Robert G. Way, *Quarterly
Journal of the Royal Meteorological Society*, Volume 140, Issue 683,
pp.1935–1944, July 2014 Part B. It is available online without charge
from onlinelibrary.wiley.com.

64   *A series of Freedom of Information requests*   These were reported in an
Independent article by Tom Bawden of 30 October 2013.

64   *The Vikings*   These Greenland settlements were never self-sustaining
and when their trading links with Scandinavia died out in the
fourteenth century, and they had been weakened by the ending of the
Medieval Warm Period, they were abandoned. For more see the article
by Günther Stockinger in *Der Spiegel* of 10 January 2013.

69   *three-quarters of people in Britain were in favour*   The poll on circus
animals was conducted by YouGov in July 2013.

6. Taking to the Streets

76   *But the tuition fee pledge*   The pre-election position of the Liberal
Democrat leadership was exposed in the *Guardian* in an article by
Nick Watt, published on 12 November 2010.

7. Power for Sale

93   *In part, this was BAE's famous lobbying power*   Many writers have
charted the influence of business on government with different
degrees of outrage, from the more detached Anthony Sampson (whose
Anatomy of Britain was one of the first in the field) and Jeremy Paxman
(*Friends in High Places*) to the more engaged Ferdinand Mount (*The
New Few or a Very British Oligarchy*), Owen Jones (*The Establishment:
And How They Get Away with It*) and George Monbiot (*Captive State*).

95   *The route of choice these days*   For more on secondments into
government see the Freedom of Information request on inward
secondments to BIS (Ref: BIS/FOI/14/0773) available on the gov.uk
website.

96   *It wasn't chance that horsemeat*   The horsemeat scandal is explored
further in an article by Felicity Lawrence published by the *Guardian*
on 15 August 2014 and in the Westminster Hall debate of 2 April
2014 (see Hansard, column 233WH).

8. Climate Change and the Politics of Hope

103   *'Why didn't we save ourselves . . .'*   If you haven't seen it, the film *The
Age of Stupid* is one of the best explorations of the reality of climate
change and our responsibility to act now. For more on the health
effects of action on the ozone layer, the World Health Organisation
has a comprehensive briefing as part of a series on the effects on
human health of global environmental change (www.who.int).

109   *This was shortly after the* Deepwater Horizon *disaster*   The *Deepwater
Horizon* drilling adjournment debate was on 18 November 2010 (see
Hansard, column 1157).

110   *which could then turn into potentially stranded assets*   I am not the only
one to raise the question of stranded assets: Archbishop Desmond
Tutu put it in very clear terms (see the *Observer*, 21 September 2014):
'The fossil reserves that have already been discovered exceed what can
ever be safely used. Yet companies spend half a trillion dollars each
year searching for more fuel. They should redirect this money toward
developing clean energy solutions.'

115   *A steady-state economy is one*   For more on the steady-state economy,
see the work of Professor Herman Daly and Professor Tim Jackson's
Prosperity Without Growth (Earthscan, 2009). Also, the New Economic
Foundation has a wealth of solid research on the steady-state economy,
while the think-tank Greenhouse has an excellent 'Post-Growth'
series. The line '. . . buying things we don't need . . .' I first heard in an
excellent 2013 TED talk by Professor Tim Jackson; and there's a similar
sentiment in the 1999 film *Fight Club*. I don't know the original source.

9. Heat, Light and Homes

123   *'To be truly radical . . .'*   The quote from academic, novelist and campaigner Raymond Williams is from *Resources of Hope*, published in 1989, a year after his death.

123   *exposure of the financial markets to 'high carbon assets'*   You can read the whole of my Adjournment Debate on high carbon assets in Hansard (18 December 2012, column 821). A free summary of the report on Zero Carbon Britain is available from zerocarbonbritain.org.

126   *because 'green levies' were putting up their bills*   For more on Green energy levies, you can listen to the report on BBC Radio 4's *The World Tonight*, broadcast on 29 November 2013.

127   *The hearings held by the Environmental Audit Select Committee*   The Environmental Audit Select Committee report on energy subsidies was published on 27 November 2013, as was the accompanying volume of written evidence.

127   *the deal was described as 'economically insane'*   The reaction of Liberum Capital to the Hinkley Point subsidies are reported in a *Guardian* article by Sean Farrell, published on 30 October 2013.

135   *I brought these proposals together*   The Housing Charter is available from www.carolinelucas.com.

137   *Alan Simpson, the former Labour MP*   The report by Alan Simpson for FOE is available from communityenvironment.org.uk.

10. A Tale of Two Policies

139   *'Drug policy has been failing . . .'*   David Cameron called for fresh thinking about drugs policy in 2002. Unfortunately, by 2012, he had changed his mind, claiming 'We have a drug policy that is working in Britain.'

141   *even a majority of* Sun *readers agree*   The poll on drug use for the *Sun* was published on 8 July 2012, under the headline 'Legalise Drugs Use Say Brits In Poll'.

143   *And in 2011, I invited 'Safe in the City'*   The report of the Independent Drugs Commission for Brighton and Hove was published in January 2013 and is available from safeinthecity.info.

146   *Churchill put it more poetically*   Winston Churchill's 1909 speech on the taxation of land value is available in full from www.landvaluetax.org.

150   *LVT has been nudged up the agenda*   I worked with Andy Whiteman on a report examining the practicalities and benefits of land value tax, which is available from andywightman.com.

11. Foreign Adventures

152   *'Shall we have womanly times . . .'*   I have yet to see the oratorio
'Or Shall We Die?' (libretto by Ian McEwan and music by Michael
Berkeley) but something about this line from the chorus has lodged in
my mind.

12. A Modest Proposal

166   *'Well-behaved women . . .'*   The phrase about well-behaved women first
occurs in a study of Puritan funeral services by the historian Laurel
Thatcher Ulrich and became so well known that she herself used it as
the title of her 2008 book on influential women in history.

175   *There will be more female doctors in the UK*   The *Daily Mail* article on
female doctors was published on 2 January 2014.

13. Arrest

180   *'Hope just means another world . . .'*   This quote by Rebecca Solnit is
from her 2004 book *Hope in the Dark*.

181   *So why should so many of the citizens . . .?*   A lot of local and
national groups have campaigned against fracking, including 38
Degrees, Greenpeace and No Dash for Gas. Frack Off has lots of
background on the technology and risks: frack-off.org.uk. The case
for fracking is made by Cuadrilla here: www.cuadrillaresources.
com. For the views of local residents (82 per cent against fracking),
see the results of the referendum held by Balcombe Parish Council
(balcombeparishcouncil.com).

183   *Cuadrilla's Francis Egan admitted as much*   The views of Francis Egan
on fracking were reported in an article by the BBC's Louise Stewart,
published on 6 November 2013, and in evidence to the House of
Lords Committee on Economic Affairs study of the economic impact
of UK Energy Policy of Shale and Gas Oil published on 8 April 2014.

186   *It happened to the village of Kings Cliffe*   For more on the imposition of
a nuclear waste dump at Kings Cliffe over the wishes of local people
see www.kingscliffewastewatchers.co.uk.

14. A Parliament that Works

193   *'If one walks around this place . . .'*   The words of the epigraph come
from a wonderful speech that Tony Benn delivered in the House in
2001 and which is worth reading in its entirety. It is in Hansard (22
March 2001, column 506). The plaque is the one I mentioned in
chapter 1 and is also featured in the Parliament website's piece on the
suffragettes.

194   *The history of parliamentary reform*   The course of parliamentary reform can be traced in any good English history, though Eric Hobsbawn is probably still the foremost historian to cover these issues.

195   *would be to allow MPs to vote electronically*   The many pros and few cons of electronic voting are covered in my report 'The Case for Parliamentary Reform', which also covers some of the other themes in this chapter and has references to further sources and debates.

198   *Explanatory notes are produced*   Hansard (the official record of parliamentary proceedings, separate from the Hansard Society) has the full text of the debates on explanatory amendments (6 November 2013) and on sustainable farming (12 November 2010, column 547).

199   *The Sustainable Livestock Bill*   For more on the Sustainable Livestock Bill, see Hansard (12 November 2010, column 549 onwards).

204   *each Member should be subject to recall*   On the recall of MPs, there is my article in the Huffington Post on 3 November 2014.

205   *One measure of this challenge*   The annual 'Audit of Public Engagement', published by the Hansard Society, is an invaluable guide to the decline in public respect for politics, though there is less on what could be done about it. Russell Brand's book *Revolution* provides more of the passion and though I don't agree with all his remedies he has drawn many people into the debate.

15. A Valuable Prize

209   *The world continues to offer*   The quotation from F. E. Smith (or Lord Birkenhead, as he became) is from 'Idealism in International Politics', Rectoral Address at Glasgow University (7 November 1923) and 'glittering prizes' has become a byword for the use of politics as a ladder for personal advancement. (The sooner we return to thinking of political office not in career terms, but the good you can do with it, the better.)

212   *The main one is called the canvass*   The Liberal Democrat internal 'Orange' guide to political campaigning sets out these traditional canvassing and other practices. Although not formally published, there are copies circulating on the Internet. The Electoral Commission recommendation that the system of deposits be abolished or reformed is summarized in their consultation paper on standing for elections in the UK, published on 17 September 2013.

219   *The government was holding a referendum on AV*   The debate on the AV Referendum was held on 12 October 2010. You can follow the debate in Hansard (column 256).

16. The Progressives

224   *invited to speak at a Compass debate*   Compass (www.compassonline.
org.uk) is the best place to explore current thinking about progressive
alignments and collaboration, as most of those involved in these
debates have contributed.

233   *An example was the Royal Sussex Hospital*   On conditions at the Royal
Sussex Hospital, and why new investment was so urgently needed, see
the report from the Care Quality Commission's Brighton and Sussex
University NHS Trust listening event published on 2 April 2014.

234   *from this came the idea of a campaign*   For more on the 'Let Brighton
Bid' campaign see www.wiredsussex.com and the Brighton *Argus*
www.theargus.co.uk.

17. Sovereignty

236   *'Lasting peace can be based . . .'*   This quotation has a double
significance for me: it comes from chapter eleven of Jonathon's book
Seeing Green, which inspired me to join the Green Party; and was also
picked out by Petra Kelly in the foreword she wrote for it.

236   *George Osborne announced*   George Osborne's statement on Chinese
investment was reported by the BBC and others on 17 October 2013.

238   *The North Atlantic Treaty Organization is an example*   For more on
NATO expansion and parliamentary scrutiny see *Enlarging NATO:
The National Debates*, edited by Gale A. Mattox and Arthur R.
Rachwald.

243   *Transatlantic Trade and Investment Partnership, or TTIP*   For more on TTIP,
see the Corporate Europe Observatory website corporateeurope.org
and the 'background' section of the website stopttip.net.

2457   *Take the extradition treaty we signed*   The various controversies over the
US–UK extradition treaty have been set out in a House of Commons
Library briefing note (SN/HA/4980) available from the Parliament
website.

18. Trial

251   *On the night of my arrest*   The way environmental protesters have been
dealt with by the police and courts could have a chapter of its own. I
haven't, for example, discussed how the police have used undercover
officers to spy on campaigners, or the use of 'creative' interpretations
of the law to try to prevent legitimate protests from going ahead. Nick
Broomfield has made a documentary about the Kingsnorth protests
published by the *Guardian* website on 31 May 2009. The *Guardian* also
has a powerful interview with one of the undercover officers, Mark
Kennedy, published on 26 March 2011.

255   *To E.ON's fury*   And E.ON's approach to the government over Kingsnorth is exposed in an article by James Ball in the *Guardian* on 19 February 2013.

257   *The worst moment was listening to the judgement*   A copy of the judgement in my own trial can be found here in a blog post of 17 April 2014 on drillordrop.com. And you can watch our statements after the trial was over on YouTube.

19. Into the Unknown

262   *'Another world is not just possible . . .'*   Arundhati Roy's quote is from a speech she gave at the World Social Forum in Port Allegre on 28 January 2003.

266   *Reshape our society*   Someone who has thought more than most about the relocalization of our societies is Colin Hines. His book *Localization: A Global Manifesto* (Earthscan 2000) remains a stimulating exploration of the issues.

Further Reading

There is so much more I would like to say about Green politics, but a book about reforming Parliament isn't the right place. Instead I can recommend some books that have inspired me or helped shape my thinking about economics, society or development. As well as those mentioned in the main text, these include Rachel Carson's *Silent Spring* (1962) and Jonathon Porritt's *Seeing Green* (1984), which inspired me to become involved in Green politics. On the alternatives to traditional economics, I would recommend Herman E. Daly's *Steady-State Economics* (1991), Andrew Simms's *Ecological Debt* (2005), *The New Economics* by David Boyle and Andrew Simms (2009), and Tim Jackson's *Prosperity without Growth* (2010). On the wider social effects of inequality and injustice, there is Andrew Dobson's *Green Political Thought* (2007) and *The Spirit Level* (2009) by Richard Wilkinson and Kate Pickett, while Richard Murphy's *The Courageous State* (2011) sets out some inspiring thoughts about how we can find collective solutions to these and other crises, and Sara Parkin, in *The Positive Deviant* (2010), shows what we can do to challenge accepted thinking in our own lives. For more on the current environmental and social challenges of energy and consumption, there is Jeremy Leggett's *Half Gone* (2006) and George Marshall's *Carbon Detox* (2007). Naomi Klein's *This Changes Everything* (2014) brings the story of how big business has tried to derail action on climate change up to date; and, finally, Rebecca Solnit's *Hope in the Dark* (2004) shows how the human spirit can overcome adversity and bring about change.